MW00929369

Are We Walking To Alaska?

To Marissa - thanks of many kinds for the great service

JoAnn Dunlap Bayne

JoAnn Dunlap Bayne

walkingtoalaska@gmail.com

Cover photo

Jenny (partial face), Me, Unknown Little Girl, Jeff (with cast and black eye), our mom,

Jimmy in back, Edna Barr (partially hidden)

Copyright © 2011 JoAnn Dunlap Bayne

All rights reserved.

ISBN: 1460951379

ISBN-13: 978-1460951378

DEDICATION

To My Wonderful husband, Don – he read the very first draft, all in one night – was with me each step of the way and has always been my biggest fan.

To our children – Beccy, Jason, Rusty, Jamie, Lori and Jay – my true inspiration and joy!

To my grandsons, Ben Bayne-Davies, Jahn-Zyel Valenti and Donnie Ray Bayne– may they find life always an adventure.

To my dear brother Jimmy, who protected me always!

To Nancy Cox – whose joy of life encouraged me to find the joy in my childhood.

To Ruthellen Shelton – my fourth grade teacher – who encouraged me to read, and told me I could do whatever I put my mind to.

Contents

SOUTHEAST ALASKA

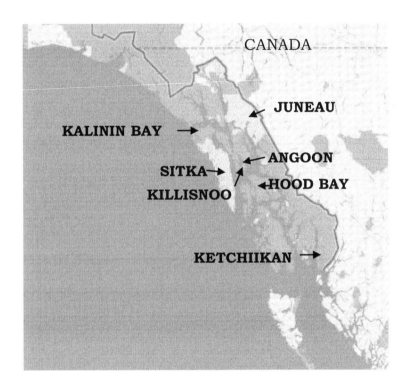

CANADA

JUNEAU

KALININ BAY →

ANGOON

SITKA →
KILLISNOO

← HOOD BAY

KETCHIIKAN →

**ALASKA STATE
FLAG**

STATE FLOWER

FORGET-ME-NOT

1
BEFORE ALASKA

I remember a lot of happy things from my first six years of life. I remember things about California, like long summer days swimming in the creek behind our house, the little crawdads that would gently pinch your toes, gathering wire baskets full of eggs from the long hen houses down by the creek, corn growing taller than the sky in the garden beside our house, long car rides at night and mountain lions in the woods to make you shiver with delightful fright, swimming in the American river and Dirdle bugs in the soft warm dirt, walking to church along a hot road, playing with my brothers in the shady backyard on a hot summer day, a snowman one strange, very cold winter . . .

But this story is not about California. It is a story about Alaska. About a time when everything seemed new and different in my life, when I was a young child, an adventure to a far-away land. An adventure to Alaska, before it became a state.

There were five people in our family; our dad, our mom, my oldest brother Jimmy and my little brother Jeff, just a year younger than me. Our dad was tall and had very curly hair. He worked in a slaughter house and meat market in California. They cut up meat to sell for customers that would come into the meat market. He wore a white shirt and a big white apron, which was awful dirty by the time he got home every night.

Our mom was short, though she seemed tall to me, with black hair. She stayed at home with my two brothers and me, and also took care of hundreds of chickens.

There were long, long chicken houses out behind our house, between our house and the creek. Our mom also made a giant garden, full of corn and tomatoes and watermelons. She would hoe the weeds and water the wonderful plants. I was always anxious for the watermelons to get ripe enough to eat.

All the chickens in the long chicken houses were hens and laid eggs. Our mom would gather up the eggs in large wire baskets. Then she would carry them to the house and wipe them off if they were dirty. She would sort them by size and then put each egg on a little stand with a light below it. She called that candling the eggs. She was looking for anything in the egg that would make it a bad egg and if she found a bad egg she would put it aside.

She also took out the very smallest eggs, as the stores didn't want small eggs. After the eggs were candled she would put them all back in the wire baskets and carry them out to the driveway in front of our house. Later a big truck would come to pick up the baskets of eggs to take someplace mysterious to us kids, where they were put in cartons and people could buy them at the stores.

We never had to buy eggs, as there were always enough small eggs to use for our cooking and eating. We kids were not allowed in the chicken houses very often, as our mom thought we might frighten the hens if we moved too quickly or spoke too loudly, and then the hens would fly up in fright and might break some of their eggs.

One day I got tired of sitting in the back yard, waiting for our mom to come back up to the house with the eggs, and I went looking for her. I wasn't sure which chicken house she was in, so I walked up and down, listening to see if I could hear where she was.

I finally heard the hens clucking a lot and figured our mom was nearby gathering eggs. The hens would squawk and carry on whenever their eggs were removed from their nests. I called to our mom, but she didn't hear me, so I jumped up a little bit and waved my hankie to catch her attention. I did catch her attention, and the attention of several hundred chickens, and then I really was in trouble.

The hens flew up in fright from seeing the hankie waving in the open spaces at the top of the chicken house walls and broke many of their eggs. Not only did our mom have to clean up the mess, but she had to account for all the broken eggs. I was in serious trouble that day, and I never went looking for her at the chicken house again. Instead I would wait under the big tree in the backyard until I saw her coming across the creek and then I would run down the dusty path to meet her.

In the spring of 1951 when I was 5, I remember being very sick while we were still in California. Our dad would carry me out to a big bed under a tree, where I would lie for hours, watching the birds hop in the bushes, listening to their twittery talk about their day, watching hawks flying in big circles over the school house that sat on a hill above our house, listening to see if anyone was coming to talk to me, napping most of the time. I would sleep a lot, and I couldn't walk to the bathroom or back in the house, I had to be carried everywhere. When I would wake up I would realize that I was outdoors in my bed, not the usual place for my bed. I would wake slowly, thinking of birds hopping on my bed, of flowers sifting down from the trees above me, of many wonderful things in that time between asleep and awake.

I remember being too sick to care that I couldn't go to the creek with my big brother Jimmy, or to the backyard to sit under the big shade tree and watch the rows and rows of chicken houses where our mom gathered huge black wire baskets full of eggs for the truck to pick up each afternoon. I would hear Jimmy and our little brother Jeff playing in the back yard, and wonder if they would come in the front yard so I could watch them, but I didn't care that I could not get up out of the bed.

After many weeks in bed, when I was feeling some better, I remember getting up and starting to walk again. I fell down and got up again, and again. I didn't cry, because crying was not allowed in our family; we must be brave. I would hold onto the side of the bed to steady myself, taking tiny steps at first, then bigger and bigger steps until I was walking again. After a very long time I was almost back to normal, happily running clumsily about in the yard, playing with my brothers, watching the garden grow in the warm California sun. I had learned to walk again and I was happy.

We would run through the soft, dry dirt, down to the creek and jump off the bank into the cold, refreshing water. We'd splash and swim about and sometimes Jimmy would climb up the bank and grab the rope that hung from a big tree. He would run a little ways while holding onto the rope and then would swing out over the creek and drop down into the water, splashing us all with the jump. I wished I was brave enough to do that, but I was too small and Jimmy wouldn't let me try anyway; he always protected me from danger.

Then one spring day our lives changed. Our mom told us that our dad was going to go to Alaska. She said he would be going first and we would go later. I didn't have any idea what or where Alaska was, but I knew that if I had to walk I'd never make it, and for many days and nights that worried me. I could run down to the creek, I could run up the hill to the schoolhouse, I could even walk down the road to Leona's house, with a couple times of resting on the way, but if it was farther than that, I wasn't sure I could do it.

I was afraid that I wouldn't be able to keep up with the others as we were walking to Alaska. My mind buzzed with ideas about what Alaska would be like, but I could only make up things in my head, as no one told me what Alaska was like. The farthest away I could remember going was to our Grandmother's house, in our car, and I liked going there, so perhaps I would like going to Alaska.

We had big dinners at Grandma's house, with bowls heaped full of food, cookies that almost spilled out of the cookie jar, and in the summer there were fresh fruits and vegetables to pick from the gardens. I decided that if that was what Alaska was like, then I would like Alaska, if I could just get there.

Our Grandma and Grandpa had a big house, a shed and a very big yard. In the yard they had an empty oil barrel with a saddle on it – and we loved to play horse riding on that barrel. Sometimes Jimmy would help me or Jeff up on the saddle and he would climb on and we'd ride double. Once in a while all three of us would get on the barrel with the saddle, but it was very crowded and pinched our legs if all three were on there. When our cousins would come on the same day that we were there, we would take turns playing on the saddle.

There was a big porch swing to sit in and a tire swing on one side of the yard. There were grapes in the backyard and we could pick some if we were very careful – and we were always very careful. Grapes fresh from the vine, and warmed in the sun were the best grapes I'd ever eaten.

There were also flowers growing in Grandma's yard, tall hollyhocks and sweet peas and zinnias. I loved the hollyhocks the best and we would sometimes pick a few of the blossoms and make hollyhock dolls to play with. In the warm California sun the hollyhock dolls didn't last long and we would lay them under the sweet peas to rest while we ran off and played with something else fun at our Grandma and Grandpa's house.

Soon I had something else to think about: we all got the mumps - my older and younger brother, and me. We all stayed in our beds, with the curtains drawn, sipping very carefully from a glass of juice or water, and sleeping long days and nights.

At about the time we were puffy and sore with the mumps our dad began making his plans to leave for Alaska, but at this point I didn't think about it much - I was too busy feeling funny and achy when I swallowed, and feeling a certain delight in pushing on my puffy face to see if the swelling was going down. I had never seen such a thing before - a face that you could push on and leave a dent, so it entertained me quite a bit. By now I could stand a lot of pain and didn't seem to mind the sore face as much as my two brothers did.

After days of planning and checking supplies, our dad packed up his bags and was ready to leave for Alaska. He hugged us all goodbye. He left with a big brown suitcase and a duffel bag (which I thought was called a "double" bag) and waved to us three puffy kids and our mom as he drove up the hill and out of sight in our only car.

I was now positive that we would be walking to Alaska, since he had taken our car with him. Earlier, one late night I heard him tell our mom he would sell the car before he got to Alaska. I hoped someone would bring their car to take us to Alaska, but I thought that if the others were walking I'd try hard to walk too, although I had no idea how far it was to our Grandma's house, and certainly no idea how far to Alaska. I knew I could not walk to Grandma's house without help – and I hoped we weren't really walking to Alaska, but I could think of no other way to get there, since our dad had taken our car and was going to sell it, and even if he had left it with us, our mother did not know how to drive a car.

After our dad left for Alaska we began to get ready for our part of the trip to Alaska. It took a long time, selling furniture and packing our things into small suitcases. We three children each had one suitcase and our mom had two, and we could only take what would fit into our suitcases. She told us we must be brave and strong, and we had to be able to carry our own suitcase or she would take things out of it to make them light enough.

I wanted to take my doll, Bunny, in my suitcase, but I knew that if I couldn't carry the suitcase our mom would leave Bunny behind when the suitcase became too heavy for me. Bunny was almost 2 feet tall, and would take up most of the space in a suitcase that a six year old child could carry. So I told Bunny I would leave her in California and told her that someday I would come back for her when I was bigger and stronger and braver. Most nights I cried myself to sleep, thinking about leaving Bunny behind, though I never let anyone hear me, for we were supposed to be brave in our family.

Before we left for Alaska were each allowed to choose a few things to leave at our Grandma's house, and the only thing I picked was my dear doll, Bunny; she was the only thing I owned. Our grandma had made

Bunny and given her to me on my sixth birthday, just that year. Bunny had long brown braids, embroidered eyes, nose and mouth, and pretty ears and even separate little fingers, made lovingly by our Grandma.

My cousin Cookie turned seven just five days after my sixth birthday, and we always had a shared birthday at Grandma's house. That year we had been given our choice of one of all the rag dolls in the big baby crib at Grandma's house. Cookie (later we used her grown-up name of Linda, but she has always remained Cookie in my heart) picked a doll with blond braids and blue eyes, I chose Bunny, with brown hair like me, and blue eyes. We all went out into the yard and lined up for pictures. My two brothers and Cookie's younger sister were there, and our Grandma took a photo that day of both of us with our new dolls.

At our birthday party each year our Grandma would make us a shared cake. She cut a round layer cake in half and turned the halves so the rounded sides touched, forming a butterfly. Half the cake was for Cookie's birthday and half was for mine. Grandma would decorate the cake with colored frosting and candies on the butterflies wings - a happy memory of early birthdays with our Grandma. I loved sharing a cake with my cousin – it made the day even more special.

So I was happy that Bunny was going back to Grandma's house to stay while we went away. I knew Grandma would take good care of her for me. It was hard to leave her for the last time, but Grandma said she would let Bunny sit in the crib with all the other rag dolls that she had made, and that made me feel better. At least Bunny wouldn't be as lonely as I was.

I don't remember what else the others chose to leave at Grandma's house, except for our large dining room table, chairs and buffet. There must have been other things that were left but none that I can remember, except maybe Jimmy's big bike. He was several years older than me and had a bike called an English racer. It had skinny tires and was very tall. Too tall for a little girl like me, but just the right size for a big boy like my brother Jimmy.

One day at our house in California Jimmy had been riding his big bike very fast down the hill to our house. He went a little too fast and couldn't make a turn where the road curved to the left and he rode right through a barbed wire fence. He scratched his face and arms and legs and his bike was bent very badly. He got some tools and fixed his bike, and soon his scratches were all gone. He rode his bike up and down the long hill many other times without going into fences after that.

The last day before leaving for Alaska our mom went through the house, checking each space to make sure we had left nothing, and checking to see that all was clean. We walked through the empty house, making sure there was no dust anywhere and closing the doors behind us as we finished inspecting each room. It looked very strange to not see our chairs and tables and beds in the house any more. Someone had come with a big truck earlier in the day and had loaded everything up on top of the truck. I watched as each piece of furniture went up on the truck. I wondered where it was all going, but I didn't ask questions. I didn't like to see our things going up the hill in that truck so I ran into the back yard and sat under the big tree until I couldn't hear the truck anymore. I didn't know where the truck was going, but I knew not to ask questions at a busy time.

2
NORTH TO ALASKA

At last all the work was done and we set out for Alaska. Our mom and her friend Leona made some sandwiches, wrapped them in waxed paper and put them in a shoebox with some apples and a cookie for each of us. I was very happy when Leona drove us to the bus station. Leona's kids, Wayne and Susan, rode with us. We got on a big bus and pushed our suitcases into the space below the big seats and Jimmy held the shoebox with our lunch. I knew then that we wouldn't be walking to Alaska, and I was quite happy about that, as my legs were tired that day and I didn't want to walk.

As the bus left the station we could see Wayne and Susan and Leona standing there waving to us, getting smaller and smaller as we drove away. I watched until the bus turned the corner and I could no longer see them. We rode for a long way on the bus, but even after a day of riding we weren't in Alaska.

My brothers and I ate our sandwiches that our mom had brought for us, and we got a drink of water from a jug of water that she carried, and we ate our apple and cookie. I wasn't really hungry enough for a whole apple so I gave the rest to Jimmy and he ate it all. Then we covered up with our little blankets from our suitcases and went to sleep. The bus went on and on, until the next morning when it was light again and we got off the bus. We all took our suitcases with us and walked down the street to the train station. I was concerned that we needed to take our shoebox with us, but our mom said it was empty and we wouldn't need it anymore. I wondered how we would get enough food for the rest of our trip.

At first, after we got off the bus, I thought we were going to have to walk the rest of the way to Alaska, and my legs still would get very tired if I walked a long way, and I didn't know how far it was to Alaska. Our mom didn't tell us where we were going after we got off the bus, she just told us to come with her. I was happy when we came to a train station and climbed up on a train and found four seats together.

Two of the seats faced toward the front of the train, and two toward the back. We sat down and a man in a suit and a fancy hat with a shiny badge on the front of his hat, came along and took our suitcases and put them in a rack above our heads. Before he put them up, we got our blankets out of our suitcases. He told us that the train had pillows if we would like one, and I did want a little pillow.

The train bounced along and swayed back and forth like a boat, and I was just happy that we wouldn't be walking after all. Jimmy wanted to sit by a window, so our mom let him sit there and I sat next to him, and we took turns sitting by our window. I loved to watch all the houses and trees go swooshing past as the train traveled along. When I wasn't looking out the window I would lie down on the seat with the little pillow and my blanket and rest. The rocking train made it feel like I was in the hammock at Leona's house - back and forth - back and forth. Jimmy didn't like to lie down because he said he got sea sick. I didn't know how he could be sea sick if we were on the train, but I believed him and tried to imagine the train being on the ocean.

We ate sandwiches for breakfast that day, ones that our mom had bought from a man at the train station. I didn't like mine; I wanted an egg and toast for breakfast! But it was what there was to eat, so I ate some of it. Jimmy liked the sandwiches, and was still hungry after he ate his, so I gave him the last half of mine to eat while I looked out the window at the houses and trees. Jimmy munched the sandwich and said it was the best sandwich he had ever had; I think he was just really hungry, because I liked the sandwiches our mom made much better. There were no apples and no cookies this time – just sandwiches, and a drink of water from a paper cup at the back of the train car.

We had to wait our turn to get the water. We would take a small paper cup from a cup holder and put it under the little faucet and fill our cup with water. I had never seen this before and loved to fill the cups. Jimmy let me fill his cup. Jeff tried to fill his cup but he spilled some water and Jimmy helped him wipe it up with a paper towel. Jimmy always helped when he could.

Before we would get to Alaska our mom said we would stop and see our relatives. First we went to see Cookie and Aunt Maxene and Uncle Jay, and Cookie's little sister Cathy. I adored Cookie, for you see, she had big red hair, all curly and puffy and soft, and I thought if you had red hair that surely you could be as brave as you needed to be. She was almost a year older than I was and knew many interesting things, like how to ride a horse, and how to play jump rope. Most of that visit was spent playing in the back yard with our wonderful cousins. They had some plastic horses that we would play with in the grass and dirt of the back yard, making the horses fly and swim and dance - they were magical horses. We would play paper dolls and some board games until it was time to go indoors for dinner.

One afternoon Cookie and I went to town with our moms, and at one stop we got ice cream cones, Aunt Maxene's idea. I licked and slurped mine up, it was so cold and sweet and delicious, but Cookie ate hers slowly, just barely keeping the drips from running down the cone. She carried it carefully in the back seat of the car, holding a napkin under it so it wouldn't drip on the car.

She said that she had to save part of it for Cathy, who had been napping when we left and would be sad if she didn't get a taste of ice cream. I thought that was the most wonderful thing for a sister to do, and always after that, wished I had a sister too. I thought it would be great to be the big sister to a little sister, though I was already a big sister to Jeff. And Jimmy was a wonderful big brother, though he didn't like to play dolls and tea party very often, so a younger sister would have been the best thing, I thought. Jimmy was very protective of me and I was glad that I had a big brother to watch out for me. And Cathy loved her ice cream cone.

We stayed a few days with the cousins and had a good time. Once, while we were at our cousins' house, we visited a lady who was a friend of theirs. She was tall and had a lot of gray hair that she twisted up into a tight bunch on the top of her head. I thought it looked like a hat. She made big pots of coffee all throughout the day and when the coffee was done she took the coffee grounds outside and poured them on the dirt under a huge tree. I don't remember her name, but she called my brother "Jiminy" and that made me giggle. Jimmy liked to be called Jiminy too. Sometimes I would call him that, but not where our mom could hear, as she would make us use his real name. Not his James Melvin, Jr. name, but his Jimmy name. I liked *Jiminy* best.

The lady told me that the secret of making the tree so tall was that it loved coffee, and so she gave it some every day. I thought it was pretty smart of her to know what that tree liked, but didn't know how the tree had told her! For a little while that afternoon I sat under the tree, hoping it would tell me something. But I listened so hard that soon I was fast asleep - and if the tree said anything, I missed it. But it gave me a very good nap, snuggled up against one of its big roots, with the leaves for a roof, and birds hopping in the branches.

Soon it was time to say good bye to our cousins and we got back on the train. Again we had a shoebox packed with sandwiches that Aunt Maxene and our mom had made, wrapped in waxed paper. And there was a special treat, small pieces of apple pie, also wrapped up in waxed paper. Later in the day I could hardly wait to finish my sandwich so I could have some apple pie, but by the time I had eaten the sandwich I was barely hungry for apple pie, so like a good big brother, Jimmy finished the pie for me. He liked to help that way.

The train took us to Las Vegas to see Aunt Herma (our mom's sister) and Uncle Kenny , and our cousin Mike, who was just a little younger than Jimmy. He didn't have any brothers or sisters. They lived in a very long house, with more rooms than I had ever seen. There was soft green grass growing in their front yard, but all the land around the outside of the neighborhood was dry and brown. There were no trees, and almost no plants. I had never seen such a place before. It was very hot in the daytime, so we played in the shade. Aunt Herma told us that they lived in the desert, where it hardly ever rained and got very hot in the summer. I could tell the hot part was true.

When we went into their house I was surprised to see that they had a huge branch hanging on their living room wall, I had never seen a branch in a house, It was shiny and red and smooth and Aunt Herma told me it was a manzanita branch. It didn't have any regular leaves, but was pretty to look at because it was shiny, dark red, and someone had attached gold leaves to it in places along the branch.

At night all of us kids slept together on the floor in the living room with Aunt Herma and she had to keep telling me not to wiggle so much, but I had never slept on a floor before, nor in a room with a big branch on the wall, and I wanted to look around. Finally sleep, and I suppose Aunt Herma was glad that she didn't always have to sleep on the floor with a bunch of wiggly kids!

In the mornings Aunt Herma and our mom would fix breakfast for all of us. One day we had fried eggs and Uncle Kenny did the most astonishing thing - he put ketchup on his eggs. He said it was delicious and so I tried it, but I found that I liked my eggs without ketchup, and with toast dipped in the soft yellow yolk. For lunch we had hot dogs with sauerkraut - and it was sour! I had never tasted it before and decided that I would eat my hotdog plain.

We spent several days there, instead of going on to Alaska as planned, because our dad was very ill with the mumps that he had caught from us kids just before leaving for Alaska. He wouldn't be able to meet us at the planned time, so we had to wait awhile before leaving for Alaska.

While we were visiting our cousin Mike, we played games during the day, from a box full of board games, and I wanted to learn how to play all of them. There were dice and little people for the games, as well as paper money and some cups to shake the dice in. Our cousin Mike, though a little older than me, was nice and always let me tag along whenever he went someplace and played games with me whenever I asked.

Sometimes we would go across the street and play with a girl named Holly Berry and I thought it must be delightful to have such a pretty name, especially at Christmas time. She had a fancy bedroom with fluffy pink curtains and pretty soft pillows on her pink bed. I had never seen such a pretty bedroom and loved to just sit on the soft rug on her floor and look at everything. I hoped that in Alaska I would have a pretty pink room like that.

Finally it was time to move on, so our mom bought more train tickets and we rode on the train to Oregon. I wasn't sure what Oregon was, or how far away it was from Alaska, but I did like riding on the train and eating sandwiches some days. Aunt Herma had stopped at a small restaurant and gotten sandwiches and cookies for all of us to eat for our lunch that day. They were packed in a pretty pink box. I thought we were going to go right to Alaska on the train, but we had one more stop to make. And sandwiches in the pink box to eat.

When we still lived in California, before we left for Alaska, we would eat sandwiches at a restaurant in a town called Placerville. Every Thursday our mom and Leona went on a shopping trip to town and all of us kids would pile in the back of Leona's big black car for the trip. Five kids in the back seat was a little bit crowded, but we didn't care, we were going to town and we knew that after our moms were done shopping we got to go to Bob's Restaurant and have lunch.

I would always get a tuna sandwich with potato chips and a chocolate milkshake. Jimmy would get a hot dog and potato chips and a chocolate milkshake, and some days we would share the milkshake. Jeff always got just a peanut butter and jelly sandwich and Wayne and Susan got toasted cheese sandwiches with potato chips and a strawberry milkshake. I was the slowest eater and they always had to wait for me to finish.

The tables had little jukeboxes on them, you could put a nickel in one and play a song, and Leona would always play the song, *Slow Poke*, while I finished up my sandwich. Then we would pile back in the car for the ride down the mountain to our homes and the next thing we knew, or moms were waking us up to go inside. Leona would drop us off at our house, where Jimmy and Wayne helped to carry the groceries into the house, then Leona and her kids would drive up the driveway to go home and our mom would start fixing dinner.

For dinner on the train on the way to Oregon our mom bought sandwiches from a man who stood outside the train with a tray of sandwiches. Our mom stepped off the train and picked out sandwiches for us to eat. The sandwiches we got on this train tasted much better than the sandwiches on the last train. There wasn't much to do on the train except eat our sandwiches and watch the scenery out the window. Sometimes another passenger would walk past and talk to our mother, but they never talked to us kids, just patted us on the head. Jeff liked this, but Jimmy and I thought we were too old for patting on the head.

We got off the train in Oregon, after a long trip from Las Vegas, and our Uncle Carl was there to meet us. He was our mom's big brother. He had a very large black car and took us to their house, where our Aunt Wilma was fixing a big dinner of fried chicken and mashed potatoes and biscuits. We all ate a plate full of the good food, and it sure tasted better than the sandwiches had. For dessert Aunt Wilma had made a big chocolate cake and Jimmy and I got to share a piece. He would take a bite, then I would take a bite. We each ate from the opposite sides of the cake until we got to the middle frosting. I let Jimmy eat all the frosting from the middle because he had been outdoors helping Uncle Carl with some chores, and I thought he deserved extra frosting – and I didn't really like frosting anyway.

Again we stayed for many days, waiting for our dad to get well. Our aunt and uncle didn't have any kids, but Aunt Wilma did have a wonderful doll from when she was a little girl. She went to the attic and brought down her doll, with its trunk full of lovely hand stitched clothes. She told me about her mother and grandmother making the doll clothes when she was a little girl. She said she would sit on the floor as they stitched and wait for each new piece of clothes to be finished.

I was allowed to take the doll and her trunk out on the big front porch and play with it. The porch was at the top of many, many steps and I sat on the porch with my feet on the first step. The doll had blond curls and tiny little shoes that buckled and unbuckled. I took all the clothes out and looked at each one - the little dresses with ribbons and bows, the sweaters that Aunt Wilma's grandmother had knit for the doll, and warm flannel pajamas.

There was even a red coat and hat for when it was winter. I would sit on the wide porch and play with the doll and her wardrobe for hours. I would make up stories to go with the different outfits. I whispered messages to her to give to my doll Bunny if she ever did meet her, and was very sad when Aunt Wilma said she had to put the doll back into her trunk and back into the attic when we left. I was sure that if she was left out she could have gone and found Bunny for me, and told her how much I missed her.

3
ALASKA AT LAST

After Oregon I don't remember any more relatives, just another bus trip! And then we came to a place with lots of airplanes. I had never seen an airplane up close before; I had only seen them in the sky, and they were much bigger than I had imagined. Jimmy told me that these were small planes, but they seemed very big to me. We climbed up the little stairs to the airplane and sat down in seats. Jeff and our mom sat in two seats next to each other, and Jimmy and I sat across from them in two more seats next to each other.

Jimmy sat by a little window, and could look out. I was too short to see out the window, but later Jimmy let me crawl up on his lap and kneel on his legs so I could see out. He told me that we were high in the air, and down below us we could see tiny roads and little houses, and sometimes a very small river. Jimmy would patiently answer all my questions and he never told me that they were silly questions.

We flew for a long time, though not as long as the time on the train, and landed at a smaller airport with smaller planes sitting about. I asked Jimmy if the planes got any smaller and he said some planes are so small that only one person could fit in them – I didn't believe him.

We climbed down from the big airplane and carried our suitcases to a plane with funny things hanging down from the wings. Jimmy told me that those were pontoons and they were for landing in the water. I wasn't sure I liked that idea, and I didn't really know how much water we would be landing in. We sat on a long bench in that plane, next to each other in a row and the plane roared up into the sky. This plane did not go as high as the first one and we got a better look at things, though mostly we saw trees and water. One time Jimmy said he saw a bear and tried to help me see it, but I guess I didn't know exactly where to look. Jeff wanted to see the bear too - but we never did, only Jimmy.

We landed in a town called Juneau in the small plane, on the water. It hadn't been as scary as I thought it was going to be, to land on the water, though the water did splash up over the windows at first, but Jimmy held my hand so I wouldn't be too frightened. Jeff climbed up on our mom's lap because he was afraid of the noise from the plane and the water. The plane floated along in the water for a little ways and came up to a float by the dock and we all climbed carefully out and walked into the small office building.

There were people all around in the Juneau airport. I remember one lady asking for a plane to Hoonah, but I thought she said "tuna," and I could not figure out how you could get a fish by being in a plane! We had flown much too high and too fast to catch any fish, even in the second smaller, slower plane. I had seen our grandpa catch fish in the lake in his little boat in California and I knew that you had to be close to the water to catch a fish.

Most of the planes in Juneau were much smaller even than the one that we had come in, and they floated on the water. They looked sort of like water bugs that could skate along on the top of the water. I was beginning to believe Jimmy that the planes would keep getting smaller and smaller and I wondered where we would all sit if we had to ride in smaller and smaller planes before we finally got to where our dad was.

I hoped that we wouldn't fall into the water when we tried to get on those small planes. We had been on land when we got in the first airplane, and even though the second plane had landed in the water in Juneau, it seemed much safer because it was bigger. The pontoons on the smaller planes were at the bottom of the plane, instead of hanging from the wings like on the plane we had just flown in. The pontoons were like stilts for the plane to stand on the water.

We climbed onto the pontoons of the smaller plane, and had to balance carefully because the plane tipped a little bit. We climbed on one at a time and went up a tiny ladder. There was just enough room for the four of us and the pilot who flew the plane. He picked Jeff and me up and put us right inside his plane as we stood at the top of the tiny ladder, and told us to sit on the little seat in the back. He had put our suitcases behind the seat, and under, where our feet went, he had put some wooden boxes full of "supplies."

Jimmy had read the words to me when the boxes were being loaded into the plane. I didn't know what supplies were and I wanted to peek in the boxes, but they were nailed shut, so we just put our feet on them and waited. Then Jimmy climbed in and sat on one of the boxes and our mom sat in the front seat, next to the man.

We had gotten our coats and hats out of our suitcases because it was very cold in Alaska. We had been used to running around in our sun suits in the sunshine in California and weren't used to rainy and windy weather. It felt good to have our coats on and I had, instead of a hat, a nice scarf with flowers on it to tie under my chin. Jimmy and Jeff had knit hats that our Aunt Norma had made for them before we left California.

The pilot started the plane – it sounded a little like a lawn mower to me. The propeller was on the front of the plane right in front of the pilot and it whirred faster and faster. Some men on the float untied the rope from the pontoon of the plane and pushed on the plane with their foot to get us out away from the float. We drifted a little ways and then the pilot revved up the engine and it pushed us along on the water until we were out in the bay, away from the buildings and boats.

We bumped along on the water for a little bit, then the plane starting going faster and faster, and got louder and louder, and suddenly we bounced one last time and were flying high into the air! It was quite different from riding in the other planes. Sometimes we were just above the water and it seemed we could reach down and touch it – if the windows opened. Sometimes we would be just over the tops of the trees and then the pilot would dip down and be close to the water again. He would point out things for us to look at – big trees, lakes, rivers and once he showed us some whales swimming in the water. Even though most of the whales' bodies were below the water we could see them very clearly.

We were on our way to Angoon, where our dad had been staying with friends until he was well. Our dad had bought a fishing boat when he first came to Alaska, and it would be our home for a few months. He hadn't been able to go fishing yet though, because he had been sick for a very long time.

The tiny plane landed with a splash on the water and the pilot moved it up to a floating dock, which was at the end of a very long, wooden walkway leading up to a house on the edge of the beach. Several people were on the float and someone hooked a rope onto the pontoon of the plane and tied it tightly to the float so the plane wouldn't drift away. We could see our dad standing on the dock and Jeff was waving to him. They opened the door and cold air rushed in, making us shiver. I could smell a strange smell and asked Jimmy about it – he said it was the smell of the ocean and the beach – I liked the smell.

First the pilot climbed down out of the plane, then our mom and Jimmy. Jeff and I were afraid to climb down the ladder so the pilot reached up, got us out of the plane and put us on the float, which was tipping a little from all the people walking about. Our dad was there and some of his friends and it seemed everyone was talking all at once.

After we all got out of the small plane, all of the supplies and our suitcases were unloaded out of the plane and stacked on the float. The pilot did not stay long, he said he had other trips to make and wanted to be back to town before night, as the small planes don't usually fly after dark. We watched as he floated the plane out to the middle of the bay and then took off. I was surprised at how fast he got the plane way up in the air. I stood waving to him as he flew off.

Everything that had come in the plane was carried up the long walkway - most of it went to the house at the end of the wooden walkway and some of it was put in a shed to be taken to a store. I didn't see a store nearby so someone must have been coming to pick up the supplies for the store. I also didn't see any roads so I wondered just how they would come.

We started off down a long path to the boat our dad had bought. The boat he bought was named *Mikey*, and it was a small boat, but it felt very big to me, compared to the small boat our grandpa had in California. Our dad's fishing boat was only 20 feet long and about 8 feet wide, with a cabin and quarters below, which is what the downstairs is called in a boat, and we surely were crowded. The quarters were for sleeping and eating, and for us to sit in during the day if we couldn't be on deck.

We put our suitcases below – our dad said that we "stowed" them, which is boat talk for putting things away. We inspected all the different things in the boat – amazed at the small stove and the little round windows, which were called portholes. It seemed like we would be living in a dollhouse. After living in sunny, warm California on an egg ranch with lots of garden space and a big river nearby to swim in, it was a big change to move into a small fishing boat, and it was even colder on the boat than it had been in the plane.

We never wore life jackets while on the boat, but we also wouldn't dare to go near the edge of the boat. Our mother was very strict, and if she told us to stay below, or to sit down quietly, we didn't think to do otherwise.

Meals were cooked on a small black stove on the *Mikey*. It looked like a wood cook stove but used fuel oil that was stored in a small tank on the boat. There was a little gauge in the pipe for the fuel oil and we could see how much was left. Every morning I would look at the gauge to see how much there was. Our mom cooked all the same kinds of food on the boat as we had eaten in California, except that we never had chicken to eat, and we now began to eat fish. I liked the fish a lot. She kept the stove very clean and shiny by scrubbing it with a big gray brick every day. Then she would rub a wet rag over the top of the stove to make sure it was as clean as could be.

To cook, she would take a little round lid off the top of the stove, and place the pots or skillet over the hole where the lid had been, right over the flame. She had a little handle that fit into the stove lids and lifted them off. The handle hung on a hook beside the stove, and it would swing back and forth when the waves got big. The bottom of the stove lids were all black and sooty from the fire inside the stove, and as she lifted them out, she placed them carefully in a rack under the stove to keep the soot from getting all over the boat. When she finished cooking she would put the little lids back on the stove and sometimes, before she got the lids back on, I could see the fire down inside the stove. The stove had a little metal fence around the top edge of the cooking surface, so when there was a storm and the *Mikey* bounced up and down, nothing could slide off it because it was stopped by the little fence.

There was a very clever little table that our mom folded down from the wall when we ate, and folded back up against the wall when we were finished so there would be more room in the small cabin of the boat. The table had a wooden leg in the center of the outer edge that swung down from under the table. We would prop the leg against a small peg that we put in a hole in the floor, to keep the leg from sliding out from under the table while we were eating. If we forgot to put the peg in the floor the table leg might collapse, and then everything on the table would fall to the floor of the boat. This didn't happen when we were on the boat but our mom warned us to be very careful about always putting the peg in the hole, and we were.

There were no chairs to put up to the table and there wouldn't have been room for them anyway. Our mom would put the food on the table and then fill our plates and we would sit on the floor by the bunks to eat - or if it was nice weather we might be allowed to sit out on the deck and eat. Jeff didn't like to eat on the deck so he would stay below and eat with our mother.

Everything in a boat has to be fastened down and closed tight when the boat is out on the ocean, or things might fly around in rough weather. The cupboard for the dishes had latches on them that were so strong I couldn't open them. The latches twisted open and shut and my fingers weren't strong enough. Cups hung on hooks in the cupboard, and clanked together when the boat rocked in heavy storms.

Everything else was kept in drawers with strong hooks on them, and each day before we got under way all the dishes and pots were put back in their cupboards or drawers and each was checked to make sure it was tight. This was often Jimmy's job because he was big enough to reach the cupboards and strong enough to work the latches.

I would hand him cups and plates to put in the cupboards, and then the silverware, which slid into the drawers. He would close each cupboard and drawer very tight, then he would turn to me and ask "Is everything done?" I would look at each latch and tell him, "Yes sir, it is all done!" Then he would salute and say, "Full speed ahead, captain!" which made us both laugh. Jeff didn't help with the chores on the boat.

We kept our little suitcases near the bunks, which is what you call beds in a boat, and opened them only to take out a fresh change of clothes. Things had to be kept very neat in such a small space or we would not have been able to find anything. The boat was so small that we could lie in our bunks and reach our arms out and touch the other side of the cabin, or a brother if he happened to be in the way.

We put our dirty clothes in a small box that our mom kept under one of the bunks. We couldn't change our shirt and pants every day because we would run out of clean clothes too fast, so we were very careful not to get our clothes too dirty. When the wooden box was full of dirty clothes, our mom would wash them in a big gray metal tub on the back of our boat.

Our dad would go ashore in the little skiff that was tied on behind the *Mikey*. A skiff is a small rowboat that is tied to the back of a boat and is there for emergencies and for rowing ashore. If there is an emergency and you have to leave the boat you can climb down into the skiff and row away. Some boats would carry their skiffs up on top of their booms, but most let them follow along behind. If the weather gets rough the skiff is pulled up out of the water and kept on the boat so it won't get broken from banging against the boat in the waves.

Our dad put a large metal barrel in the skiff, and he and Jimmy would row to the shore where they knew there was a river coming down onto the beach. They would find a deep place along the river edge and begin to dip water up with buckets, and carry the full buckets to the barrel in the skiff. They always went when the tide was going out, so the ocean water would not mix with the fresh water from the creek. It might take them an hour to fill the barrel, especially if they had to carry the buckets of water very far.

Then they would row back to the *Mikey*, and Jimmy would dip buckets of water out of the barrel and hand them up to our mom. She would carry them to the stove on the boat and heat the water for washing clothes. Then she would carry the pails of hot water to the gray metal tub, sitting on the back of the boat.

When the big gray tub on the back of the boat was full of hot water, our mom would slice some soap from a bar into the water to melt, and stir the water around to make suds. In would go the light-colored clothes, and sometimes I got to push them under the water with a wooden stick. Our mom had a washboard that had a wrinkled metal surface for scrubbing, and she would put soap on the wet clothes and scrub them on the washboard until they were clean.

Into another tub they would go for rinsing, and Jimmy would hand up more buckets of cold water for that. Slosh, slosh, slosh went the clothes in the rinse water. I would poke and poke at the clothes with my wooden stick to get all the soap out, and then our mom would wring most of the water out and put them over some clotheslines that our dad had strung up on the deck of the *Mikey*.

Sometimes we had to watch for wind, because it could blow the clothes right overboard into the ocean! When that happened, Jimmy would go after them in the skiff, and they would have to be rinsed and hung up to dry again. It made me laugh when Jimmy would chase the clothes about in the water - he used a long pole to dip them up out of the ocean to put them in the skiff.

It took most of the morning to get the water and wash the clothes. When our mom was finished, she would bake a chocolate cake, and we would sit on the bunks or if it was nice out, on the deck, and eat chocolate cake for dinner. That was my favorite dinner in the world, a big slab of chocolate cake. If Jimmy was still hungry I would pick the frosting off my cake and let him eat all the frosting. He always did.

We didn't have toys on the boat, and there wasn't even enough room for books, and our mom didn't like us to have books, so we entertained ourselves by softly singing songs, or making up silly riddles.

One day Jeff asked Jimmy to get him some bread and butter out of the cupboard. Jeff spread the butter on two slices of bread and went up to the wheel house and asked our dad to bend down. When he did, Jeff slapped the slices of bread on our dad's ears and said, "What did I give you?" Our dad looked surprised and asked what it was, and Jeff said, "an earwich!" Our dad laughed and then he and Jeff went out on the deck and tossed the bread to the seagulls. It was rare to hear our dad laugh, and even rarer that he would go out on the deck with one of us kids if it wasn't for fishing activities.

In rough weather we needed to stay below deck so we didn't fall over the side, but on calm days we went up on deck to see the scenery. Our dad taught us the names of the birds, fish and animals that we saw. Sometimes we would see brown bears walking along the beach, and he told us stories of how the bears slept all winter long. I thought they did that because their moms were extra strict and made them stay in bed! I couldn't imagine sleeping all winter long. The bears would sometimes jump and splash in the water. This looked like a lot of fun, because I remembered swimming in the warm river in California, but this was ocean water, and I soon found out that the water tasted salty and was very, very cold!

Once or twice we saw a bear in a creek catch a fish, but usually the *Mikey* was too far from the shore to see it well. We had a pair of binoculars, and if we were very careful with them, and kept the strap on our neck, we could use them to look at things. It was fun to see things up close, and the binoculars became my favorite toy. When we had to be below I would look through the wrong end of the binoculars to make things seem far, far away. It made the inside of the boat seem much bigger if you looked through the wrong end of the binoculars - and a pesky little brother seemed farther away too.

Seagulls would follow the *Mikey* when our dad was fishing, because they liked to get the parts of the fish he threw overboard after he cleaned them. Jimmy was usually in charge of cleaning the fish, and he would toss the fish guts high in the air so we could watch the gulls fly up and catch them before they hit the water. The seagulls would fight and squawk and beat against each other with their wings to get the most. They would eat just about anything that you would throw to them, and we were sometimes allowed to throw scraps from food overboard, so there was often a big flock of seagulls around our boat.

On good fishing days the flock would be so big and loud that it would cause other fishermen to come near our boat to fish, to see if they could catch as many fish as our dad was. On those days our dad would tell Jimmy not to clean the fish until later, so others would not see how good the fishing was and wouldn't follow us. And sometimes when he wasn't catching a lot of fish he would have us throw food to the seagulls, then the other boats would follow us until we stopped throwing food, and our dad was slip away to another spot where he would find fish, and the others were still trying to catch fish in the first spot.

We saw other things besides fish; one time, along the shore, we saw a herd of about twenty deer. Our dad said that when you ate deer meat it is was called venison, and that it was very tasty. He told Jimmy he would take him deer hunting after we got settled in a house. We were very excited to think about having a house again. The boat was fun but there was no room for running around.

4
A NEW HOME

Our dad fished for salmon and halibut during the spring and summer, but not in the winter. After a few months of living on the *Mikey*, when fishing season was over, we moved into an empty store building at Kalinin Bay, which was a fishing village that was empty during the winter months.

The house was a very big building, and seemed even bigger after the cramped spaces of the *Mikey*. We lived upstairs, and the empty store downstairs was our play room, as well as laundry room for drying clothes in the winter. There had one time been a big store in the building, but nothing at all from the store was left except the shelves and a big counter, and a big brown stove for heat. Our dad was paid to be the watchman of the area, I suppose making sure that there were no robbers, but as we saw almost no one else the entire winter I don't think there was much chance of that, and Kalinin Bay was a long way from any other town.

There were no stores in Kalinin Bay so we had to bring all our food with us, as well as blankets, cooking pots, dishes (all from the boat) and our school books. There were no other people at Kalinin Bay, and no school, but we still needed to go to school. Our mom had written to Calvert Correspondence School in Pennsylvania. They sent us schoolbooks to use, and we had lessons at home all winter long, just as if we were in a regular school. Our mom was the teacher and would give us lessons. We would sit in the downstairs storeroom, in front of the big oil burning heater, and read and write.   I learned to read and write that year. I was in second grade. and was so impressed that when I made marks they made sense. I used to make books for my dolls when we still lived in California. When I would make a book for them to read I would just make marks of any sort and pretend they were writing, although I knew how to write the word LOOK, with eyes where the Os were, so my doll's books were full of the word LOOK, along with my other scribblings.

Now I could really write, and I used every spare scrap of paper I could find to practice writing. There wasn't much extra paper around so I would sometimes use the labels off the cans of food, turn them over, and write on the back. I had to wait until the cans were empty, of course. There were bits of glue on some of the labels and I had to cut that part off because the pencil wouldn't write over the glue. I tried to cut very carefully so I would waste as little paper as possible. I would fill the labels as fast as I could get them, so I never had any extra paper sitting about. We had to send our school papers back to Pennsylvania to be graded, so I couldn't write on the back of them.

I made lists of everything. Lists of the animals we saw, lists of food in our storage space, lists of people I knew, or hoped to meet one day (I just put down every name I knew, hoping that I would meet a person with each name, sometime in my life). I kept that list for a long time and marked off the names of all I would meet, adding the names of people I would meet whose names were not on my list. I started with simple names, like Mary and John and Sally, and of course all the names in my family, Neal (grandpa) Harriet Hazel (grandma, she had two names so I listed her twice) James, June, Jimmy, Jeff and me of course – and cousins Linda, Cathy, John Paul, Sidney, Barbara, Sally, Thomas, and April Sue and my granny, Ina. And friends, Carl, Peg, Hunter, Christine, Victoria, Paul, Gerry, Cracker, Tom, Kyra, Harry; the lists went on and on. I would fill as much paper as I could with my lists.

I made lists of flowers, lists of fish, lists of dishes, trees, birds, animals and toys. I adored writing. Many times I would have to ask Jimmy to spell words for me. I would fold the larger scraps of paper into tiny booklets and make up stories so that my doll Bunny could read them when I got her back someday. Some of the books had titles: "The Quick Little Fish", "Rowing The Boat to China" and "Ravens Have a Party". I kept the booklets in a small wooden box that I kept under my bed, being careful to not leave them lying about or our mother would have thrown them in the stove and burnt them up. She didn't like anything out of place, so I was very careful with my lists and booklets.

I remember some winter mornings in Kalinin Bay waking up to find ice on the windows and in the glass of water on the little table at the end of the room. We would jump up and dress quickly so we could get out to the warm stove in the other room. Our bedroom door was always kept shut, and there was no dressing in front of the stove for us. We had to be brave. I would wiggle my clothes on under the blankets, trying to keep my fingers and toes from getting cold as I was getting dressed. I always put my shoes on the floor right by my bed before I went to sleep, so as soon as I got my socks on in the morning I would stick my feet into my shoes and run to the stove in the kitchen. Jimmy would jump out of bed and jump up and down and up and down as he got dressed, trying to keep warm.

Jeff was allowed to take his clothes out to the big room and stand by the stove and get dressed. Before Jimmy and I could run out to be near the stove we had to fold our pajamas up and put them under our pillows and spread the big black scratchy blankets neatly on our bed. I had to spread the blanket on Jeff's bed, and Jimmy would go out and get Jeff's pajamas and fold them up neatly.

The third room upstairs was called the "bathroom" although there were no bathtub in it, and I don't remember bathing there! We kept our supply of food on shelves in that room. Because we were going to be in Kalinin Bay all winter, our dad had brought a lot of food: cans of vegetables and fruit, bags of flour and sugar, peanut butter in one gallon metal cans and many packages of butter. Our mom had to plan meals carefully so that the food would last a long time, in case we didn't get to town in the winter.

You had to step out into the freezing hallway to get to the "bathroom" to get food for meal time, and I could move pretty fast between there and the warm kitchen when I was sent for food in the winter. Our mom would give us a list of things to get out of the "bathroom", but she never wrote it down, she just told it to us, and we would run to the "bathroom" pick the items off the shelves, and hurry back to the kitchen, our arms full of delicious things to eat. Coming back into the big, warm room was exciting – it was like coming indoors from being out in the snow because it was so cold in the hallway between the "bathroom" and the big room, and we weren't given time to put on our jackets when we were sent to get food.

Life was very hard for our parents, with no running water and just a small oil burning stove to cook on in the kitchen area, which was also our only heat upstairs.

There were three rooms upstairs. One was a kitchen and living room, with the big bed for our mom and dad in one corner. That big bed was also our sofa. There was a table with chairs and some small shelves for cupboards and the cook stove. There weren't enough chairs for all of us to sit on so Jimmy and I sat on wooden boxes - tipped up on the end so we could reach the table. We didn't mind sitting on the wooden boxes, except when we wiggled too much and got a splinter in our behinder.

There was a smaller table in the kitchen for a wash basin for the dishes and a shelf for putting the wet dishes on so they could drip. There was a spot under the smaller table for two buckets. One had fresh water in it and one was for dumping the dirty water into after the dishes were washed. Jimmy's job was to carry the clean and the dirty water buckets up and down the stairs. And he had to be very careful not to slosh the water on the stairs.

One time he wanted to throw the water out the window, but our mom said no - that it would just splatter against the house and freeze there, or it would make a patch of ice that we might slip on, so he lugged the bucket of dirty water downstairs and poured it onto the beach.

Many of the walls in our Alaska house were not smooth like those in the house in California. They were just bare wood and sometimes we could feel the wind blowing through the cracks. Our mom would make some paste out of flour and water and take old papers and paste them on the walls where the cracks were – to try and keep some of the wind out. If the cracks were big, and many were, she would put many layers of paper over them, pasting them on one at a time until they were thick enough to stop the wind. Sometimes she would take some rags and stuff them in the cracks first, before she pasted the layers of paper on.

The second room was long and narrow, and was a bedroom for all three of us kids. Our beds were placed along one wall, with the foot of one bed at the head of the next, like railroad cars, with just a small space between the beds. We didn't bring the beds with us - they must have been left there by the last people to live in our house above the store. The beds had striped mattresses on them, and big, thick, scratchy, black wool blankets.

When we made our beds we had to be careful not to scrape our hands against the bare boards of the wall or we would get many painful splinters, which our mom would pull out with her tweezers and then put iodine on our hands, which stung really badly, and it colored our hands red.

Our mom baked all our bread in that little stove. It was a small stove with a tiny oven, just big enough for one loaf of bread. She would make enough bread dough for three or four loaves of bread. The dough always smelled good and we knew we'd have fresh warm bread for lunch. Mixing bread dough was a big job and we kids were not big enough to help. Our mom would mix the flour and water and other good things together in a very big bowl.

When the dough was stiff enough she would dump it all out on the table, which had a layer of flour on it, and she would punch and push and knead the bread until it was smooth and silky feeling. Then she would clean out the big bowl, spread a thin layer of shortening on the inside of the bowl and put the soft bread dough in the bowl. She would turn it over once so there was shortening on all the sides of the bread dough and then put a clean dish towel over the top of the bread.

She set the bowl close to the little stove, just close enough for it to be warm and the bread dough would rise and rise, getting bigger and puffier. Jimmy and I liked to watch for the bread dough to get all the way to the top of the bowl - then it was time for our mom to make loaves of bread from the dough.

Our mom would carefully wash her hands and then push and punch at the big puffy bread dough until all the air was out of it, like a popped balloon. She would divide the dough into four parts - cutting it apart with a sharp knife. She said if she tore the dough it would be ruined and we wouldn't have any bread. Each piece of bread dough would go into a bread pan that had shortening also spread all around the inside, so the bread wouldn't stick to the pans. One pan would be covered with the dishtowel and placed near the little stove, to rise and get big enough to fill the bread pan. The other three loaves were set out in the cold hallway to wait their turn, under another dishtowel. Then she would scrape the flour off the table and scrub it until it was clean.

When the dough in the first pan was just above the top of the bread pan, our mom would stick her elbow a little way into the oven and she could tell if it was hot enough to bake the bread. I didn't know how she could tell, but I knew that I didn't want to stick MY elbow in the oven. Into the oven would go the loaf of bread and soon we could smell it cooking. Halfway through the baking time, our mom would open the oven and look at the bread. If one side was browner than the other, she would turn the bread around so it would bake evenly. The fire that heated the stove was on the left side of the oven and so that side baked things faster than the right side.

When she had put the first loaf of bread into the oven to bake she would bring in one of the loaves from the cold hallway so it could sit by the stove and warm up and rise, to be ready to bake when the first loaf came out. At long last, the first loaf was done and the smell was heavenly. Our mom would take the loaf of bread out of the oven, spread margarine all over the top of the bread and tip it out onto a clean dishtowel on the table to cool.

If our dad was home he would take a big sharp knife and cut off two slices of bread. He never ate the first slice - he called it the heel and he didn't like it. The heel was almost all crust and it was my favorite - and Jimmy's too. We would spread margarine on our slice of bread and share it. Jeff didn't like the fresh bread so if he was hungry he would get a cookie. Jimmy and I would rather have the fresh warm bread than a cookie. Sometimes we would get to spread some Salmonberry jelly on the warm bread.

There were no water faucets in our house, so for water, our dad would carry in ice to melt on the stove in the winter. He got this ice from the frozen waterfall a long ways down the beach, and he carried it to the house on a contraption he had made from a very thick branch and some rope. He put the branch across his shoulders and attached a short rope at each end, with a big hook on the ends of the ropes. He would fill large buckets with ice he had chopped off the waterfall, hook the buckets to the ropes and carry that ice through the deep snow. When he got it home, we would carry big chunks upstairs in a big dishpan to melt in a pan on the stove.

In the summer he carried fresh water from the waterfall when he was there, but he was out fishing a lot so our mom would take the buckets and go to the waterfall and come back with fresh water. She couldn't carry as much water in the buckets as our dad, so she had to make more trips. Sometimes Jimmy would carry some water too, if he wasn't out on the boat with our dad.

Since we had no regular electricity, we had no refrigerator to keep our food cold like we had in California. Our refrigerator was a box attached to one window on the outside of the house. We would slide the window up and reach out to get something cold, and slide the window down again. Even in the summer some food would stay cool in that window box.

We would put the plate of margarine in the window box, and canned milk, if there was some left after it was first opened. We had no fresh fruits or vegetables to keep in there so it didn't have to be a very big box. If there was some food left from dinner our mom would put it in a small dish and cover it with a plate and save it in the window box and we would have it for lunch the next day.

Even without a refrigerator we could still have ice cream, made in an old hand cranked freezer, but only in winter when our dad would bring in extra ice from the waterfall. He would tell us to get ready for ice cream because he was going for ice. He would carry in extra buckets of ice and Jimmy would crack it into pieces with a hammer. He would put the big chunks of ice into a burlap bag and smack it over and over with the side of the hammer. If some of the pieces were still too big he would put them back in the burlap bag and smack them again.

Our mom would cook up the custard for the ice cream while they were getting the ice ready. She would cool the custard for a while in the window box and then pour it carefully into the tank of the ice cream maker, put the paddle inside the tank and put the lid on. Ice and rock salt were packed all around the tank, which was placed in a wooden bucket with a crank on it.

Jimmy and I would turn and turn the old freezer's big round wheel in the big store space downstairs until the ice cream began to freeze. We didn't crank fast though, because then the custard wouldn't freeze, it would just slosh around and not spend much time touching the cold sides of the tank. As it froze more the crank was harder to turn and finally our dad would come downstairs and do the last 5 minutes of hard cranking. Sometimes Jimmy or I would stand on top of the ice cream freezer to hold it steady so our dad could crank it.

At last it was finished and our dad would scrape all the ice and salt away from the top of the tank and carefully pull off the lid and paddle and scrape the ice cream off the paddle back into the tank. We kids were given the paddle and we took turns licking it and tasting the delicious cold ice cream. Sometimes a little salt would get on the ice cream on the paddle and we loved to lick that part.

Our dad would carefully put the lid back on the tank, cover the hole in the top where the crank had fit with a teacup and pack more ice around the tank until it was all covered. We had to wait at least a half hour, sometimes more, until he said the ice cream was hard enough. We would then carry big bowls and one large spoon downstairs and fill up the bowls with ice cream and then carry the bowls of cold ice cream up to the warm kitchen to enjoy.

Our mom had put the bowls in the window box to get cold so the ice cream wouldn't melt fast. Sometimes she would make chocolate syrup while the ice cream was being cranked and we would pour the hot chocolate sauce over the cold ice cream. I loved winter time!

We made our own fun in Kalinin Bay, as we hadn't brought any toys with us. They were considered unnecessary and took up space that would have been needed for food and other supplies on the boat. I don't know where some things came from; perhaps someone had left them there from the summer, but we had the ice cream freezer and a tricycle, and of course our beds and the stove.

5
OH! THE THINGS THAT HAPPEN

My brothers and I would often play on the dock, near the house, the part that was over the beach. When the tide came in there was water under that part of the dock, but with the tide out there were boulders right under the dock, and a sandy, gravel beach nearer the house.

One calm day our mom and dad went up the bay in the skiff to catch crabs for fresh meat for dinner. Jimmy was in charge of watching Jeff and me while they were gone and I was driving the tricycle around on the dock that day.

I was very good at turning and decided that I needed to be able to back up too, like I had seen cars do, while turning around in a small space. So I practiced and practiced, while Jimmy and Jeff played on the beach nearby, under the dock. They were running back and forth and having a great time building roads on the beach, and I turned a bit to watch them, and my backing up was not as good as I had thought, for all of a sudden I felt one back wheel going off the dock, and then I was falling onto a pile of big boulders, head first.

Jimmy came clambering up the rocks to where I was. My head hurt and I was crying and Jeff was standing on the beach crying really loudly. Jimmy helped me to crawl back off the rocks and he helped me up the stairs. I was a little dizzy and Jimmy made sure that I didn't fall down the stairs. He told me lie down on my bed. Then he walked up the bay to find our mom and dad, and Jeff stayed with me and kept worrying that I would bleed to death before they all got back, and kept telling me so, over and over. When you cut your head it can bleed a large amount, even if it is not a really big cut, and this one seemed to have Jeff extra worried.

He sat on the floor by my bed and cried and cried. I wanted to help him not to cry, but if I moved my head it hurt worse and I felt sick, so I just lay there, wishing Jimmy would find our mom and dad soon and bring them back so they could help Jeff stop crying.

I finally slept for a little while, but Jeff kept waking me up to ask if I was dead yet, and then he would start crying all over again. After what seemed like a very long time, our mom and dad came running. My head was split about three inches from the top towards the back of my neck, and matted with hair and blood. There are no doctors nearby and we were a very long ways from town.

For emergencies our dad had a two-way radio. With a two-way radio you can send a message out to someone else with the same kind of radio and if they have their radio on they can hear your call. You hold a little button down and speak into a microphone that you hold in your hand, and after you are finished speaking you say "over" so the other person knows that it is their time to hold the button down on their microphone and talk to you. When you are completely done talking and ready to shut down the radio you say "over and out" and the other person says "out" so you both know you are done talking.

Our dad called for the doctor in Sitka, the nearest town. Someone in Sitka had their two-way radio on that day and ran to find the doctor. It took a while to find the doctor because he was visiting a sick person in their house and they had no telephone. When they finally found the doctor he rushed to the house with the two-way radio and talked to our dad.

By now I was sitting up in a chair so our mom could see the wound on the back of my head, and as the doctor gave instructions on the two-way radio our mom did what he told her to do. He told her how to clean the wound, how to cut the hair off, and how to use a mixture of alcohol and vinegar to numb and sanitize, the area and how to stitch it all up with sewing thread and a needle. She first cut off the matted hair on the back of my head as closely as she could with scissors, and cleaned it with the solution of alcohol and vinegar that the doctor told her to use. Well it may have sanitized it, but it surely didn't deaden it. But, once again, as we weren't allowed crying and must always be brave, I managed to keep the family tradition and didn't cry until late that night in my bed, when my poor little head felt like it would explode.

Next she used our dad's razor and shaved the spot on my head where it was bleeding. Then she took a sewing needle and thread and dipped them both in the alcohol and vinegar to clean them. The doctor told her to be very careful not to breath the fumes from the mixture or she would get dizzy and sleepy.

She took the needle and thread and stitched up the wound - each time she poked my head it felt like the needle was going right through my head - but still I didn't cry, because I didn't want to get slapped for crying. When she was finished she put a shower cap over my head so I wouldn't get lint from the blankets in the wound and I went to lie down on my bed again. I had to lie on my side because it hurt too much to have the back of my head on the pillow. Jimmy had taken off the bloody pillowcase and put a fresh, cool one on the pillow and it felt so good to lie down, and finally Jeff had stopped crying.

For several days I wasn't allowed to play outdoors because I couldn't put a scarf or hat on my head. I stayed indoors and looked at books or took a nap on my bed. When I was allowed to go outdoors our mom put the plastic shower cap on my head and then I tied my scarf on over that. My scarf would slip down off the shower cap and I would have to stop and tie it back on my head, but I didn't mind, because at last I was able to play with Jimmy again.

When it was time to take the stitches out, our dad called for the doctor in town on the two-way radio and he told our mom how to clip each stitch so they wouldn't pull on the others when she took them out. She used some tiny scissors and clipped very carefully, but it still hurt. She then pulled each little stitch out with tweezers. Some of the thread had stuck tight in my skin and she had to pull hard. After she was done she rinsed my head again with alcohol and vinegar - stinging so much it made my eyes water, but I didn't cry. Then she put the shower cap back on my head and I went to bed, but didn't get to sleep for a long, long time that night. The next day she put a big bandaid on my head and every morning and every night she would change the bandaid. It hurt when she took it off, and I was so glad when I no longer needed a bandaid. And I never rode the tricycle on that part of the dock again!

Later that same summer Jeff was playing farther out on the dock and somehow slipped off and fell even farther than I had, and he broke his arm. I saw him fall and thought he was going to fall into the water. Jimmy ran to the house - being oldest he could run fastest - and yelled to our dad that Jeff had fallen off the dock. Here came our dad, racing down the stairs, tearing off his shirt and trousers, ready to jump in the water to save Jeff. But the tide was out and Jeff had not fallen in the water. He had gotten himself up off the big rocks that he had fallen on, and was walking on the beach, holding one arm with the other.

That sight I will never forget, because our big strong, brave dad almost fainted at the sight of a little five-year-old boy holding his arm with the bone sticking straight up out of the skin. Well, this was much more serious than my whack on the head, and they hurried to call for the doctor on the two-way radio again.

The person who answered the radio call knew where the doctor was that day and ran to get him. The doctor told them they should wrap Jeff's arm with a cloth to hold it steady and then said that he would send a plane to come out from Sitka to pick up Jeff and our mom. Jeff was crying and crying and finally he stopped when our mom gave him a sleeping pill. There was a fish-buying scow at the dock at that time and the lady on the scow had some pills. She broke one in half like the doctor said, and our mom crushed it up and mixed it with water and sugar so Jeff would eat it.

After that our mom packed a suitcase with clothes for her and Jeff to take when the plane came for them. She made some sandwiches for our lunch. Jimmy and I took our sandwiches and went down to sit on the dock to watch for the plane. When we heard it coming over the mountains we ran back to the house to tell our mom - and soon the plane was landing at the float.

The pilot said he had flown straight over the mountains instead of following the water like he usually did because it was so much shorter that way. He said he would be flying back the same way and told our dad to wrap Jeff in blankets so he wouldn't get cold. There was no heat in the little plane and they didn't want Jeff to get sick from getting too cold. The pilot helped our mom climb up onto the pontoons of the plane and then into the back seat.

Our dad was carrying Jeff and he climbed onto the pontoon and carefully handed Jeff to our mom in the back seat. Then he went back to the house and got two more big wool blankets. One to fold over Jeff and one to put around our mom so she would be warm on the trip to town. They had wrapped Jeff's arm in a clean sheet so it wouldn't move or bleed on the way to town.

After everyone was in the plane our dad untied it and pushed it out into the bay with his foot. The pilot started the engine and they went a little ways out before he roared up into the sky. We all watched from the dock as the little plane got smaller and smaller as it climbed up over the snowy mountains. Then we walked slowly back up to the house. It seemed so empty.

I wasn't sure if our mom and Jeff would ever come back and I was worried that they would have to take Jeff's arm off, but I had no one to ask about this because our mom had told Jimmy and me to not be any trouble for our dad while she took Jeff to the doctor, and I thought questions would be trouble. I didn't even want to ask Jimmy, because he seemed so worried about Jeff and I didn't want to worry him more.

Our dad fixed some dinner, but Jimmy and I weren't very hungry that night. So when it got dark we put the food in the window box, turned off the lamps and went to bed. Jimmy and I whispered a while in bed. I was so frightened but Jimmy said if I went to sleep it would seem that things were much better in the morning, and maybe the doctor would call us on the two-way radio and tell us what happened to Jeff.

I woke up early the next morning and Jimmy said that we would sweep the house and clean up the yard outside. We got dressed and as soon as breakfast was done and we had washed the dishes, we swept all the floors and went outdoors to pick up sticks and leaves off the area in front of the house. We didn't have a regular yard, but a big part of the dock came right up to our house. It was all built of wood and was very wide so we had a big space to play and stay out of the mud when it rained. Our mom called it the boardwalk.

Cleaning up kept us busy most of the morning, until our dad said it was time for Jimmy to make us some sandwiches for lunch. Jimmy made our sandwiches and he cut them into funny shapes. Then he made a puzzle of the sandwiches - some of his sandwich and some of my sandwich in each puzzle, and we sat at the window and ate our lunch. Our dad just had regularly shaped sandwiches, because he didn't think the puzzle sandwiches were fun.

We drank some milk with our sandwiches. We didn't have regular milk, just canned milk. Jimmy punched two holes in top of a can of milk with a sharp pointed ice pick and poured some milk into our glasses. Then he added water to it, and that was our milk. I didn't like it much, but I drank it because Jimmy said it was good for me. Whenever we had milk to drink I would try to get Jimmy or Jeff to drink mine when our mom wasn't looking, because I didn't like the taste of it, but this time I drank it to make Jimmy happy.

The doctors were able to fix the bone that was sticking out, and set Jeff's arm in a cast, a big plaster thing that went from above his elbow to almost all the way over his fingers. After almost a week our dad told us that the plane was coming back with Jeff and our mom. This was the first we had heard about their plans and we were very happy.

Jimmy and I swept the floors and made sure there were no dishes that needed to be washed and no leaves or twigs out in front of the house.

Then we ran down to the dock and sat on the edge and listened for the plane. We kicked our legs back and forth over the edge of the dock and sang songs while we waited. We could hear the plane before we could see it, but soon it was close and we jumped up and down and waved as it flew right over the dock. The pilot dipped the wings to say hi to us and zipped down and landed on the water.

We ran to the float and Jimmy grabbed the rope from the dock and tossed it to the pilot to tie up the plane. We saw Jeff inside the plane, sitting by the pilot. When the pilot took him out of the plane we saw that he had that big white cast clear up past his elbow, almost to his shoulder. He let us touch it, but said not to touch too hard because sometimes it hurt.

Our mom got out of the back seat of the plane and the pilot said he had to get back to town and we all waved goodbye as he taxied out into the bay and quickly flew out of sight. We gathered our mom's things up and helped her carry the blankets and her suitcase up to the house. Jeff couldn't carry anything because he had the big cast on his arm. As soon as we got in the house our mom got busy and scrubbed the floors and changed the sheets on all the beds, and then made us some dinner.

After a few weeks Jeff's arm began to heal and he could play outdoors with us again, even with the cast on. He had to be very careful not to get the cast wet or it would get soft and hurt his arm, and if he got it wet enough, it would fall off and then he'd have to go back to town to have a new cast put on. He would sometimes cry when his arm hurt; he was the only one that was allowed to not be brave and to cry. I would read him stories when he was resting on the big bed in the living room, and sometimes I would rub his back so he wouldn't cry.

After a long time, the plane came back to get Jeff and our mom and took them back to Sitka. Jeff had to get a new cast put on his arm, and the doctors noticed that he couldn't move his fingers. They told him to try really hard to wiggle his fingers but he couldn't do it. They said that in one week he would have to come back to the hospital again to have his arm re-broken and set properly so his fingers would work. They then flew back home and waited for a week, and for a third time the plane came back and they went to Sitka. This time they stayed longer than a week.

Jimmy and I had our lessons to do, and work around the house to keep us busy. Our mom had set out our lessons before she went back to

Sitka on the plane. We did our lessons in the big store downstairs. She would put each day's lessons in a pile on the counter and we would take a pile and begin to read and write. Jimmy could read the instructions so he would tell me what I was supposed to do in my lessons, and he would listen to me practice reading.

Then when I was drawing or writing he would start on his lessons. Sometimes he would read to me from his books after I had finished my lessons. We could do two days lessons in one day if we worked very hard, and so we had some days that we didn't have to do lessons at all. Jimmy had to help me with my lessons because our dad didn't like to.

While our mom and Jeff were still in Sitka, one of the ladies on the fishing boats that came to the bay had given us a model to put together. It was a life-size squirrel. Jimmy helped me to glue the sections together and we had made a plastic squirrel that was the size of a real one. Then we painted the plastic squirrel with a special glue and sprinkled some fuzzy stuff on it that came in the kit. It was gray fuzz and made the squirrel feel like it had fur on it. When we finished it we put it on a shelf behind the store counter and left it there so we could show it to Jeff when he got back from Sitka.

We never heard our mom talk of wanting to go back to the States where life would be easier, even though two of her kids had now fallen off a dock and injured themselves.

6
OUR FIRST WINTER

Often things would come up missing in our house that first winter, and our mom always said that we had misplaced things: one sock, a spoon, a small tin of tape. We would search and search for the items, but couldn't discover what could have happened to them. One day Jeff and I decided that we would look in a small side-attic storage space at the top of the stairs. There was a small door into the attic from the hallway between the kitchen and the bathroom, at the top of the stairs. Our mom had told us to never open that door, but we just couldn't resist, and our mom was out on the dock with our dad, doing some boat repairs. So for once we did something we had been told not to do.

We slowly opened the door and tried to see inside, but it was dark. We went back into the house to find a flashlight and shined it in the attic space. It was very dusty in there, and we saw some small boxes and a few big pots in there. We climbed inside the door and peeked into the boxes. They were very dusty and made us sneeze when we opened them. They were full of papers so we left them and looked at the big pots. One was so large that Jeff could stand in it. I wanted him to stay in the pot so I could draw a picture of him, but he wanted to get out. We pushed the pots aside and behind them we found a big nest made of old pieces of cloth, and some branches and paper.

There were broken shoe laces, a man's pipe, some old letters from long before we were there, labels off cans, stones and much more. The nest was about the size of a big dish pan, and very thick. It smelled dirty and dusty. We were afraid to touch it very much, because we didn't yet know what it was.

Later, when our mom came back in the house we were frightened because we had snuck around and opened the doors. Jeff told her that we had done it, and said that it was my idea. I knew I was in big trouble – but still wanted our mom to see what was in there. We showed the nest to our mom and she said that we were to leave it alone, it was a packrat nest, full of things that a packrat had gathered, that it was unhealthy to be touching things a rat had touched.

Our mom left the attic and said we were to come out and close the door and put the latch on and never disobey and go in there again. I was punished for making Jeff go in there and had to sit on a chair all the rest of the day. We wanted to look at the nest more, but when our mother told us to do something we tried not to do it; she was very strict that way. We didn't ever take the things out that we found but still sometimes Jeff and I would sneak in there to see what the packrat had added. But only after I made Jeff promise not to tell our mom.

At the bottom of the steps going to the store in the lower half of the building, there was a small room that must have been the store room for supplies at one time. In this room was a big wooden chest, about four feet high and ten feet long. We often played hide and seek and one time Jimmy told me to hide in the big box and then he would lower the lid and Jeff would look for me. I climbed in and he lowered the wooden lid. I was a very small child and could not push the heavy lid off. After a while I began to wonder when they were going to find me and I got scared. I never cried so no one knew I was in there, I just sat in the dark and waited and waited.

I would make up stories while I waited for Jeff to come and find me. Stories about a deer family, or stories about Bunny and what she might be doing in California at Grandma's house. After a long time Jimmy came back and let me out and told me that Jeff had looked and looked for me but couldn't find me, and then they had gone outdoors and found some interesting things washed up on the beach and forgot to look for me.

When he remembered, Jimmy came running back to open the big wooden box and let me out. Another time we were playing hide and seek and Jimmy said he would help me into the wooden box if I wanted, but I said that I would find a different place to hide. I surely didn't want to get forgotten again.

Jimmy had a B-B gun and he and Jeff played an awful scary game with it. One of them would hold the gun and count to five while the other ran away as fast as they could, down the dock or down the beach. Then the gun person would begin shooting, hoping to hit the runner. I didn't like that game and never let them talk me into playing. I couldn't run fast, or very far, and knew that I would have been shot many times and I didn't want that! Jeff couldn't run as fast as Jimmy, so he got a count of ten before Jimmy started shooting. They must have been terrible shots, for I never remember either of them having to have a B-B removed from their behinders. I can only imagine what would have happened if our mom ever found out about that game! They only played that game when our mom and dad had gone out on the boat and would be gone a long time.

By this time I knew how to handle a gun, but I never liked them. I started with a .22. We would walk up the beach with our dad and mom, and practice our shooting. Our dad said that we all needed to know how to shoot guns and he gave us lessons. He would set tin cans on a log and then tell us where to stand to shoot at them. Before the lesson was over we had to hit the can 4 times in a row, without missing. The .22 was automatic and I was left handed, not a good combination, as the hot shells would eject after each shot and hit my right arm. I didn't cry out , but I hated it - they burned little spots on my arm even if I wore my sweater. I tried really hard to hit the cans because I didn't want to shoot the gun any longer than I had to.

Our dad was very good at carpentry and that first winter he built us a pool table; he even ordered a large piece of green felt for the table top and some pool balls from the Sears catalog. He made the cue sticks and I got to help sand them smooth. Then he made a nice rack to place them in when we weren't playing pool. I don't know where he got the lumber, if it was there or he had to haul it there on his boat. He had tools in the warehouse, and he would sometimes bring them into the store and work on the pool table. It looked as good as any table we saw in the catalogs, and we spent the winter having pool tournaments.

Even our mom played, although she never played pool if there were others around. I didn't know why she thought playing pool was bad, but she often remarked that she really shouldn't be playing it. When a boat was in the harbor and the fisherman came to our house she would never play pool, only when it was just our family.

We learned to not jab the cue sticks into the felt, and were quite good at trick shots. I was small and had to stand on a box that I dragged around the pool table to make my shots. I would take careful aim and whack the ball with the pool cue to knock it into the pockets. I liked it when all the balls were in the pockets and I could go around and pick them all up. I liked the smooth, cool feel of the painted balls - and the sound of them as I put them in the rack. I always liked a good game of pool.

Another thing we played with were rivets. There were boxes full of them in the warehouses on the dock; I guess they were from making the huge oil tanks on a little hill near the store building where we lived. The rivets would be used to hold the big sheets of metal together to make the tanks. Rivets are heavy metal fasteners, larger and thicker than a thumbtack. We would take the boxes of rivets out and use them for many things, and were always careful to take them back to the warehouse when we finished. The boxes were heavy so sometimes I had to carry mine in smaller containers. My brothers liked to use them for weapons and would hurl them at each other, at me or at anything they could think of, but never at windows; they knew better!

I preferred to use them for cookies. I would put a big metal sheet that I found in the warehouse - about the size of a cookie pan - on top of an oil barrel (my stove) right close to the outside front of our store building, the one we lived upstairs in. Then I would spend hours lining up the rivets, on their fat end, on the cookie pans, rows and rows, close together, until there were hundreds of them on the cookie pan.

I remember one of those times is when I first learned what stuttering was. I was so busy with my own world and the rivet 'cookies' that I didn't hear our mom open the window and when she yelled for us kids to come in for dinner it startled me so that I said wh-wh-wh-at?' It made her laugh and she said I had stuttered. I was pretty impressed, although I wasn't exactly sure just what stuttering was at that time, or why it was so funny to her, but she did not laugh very often, so I figured it had to be good.

For our first Christmas in Alaska we had very few gifts. When we lived in California we would drive into town and find an empty lot filled with Christmas trees. We would walk around in the lot and look at every tree, trying to pick the best one. In Alaska we were much too far from town, and our dad told us that they didn't sell Christmas trees in Alaska because there were so many trees growing in the woods.

We all went into the woods behind our house to search for a Christmas tree. There were very tall trees and some very tiny trees. We were looking for a smallish tree to fit in our little apartment above the store. We talked about each tree we thought was good and finally found the right one and our dad cut it down with the saw he was carrying. Jimmy helped to drag the tree out of the woods and our dad carried it up the stairs after he shook all the bits of snow and dirt out of it. He set it in a tub on a small table and put rocks in the tub to keep it from falling over. There wasn't much extra space in our house, so we had to have a very small tree. It smelled so good, just like the woods.

We had some Christmas lights, though I don't know where they came from. I don't think our mom had carried them from California in her suitcase, so someone must have given them to us. Our dad put the lights on the tree and then we put some pretty paper cut-out ornaments on it, and some strings of popcorn. It didn't take very many things to cover the small tree. We had a power plant that our dad would turn on for special occasions and on Christmas day he went down to the shed and started it up. It made the lights on the tree sparkle and we got to have the lights on for over an hour. Then he went back down to the shed and turned off the power plant. We had opened our tiny packages and thought it was a very good Christmas. Jimmy and Jeff each got a small metal car and I got a book of paper dolls.

Our dad had gotten a duck while hunting and our mom put it in the oven with stuffing: the house smelled so good! She baked fresh bread and opened cans of green beans, cranberries and olives. After the bread was done baking she put a pie in the oven. I had never smelled a pie that smelled so delicious. She said it was mincemeat, and after dinner when I had a taste of it I knew it was my favorite pie.

While she was cooking dinner and after Jimmy and I had set the table with the lacy tablecloth, Jimmy and Jeff and I went downstairs to play with our Christmas presents. Jimmy was old enough to light the big brown stove downstairs and it warmed us up while we played.

I got a big pair of scissors and sat on a chair by the store counter and carefully cut out the paper dolls from my book. When the dolls were cut out carefully I then started with the pages of clothes. There were fancy dresses and play dresses, pajamas and robes, and even a puppy and kitty to cut out. I put each piece of clothes on the paper dolls when I had finished cutting them out, and they got to wear that piece until I had cut out another. I didn't cut them all out that day, but saved some pages to cut out for several days. I thought paper dolls were the best thing in the world.

Later that winter we got more toys, as our Grandma and Grandpa Dunlap sent us some in the mail! It was very cold that winter, with heavy snowstorms, followed by very cold days and nights. It got so cold that our boat was frozen in the ice at the dock at Christmas time and we couldn't get to Sitka to pick up the mail.

If it gets cold enough, salt water will freeze, and our boat was frozen right in place next to the dock. As the tides would come in and out, our dad would go down to the float, walking carefully on the dock and the ramp down to the float so he wouldn't slip on the ice that formed there. He put old tires on short ropes and hung them over the sides of the boat, all the way around, to keep the ice from crunching up next to the boat and damaging the hull. He would go out there with each tide, even if it was in the middle of the night, and check the boat to make sure it was safe. I would hear him in the dark of the night getting dressed and walking slowly down the steps to go check the boat. I don't know where he got all those tires; there were no cars in Kalinin Bay, and only a very few in Sitka.

One day in February our dad said we should pack a suitcase - we were going to town to get the mail. When we had brought food with us when we first came to Kalinin Bay he had figured that we would go to town and get more before Christmas, but then when the ice came we had to begin being very careful with our food so it didn't run out. We ran out of butter. When our mom would make canned potatoes for dinner, Jeff didn't like them without butter and he didn't like gravy, so our mom would spoon jam over the potatoes and he would eat them. I tried it, but I didn't like the taste of it, so just ate mine with gravy.

We packed our clothes in one suitcase for all three kids and carried the suitcase down to the boat. Our mom gathered up food to take with us for the trip, and Jimmy helped carry the boxes of food down to the boat. When everything was ready, we climbed onto the boat. Jimmy stood on the float after untying all the lines, except for the last one. As he untied the last one he jumped up on the boat, giving a push with his foot to push the boat away from the float, and we were on our way. We went below to sit on the bunks until our dad said it was ok to come up on deck.

Up on deck we saw the big mountains covered with snow and watched for seals in the water. It was very cold even though we had on thick coats and hats and mittens, so soon we were glad to go below again and watch our mom make some soup for lunch. She put some meat from a can into the pan and added canned carrots, potatoes and onions. We didn't have any fresh potatoes, but the ones from the can tasted delicious so I didn't mind. She stirred it around and then let it cook for a while on the stove. Then she mixed up some cornbread and put it in the oven just as the soup was about done.

A good meal of soup and cornbread tasted so wonderful on the boat. Jimmy and I took our bowls of soup up on deck and sat on the hatch cover to eat and watch the water for seals. Jimmy would go back in and get another bowl of soup, but I could never eat more than one bowl and two pieces of cornbread. It was cold on deck that day, but we liked to eat on the deck as often as we could, and the warm soup tasted so good out in the cold weather.

After lunch was finished and we had cleaned up the cabin we all lay down in the bunks for a nap. It was easy to fall asleep on the boat. The rocking was smooth that day and it was like being in a hammock, and we could hear the hum of the engine as we drifted off to sleep. Some days it might be very rough on the water and we would have to brace our arms and legs against the edge of the bunks to keep from being tossed out. On those days it was hard to take a nap. On the very roughest days we would sit on the floor of the cabin and put our legs straight out to touch the other side and that kept us from slipping about.

Sometimes, if our mom was not below with us, we would not brace our feet, and we would slip and slide from side to side on the floor of the boat. We would laugh and giggle, but quietly, because if our mom came down and saw us sliding around she would make us sit still again and stop laughing.

We had to make sure that there was nothing in the bunks that would fall out and hit our heads on the rough days. Our mom said it was our job to make sure of that, since it was our heads that might have something fall on them. After our nap that day our mom told us that soon we would be in Sitka, so we straightened up our blankets and got everything put back where it belonged. Jimmy always checked to see that Jeff had put his things away, and if he hadn't then Jimmy would do it for him.

It was fun to go to Sitka - we could see the houses on the shore for quite a ways before we got to the dock. We would look for people along the way, using the binoculars. Sometimes we would see a bit of the road and a car would be going by. We would each take a quick look in the binoculars so everyone could see the car. As we came up the channel we would begin to pick out the buildings that we recognized.

Soon it was time for us to go below, all except for Jimmy, as we neared the dock. I always wished I could be like Jimmy and hold the rope and jump for the float while our dad maneuvered the boat in close. Jimmy would hold the rope in one hand and jump across the bit of water between the boat and the dock. He would tighten the rope around the cleat with a clove hitch. He would later change to a tighter knot, but that one was fast for tying up the boat. Jimmy had taught me many different knots and I knew I could tie the knots, I just wasn't sure I could leap to the dock, so I would just look out the porthole and watch Jimmy tie up the boat.

At last we were docked and everything stowed in the boat and our dad had finished what he had to do and we set off for the post office. The packages from our grandparents were still waiting at the post office, along with letters and an order from Sears that our mother had sent for in the summer. It was a small post office and the post master knew that we were expecting some packages, so he set them in a back room to wait until we came to town again. There was a big pile of packages waiting for other fishermen's families too, and for the loggers who lived out in the woods.

We got our packages and letters and carried them back to the boat. Jeff carried a magazine and the rest of us carried as much as we could. Jimmy had to go back two or three more times to get everything. Our mom looked at all the envelopes that she got, and put them away until we got back home. Then we climbed off our boat and set out for town again.

Whenever we came into town there were many things our mom and dad had to do so we spent several days there. Our mom took all of our dirty clothes and sheets and blankets to a friend's house and washed them in her electric washing machine. Jimmy would take many loads up to the friend's house. We had to stay indoors while the washing was being done because our mom also washed our coats. They were the first things washed because it took the longest for them to dry. After each load of washing was finished our mom would hang the clothes on wooden racks in front of the stove to dry. She would move the clothes around on the racks, flipping them over so they would dry faster.

We slept on our boat for several nights until our mom and dad had finished everything that they had come to town to do, and one night our dad said we would be getting up very early the next morning to leave for home. Our mom put the boxes of Christmas gifts on her bunk in the boat and we had to sit quietly the whole day as we chugged back towards home, with those packages sitting on the bunk.

We desperately wanted to open our packages and play with the new toys, but our mom would not allow us toys or running about on the boat, so we would sit in a straight row, our hands folded and not much talking allowed, all the way back to Kalinin Bay. If we got tired we were allowed to crawl up on a bunk to sleep, but I was too excited to become sleepy. I could see the outside of the packages and knew what was in them. They were not wrapped in paper – they showed on the box what was inside.

My package was a big doll, and you could hold her hand and make her walk along with you. Jimmy read the outside of the packages to us so we could tell what each thing was. My brothers' package was Fort Deerborn, with men and horses, fences, and a big fort. We had those packages almost a week now, and had not been allowed to open them. We were anxious for the trip home to be over so we could finally open the packages that we had been looking at all this time, and longing to open them.

It was a long boat ride to Kalinin Bay. It is on the north end of Japonski Island, the opposite end from Mt. Edgecumbe, and I thought we would never get home so we could have our packages. There were clothes packages too, but we couldn't see what was inside of them so they weren't so tempting.

We had our breakfast and then our lunch on the boat. This time there were fresh vegetables to cook and a big piece of meat that our mom fried for our dad. We had hamburgers and vegetables for our dinner, and some potatoes baked in the little oven of the black stove. It was the best dinner you could ever have. Again Jimmy and I took our plates out on deck and ate there. We liked to have boat picnics together. Jeff couldn't hold his plate and eat at the same time, so he stayed down below and ate with our mom. There were lots of logs in the water and sometimes our dad had to slow the boat way down so he could watch closely that we didn't hit a log - so we could look at things for a longer time along the shore as we ate our hamburgers.

At last the boat pulled around the point and into our bay, and it seemed a long way up to the middle of the bay where our house was. As we neared the float Jimmy jumped off the boat with the rope and secured the boat to the float. The current was fast that day so he tied several lines to the float to keep the boat from moving back and forth while we unloaded. There were lots of groceries in the hold that our mom and dad had bought in town, as well as some Sears orders that had come, and of course, the presents on our mom's bunk.

Jimmy was strong and helped to lift the food and packages out of the hold onto the deck, and then carried them up onto the dock. We all carried what we could up to the dock and loaded them on a small cart that our dad would pull and Jimmy would push, all the way up to our house. Then we had to carry everything up all those stairs to our apartment.

The mail was put in a special box next to the table and our mom would read it all later. The food had to be put away in the storage room, each thing in its proper place. There were cans of meat, vegetables and fruit. There were huge bags of flour that only our dad could lift, and those were dumped into big tin boxes with tight lids. The flour made a big cloud of dust in the storage room when it was poured into the tin box. Sugar was also poured into a smaller tin box. There was coffee and chocolate, peanut butter in big jars, along with a big block of cheese and cases of margarine and canned milk.

One of my favorites was the big slab of bacon, wrapped in a dark waxed paper, that was hung from a hook in the ceiling. There were new bottles of cod liver oil that sparkled in the sunlight, but didn't taste good when we got a dose of it each morning. Our food room was almost packed full when we finished putting everything away. It seemed that the food would last us forever, but soon there would be empty spaces when we went to the room to fetch more food for meals.

When everything was put away, we were sent to unpack our suitcase while our mom started dinner. It took a long time for the black stove to heat up and the house was very cold because no one had been in it since we left for Sitka. Our mom fried up some of the bacon and we had fresh eggs from the store, and she made some biscuits and gravy to go with it, with regular milk from the store in town. It was a delicious dinner, and Jeff was happy to have margarine to put on his biscuit once again, because he didn't like the gravy.

Then we had to do the dishes, and make our beds with the clean sheets that our mom had washed while we were in town. Oh my, you would think that I would have learned patience by now - but I kept finding reasons to go out in the cold hallway and peek at the doll package. I was so hoping that Bunny had jumped in the box and was coming back to me! Our mom had said we would leave the gift packages out in the hallway until after everything was done for the day.

After what seemed like days we were allowed to go downstairs and open the packages and my big tall, blond doll was wonderful in her crisp pink dress and shiny shoes. She was almost three feet tall and really would walk when you held her hand. I took her carefully out of her box and smoothed her pretty dress. Her name was Samantha Sue Jeanette Penelope Redrose WiseOne, but she liked to be called Sammy Sue, and we had so very many adventures together. Jimmy and Jeff had opened their fort and were setting up buildings and fences, then they put the men around inside the fences and began to play with them. Sammy Sue and I sat on the floor and watched them. It was a very good Christmas in February.

That winter I was learning to sew and Sammy Sue was very patient with me. I would take small scraps of fabric that our mom didn't need any more and cut out clothes to sew for my doll. She would sit still for fittings for hours and hours, and only complained just a teensy when I might poke her with a pin, but then I would serve her acorn tea and she would feel better.

She loved best her pink jammies that I stitched for her; they had little white puppies on them and were quite the fashion. It was cold in our bedroom, where she had to stay when I wasn't playing with her downstairs, so I wanted to knit her a scarf and hat. Sometimes she would give me advice about my knitting, especially if I was knitting for her. I was determined to not let her out of my sight, and one day that saved her life, but I will tell you about that later.

She sat on my bed when I was not sleeping or playing with her. She liked the big black wool blankets and sometimes she would lie down on my pillow and have a nap if I was going to be outdoors for a long time. I would cover her up with a small piece of a blanket that was worn out and had been cut up into smaller pieces. She smiled and went to sleep.

That same winter there was a sight that I had never seen before. It was a cold and clear day, after a heavy snow storm, and the temperature kept dropping all afternoon. We had been playing outdoors in the snow during the afternoon, but the wind started blowing hard and finally we went indoors and peeled off our wet coats. We hung them on lines in the store downstairs to dry off and put our boots in a neat row near the stove. Our mittens, hats and scarves were placed on some wooden boxes near the stove. We moved the dry ones off and put the wet ones on to dry. We folded the dry clothes and carefully put them on a shelf so we could wear them the next time we went outdoors.

We had a nice hot dinner and our dad read to us from a magazine that had come in the mail when we had gone to town in February. Then it was time for bed. It was extra cold that night and our mom brought in an extra blanket for each of us. She had warmed them by putting them on the back of the black stove and it felt good to crawl in bed under those warm blankets. Our flannel pajamas kept us nice and snuggly warm.

Late that night our dad came in to wake us up from our sleep. He said to get bundled up for outdoors, but didn't tell us why, so we got dressed in our warmest clothes, as quickly as we could, for it was very cold in our bedroom. We put our clothes on over our pajamas and put on two pairs of socks and two pairs of mittens, as well as thick hats and scarves. We walked outside and there in the sky were big patches of colored lights, swirling and crackling and swooshing across the sky. The colors changed from pink to green to yellow and back again. They dipped down close to the trees, it seemed, and then back up high in the sky, We stood there, our teeth chattering, and didn't know what we were looking at. Our dad called them the Northern Lights and said they came from the North Pole. He said they only came on the coldest and clearest nights and that this didn't happen very often.

At first Jeff was frightened by the lights, but Jimmy said they wouldn't come down to where we were and Jeff felt better. The lights made a noise that was loud and crackling as they changed and swished across the sky and reflected off the snow. Sometimes the snow was bright pink, and then it would be a very soft green, almost like grass was growing on the snow. The lights lasted for a long time and we watched as the waves of lights came whipping across the dark sky.

We finally went back upstairs to our beds and peeled off our layers of extra clothes and folded them neatly onto our clothes shelf It didn't seem so cold inside after standing out in the frosty night time air for so long. Many other nights our dad would call for us to get dressed and watch the Northern Lights - but they were never as bright as that first night we saw them.

We often made our own toys and playthings, and the rocks and plants that we could find near our house were sometimes our toys. There was a big oak tree beside our house; our mom told us that someone had to plant it there, because oak trees don't usually grow in Alaska. We would beat acorns into mush and tried to make it taste good by adding salt water, but it was still harsh and sour so we didn't actually eat any.

We would build canals and lakes and rivers on the beach with rocks and gravel. We would use big clam shells to dig with, or a piece of driftwood that had washed up on the shore.   We would make towns and use different size rocks for the buildings. Smaller rocks were cars and trucks and bright colored pebbles would be people. After we worked on the towns for a long time the tide would begin to come in and after the next tide we would run to the beach to see if anything was left

Sometimes the large rocks would be there, but everything else would be gone. We didn't mind, and we would start all over again, planning a different town. Sometimes we would bring rocks of all sizes and stack them up in piles, or try and balance as many as we could before they fell over. We called these our rock totem poles. One day we made a long row of rock totem poles, some with three or four rocks, and one that was 7 rocks tall. We never could get 8 rocks on the stack; it would always topple over. So we rebuilt that stack to 7 rocks and left it that way.

After the tide came and left there were a few of the smaller totems left, but the big one had toppled. We also built long, snaky rock walls or just made big piles of rocks. Many of the rocks were very smooth from the tides rubbing them back and forth on the beach for so many years, and some of the rocks nearer the big boulders by the dock were sharp. Some were jagged and some were flat, and there were many things you could do with different rocks.

7
WINTER STORMS

Up on the hill in front of our house were some gigantic oil tanks - some of them almost as wide as our house. Nothing was in them now, but in the summer the big tanker boat would come to the end of the dock and hook up a hose to a pipe to send oil and gas into the tanks until they were full. In the summer the fishermen would come to the dock and buy gas for their boats and oil for their cooking stoves and heating stoves.

My brothers liked to take their little tin cars up to the big storage tanks on the hill above our house. The base of the tanks was about four feet tall, and at least twenty feet across. My brothers would prop a board against the top of the cement foundations of the tanks to the ground and run the cars down in races. They would pick boards that were the same length and lean them against the foundation. Then Jimmy would say "ready, set, go!" and they would let their cars run down the boards to the bottom. When they were done playing car race, they would take the boards back to the warehouse where they had gotten them.

One day our mom called for my brothers to come right in to the house, and they didn't get the boards put back that they had been racing their cars down. Our mom said we must stay indoors the rest of the day because a big storm was coming and she didn't want to have to hunt us up when the weather got bad.

We set to work at our lessons and then spent some time playing pool after dinner as the wind began to howl. The windows rattled and shook, and rain and then snow began to beat against the windows. We were warm because we had a big heater in the downstairs room that our dad or Jimmy would light before we came downstairs. It had a window in the front of the stove and we could look in and see the fire burning.

Coming up the bay the wind could really pick up speed, and this wind was stronger than any we had ever had before. We played in the store for a long time, with our toys and the pool table, then finally it was bed time and we marched up the stairs to wash up and get ready for bed. Late in the night, long after we had fallen asleep we heard the most horrible crash, and had no idea whatever it could be. It woke us all up, and as we lay in our beds we heard another crash that shook the house.

Our dad said he had to go and check the boat and make sure it was safe, so he put on his heaviest pants and shirt and added another shirt before pulling on his big wool coat, then gloves and a hat that snapped under his chin to keep him warm, and started downstairs. When he got to the outside door, he started to open it the wind flung it open and yanked him outside. He pushed the door closed and tried to walk to the dock to check on the boat to see what had made the crashing noise, but he only got a few steps away from the house, pushing against the wind, when we heard an awful WHUMP against the house. We thought a tree had fallen onto our house, but in a few minutes our dad came crawling slowly back up the stairs. He was very quiet and went directly to bed, without saying a word.

We were peeking out the door of our bedroom and saw him before our mom told us to get back in bed. There was blood on his face and hands and our mom heated some water on the stove and washed his face while he lay in bed. Jimmy and I had peeked out our bedroom door again and we were frightened. Our mom and dad didn't talk at all, just lay in their bed, so we climbed back into our beds and tried to go back to sleep, but we were worried that there would be another crash in the night and our dad would have to try to go back outdoors again.

I thought our dad was going to die, and couldn't figure out why he had come crawling up the stairs. Usually he would come running up the stairs!

Later he told us that when he had tried to go out the door the wind was so strong that when he got out of the shelter of the shed near the house the wind picked him up and flung him about 6 feet, back against the house! He hit the house so hard that he couldn't get back up for a long time so, he lay there until he could gather his strength and then began to crawl up the stairs.

He had tried to call for our mom and Jimmy to come down and help him, but the wind was so loud that they never heard him. In the morning, when he finally got out of bed after the rest of us had breakfast he said he was going to go out and look at the boat. He pulled back the curtain and what he saw made him sit down hard on a nearby chair. Our mom went to the window and began to shake, they were so frightened at what they saw.

One of the huge empty oil storage tanks had been blown over in the wind! It must have made the first big noise we heard, and the only thing that kept it from crashing down the hill, smashing into our house and perhaps killing us all, was the boards that my brothers had left up there the night before! The second crash we heard was another tank blowing over behind the first one, and it had stuck up against the first one that fell, so it didn't roll down the hill either.

After breakfast that morning the wind had begun to slow, so our mom sent us out to play in the warehouse on the dock, a safe place where the tanks would not hit if they did roll down the hill. We made up games and had running races and I took some paper and a pencil out to the warehouse so I could write some lists.

Jimmy climbed up to the ceiling of the warehouse and dropped rivets down on the floor to see how high they would bounce. For a while Jeff would hold a bucket and try and catch the rivets - they made a wonderful, loud noise when they hit inside the bucket - but Jeff got tired of that and wandered off to a corner in the warehouse where there were some burlap bags and he made a nest and pretended he was a chicken. He didn't really remember what the chickens in California had done, so I helped him by telling him how a chicken acted. Jimmy came by and made some chicken noises, and Jeff was happy playing in his chicken nest.

Our mom and dad spent the day hauling lumber from the warehouse up the hill to the oil tanks and building a barricade to stop the tanks from rolling down the hill. Those little boards that Jimmy and Jeff had left there the day before would surely have snapped and let the tanks roll down the hill right towards our house before long. They used some lumber that was in the warehouse, dug deep holes and put in fence posts, and built a strong wooden wall to keep the tanks from rolling. The wall was about three feet thick, so it took a long time for them to carry all that wood up the hill.

They wouldn't let Jimmy help because, they thought it was too dangerous for him to be there if the tanks started rolling. They also carried big rocks up the hill from the beach and hammered on them to make them wedge under the sides of the tanks. Jimmy helped with that by picking big chunks of rock from the beach and putting them on the edge of the boardwalk in front of our house. He was still safe if the tanks started to roll down the hill. I wanted to help too, but I couldn't lift the big rocks, so had to stay in the warehouse with Jeff.

We took turns pushing each other on a rope that hung from the rafters while Jimmy carried big loads of rocks. They all stopped for lunch and our mom brought us sandwiches and cocoa out to the warehouse for our lunch. We ate our sandwiches and she gave us blankets so we could sit on them and be a little warmer. When we got too cold we would get up and run up and down the long warehouse to warm up.

By dinner time they were finished with the fence and the rocks and we all went back in the house. Our dad lit the fire in the cook stove so our mom could cook a nice hot dinner. It felt good to sit beside the stove while she cooked, and as long as we didn't get in the way we could sit there to warm up. After that our dad would go out every night, wind or no, and check the tanks. I'm not sure what he was checking for, but it must have made him feel a little safer. He would put on his thick coat and his boots, hat and gloves and walk up the hill to the tanks. When he came back in he would say that the fence looked like it would hold for another night and we could all go to bed. No one ever came and put the tank back up on the foundation that winter.

8
TRIPS TO TOWN

Once or twice while we lived at Kalinin Bay we again went to Sitka and spent a few days there. Sometimes we would sleep on our boat, and sometimes we got a treat of sleeping at a friend's house. Fred and Gert Manley lived in a big apartment above a business in town and we would visit them. Fred was also a fisherman, but he would come home some nights and sleep at home. When our dad fished he might be gone for a week at a time.

I loved to look out the windows on the street side of their apartment. You could see down to the street and watch the people going by. I didn't know anyone from Sitka that walked by, but I liked to see all those people. We hardly ever saw anyone in Kalinin Bay - unless a fishing boat needed a place to tie up for a night or two.

The windows that looked out the back of the apartment gave us a view of the harbor and the boats coming and going. We could sit at the kitchen table and see everyone who came to Sitka in their boats.

I liked their apartment. Gert had decorated it with a lot of pretty things. In the kitchen was a yellow table and chairs that matched, with very soft seats. She had lots of pretty tablecloths that she changed after every meal. Some had cherries on them and some had flowers. They were bright colors and I liked to feel the smooth cloth.

Gert would sometimes iron while we were there, running the hot electric iron over and over the tablecloths until they were smooth and fresh smelling. She would fold them in little squares and put them in a closet with doors. It was full of the nicest towels and sheets and tablecloths. In the kitchen she also had pretty metal canisters to put her flour, sugar, tea and coffee in, and each one had a word on it so she didn't put the wrong things in.

There were pretty flowers on the canisters and bright red lids with white knobs on top. She had spice cans that matched the canisters and each had a name of a spice on it. I couldn't read the big words, but Jimmy would tell me what was in each one, and sometimes Gert would let us smell the spices. They made my nose tickle, but I liked the smell.

In the living room they had a big sofa and three fat, squishy chairs. When the adults were in the kitchen drinking coffee and talking, Jimmy and I would take turns sitting in all the chairs and then we'd both sit on the sofa together. We said when we were big we would have a house full of soft sofas and chairs. On the backs and arms of the chairs and sofa there were pretty lace doilies that Gert had made. She made them in the summer when Fred was fishing and she went along on the boat with him.

The bedrooms in their apartment had fancy beds with wooden headboards and soft mattresses. There were pretty blankets that matched the paint in each bedroom, and soft pillows on the beds. One of the beds had a lacy skirt around it, and the dresser in that room had a big mirror on it and a little chair that you could sit in to comb your hair. I thought Gert must be a queen to have such fancy things.

Whenever we went to town there was always a stop at the post office. The postmaster would hold packages and letters for the fishermen until they could get into town. On one trip we got a big box of clothes from our Aunt Herma in Las Vegas, where we had stayed on our trip to Alaska. She is our mom's sister and would send us clothes and fun things. Their younger sister, Aunt Kae, was only a few years older than I was and she lived with Aunt Herma. Aunt Kae sent me her Patty Paige paper dolls in one of the packages. I had never had such wonderful paper dolls before! The doll was made of heavy cardboard and had a little stand that made it stand up by itself.

You could change her clothes and have her standing right up there looking so fine. There were three paper dolls in the package, each one a little different from the others, and I had such fun playing with them. Aunt Kae had cut out all the clothes very carefully and there was a little folder to keep them in. I played with those paper dolls for years and years. I didn't think they should all be called Patty Paige so I gave two of them new names. They were Sally and Susan.

The boxes of clothes from Aunt Herma were mostly for Jimmy and Jeff, as our cousin Mike was more their size, but the paper dolls were enough for me. Aunt Kae once sent some clothes for me but our mom said they were clothes for fancy town girls, and not for girls who lived in the fishing villages, who needed heavy coats, boots and pants. So our mom put them in a package and gave them to Gert to give to girls who lived in town.

I saw a pink dress as she was putting them in the package and I wanted it so much. I asked if I could have it. I said I would only wear it on very special days and I would be careful not to get any dirt on it from the warehouse or the beach - but our mom said it was too fancy for Kalinin Bay, and she packed it in with all the other things Aunt Herma had sent. I went into one of the bedrooms at Gert's house and sat and looked sadly out the window. I wished I was a town girl so I could have pink dresses and pretty white anklets, and maybe a pink ribbon to tie up my fluffy curly hair.

Sometimes while we were in town we would go to a little grocery store and visit Jack and Mikey. Their little store was down past Cold Storage, near the ANB (Alaska Native Brotherhood) dock, and it was old and full of fun things to look at. Cold Storage was a big building with many companies in it. There was a place where the fishermen could sell their fish, then the fish was stored there until it was sent to the canning factories. There was also a very large grocery store in the front part of the building.

Jack and Mikey had a small freezer box that had ice cream in it and every time we would come to town our dad would buy several boxes of ice cream. We would take them back to the boat and eat them all up right away, because we didn't usually have a way to keep the ice cream frozen on the boat!

If we were staying with Fred and Gert we would take the ice cream to them and have a little party sitting at the sunny table and eating big bowls of ice cream. Gert would set out enough bowls for everyone that was there. She then divided the ice cream evenly into the bowls. Sometimes the bowls would be heaped up over the rim, so full of ice cream that it seemed like a dream. I would get big spoons from the drawer in the kitchen and pass them out to everyone with one of Gert's pretty napkins, and we would eat and eat ice cream until there wasn't a lick left in our bowls. Sometimes Jeff and I couldn't finish our ice cream, so we would give it to Jimmy and he would eat it all up. My favorite was chocolate.

9
RADIOS, BOOKS AND BOATS

I have told you that we had an electric power plant at Kalinin Bay that we sometimes ran, but usually we had lanterns and candles. We also had a battery powered radio that we could listen to. In the mornings we would listen to the 'Breakfast Club', and get up and march around the table when they played exciting songs. At night, after all of our chores were done and the dishes were dried and put away, we would listen to 'Suspense', 'Johnny Dollar' and other programs on the radio. I didn't care for 'Suspense' and would huddle under the table, feeling somehow I was safe under there until the show was over. The program was always scary and had creepy music playing that frightened me even more, but I didn't tell our mom and dad because they would have called me a baby for being afraid. Jimmy told me to try and plug my ears with my fingers so I couldn't hear the words and music.

Sometimes we would turn the big dial on the radio and listen to stations all over the world. We would stop at each station and listen for a while to see if we could understand them.   We would guess at what the language was and then go on to the next station. Our mom knew a lot about different languages and she could often tell us what was being said. Sometimes she would speak some words in the language, we liked to listen to that. If there was music playing we would listen to it until it ended and someone began to talk, then we would twirl the dial and find another song.

There was a set of encyclopedias in the house when we got there, and some nights our dad would read to us from them, starting with A and making good progress through P that winter. We learned many wonderful things from the encyclopedia.   There were stories about animals and faraway places, many with pictures that helped us to learn more about these things. On days when our dad was busy we might take down one of the books and look through the pages, hoping to find something interesting to suggest for reading that night.

If Jimmy had finished his lessons and didn't have any chores to do he might read a little bit to me from the encyclopedia while Jeff took a nap. Jeff didn't like to sit still for very long to listen to Jimmy read.

When we would get to town there would be a magazine or two in the mail for us. One year a magazine printed "How the Grinch Stole

Christmas", and our dad read that to us at Christmas time. He liked to read out loud and we liked to listen. We would all climb up on the big bed in the corner and settle down for an interesting story. We sat at the foot of the bed and our dad sat up by the pillows, so it was often hard to see the pictures, if there were any.

Our mom would not sit down while he read, but kept on about her many chores that kept her busy until bed time. She said it was the perfect time to mop the floor, as we were all up on the bed sitting quietly while being read to, and she mopped the floor several times a week. Sometimes she would get the big fat iron out, heat it on the stove and iron some of our clothes that she had washed and dried the day before. The house smelled good with the steam from the ironing and the fresh clothes.

Then the next summer something terrible happened! Our dad lost his boat, the *Mikey*, in a fire. While he was out fishing the boat caught fire and he could not put it out. He quickly got the skiff untied that he always pulled behind the boat and was able to get in it and row away from the burning boat. He lost one of the oars while getting in the little skiff and had to use the remaining one as a paddle, switching it from side to side, to get to shore of a nearby island.

He was a long way from our home, and there were no other boats around to see his boat burning. The boat soon burned to the water and then the smoke was gone. Our dad was cold and wet and had to figure some way to get the attention of a boat that might be going by. He hadn't had any time to put any food in the skiff and he knew he had to be rescued soon. He didn't have any way to catch a fish or shoot a duck. He always carried one of those little metal tubes in his jacket pocket that has a screw on lid and was waterproof, full of matches. He knew that the only way to draw attention was to make a lot more smoke, so he fixed up a big fire by gathering up wood from the beach and the woods, and when that didn't attract any attention, he made the fire bigger by burning up his skiff! He pulled the skiff over into the fire and it made a lot of smoke and he kept small branches from nearby trees that he could pull off, and some sticks from under the trees to it to make it even smokier. After a very long time a boat passing by saw the fire.

The fisherman anchored in the bay and came ashore in his skiff to see what was going on - everyone knew that a fire in a place where there was no house was a distress signal. The fisherman took our dad back to his boat, fed him a good meal and made some coffee for him and brought him to Kalinin Bay. It was scary to hear him tell of the boat catching on fire, and it made me afraid of fire for the rest of my life.

A fisherman can't be without a boat and it wasn't too long before he had his next boat, the *Ella June*, which was just a little bigger than the *Mikey*. The *Ella June* was 24 feet long and was not a double ender like the *Mikey*, so there seemed to be a lot more room on it. Our dad had to go to Seattle to get the new boat and Jimmy went with him. They rode into town one day with another fisherman and then took a plane to Seattle. Everyone would tease our mom about the new boat, as her name was June. They would ask her, 'but who is Ella?' She didn't always think it was funny.

When they were in Seattle they stayed in a hotel and Jimmy told about the big wooden bath tubs where they took their bath. He said it was smooth wood and full of hot water, up to his chin. We didn't have a bathtub, but had to take a bath in a small tin tub, with just enough water to wash in, because our dad had to carry up every bit of water to the house from the waterfall. Jimmy said he pretended that he was swimming in a big pool and stayed in the tub until someone else at the hotel wanted a bath.

The *Ella June* had to be fixed up a little, and one winter day our dad decided to haul the old engine out and put in a new one. He had all sorts of tools and pulleys and big equipment to use in the warehouses that sat on the dock near our house. He tied the boat to the dock and put a pulley out one of the big doors in the warehouse. He climbed down to the boat and tied the heavy ropes and chains around the old engine and then climbed back up the ladder to the warehouse and wound the rope around and around a winch to pull the engine slowly up to the warehouse.

He had to do it slowly because he didn't want the engine to bang against the pilings of the dock and perhaps get knocked loose and fall back into the boat. If that happened the engine would crash through the bottom of the boat and sink it. When he had the engine out he climbed back down the ladder to move the boat to a different location along the dock where he was going to get the new engine and put it in the boat. The tide was going out and the ladder up to the dock was now higher above the boat and our dad had to jump a little to get down to the deck of the boat.

There were no other people left in Kalinin Bay besides our family so he was doing this alone. He untied the boat, which was much lighter now that the engine was out, and began to push against the pilings of the dock with his arms to move the boat down. He would push against one piling, starting the boat moving, then rush a little way down the deck of the boat and grab on the next piling to pull the boat along farther. But the wind was coming up the bay and a sudden gust pulled the boat out away from the dock, with our dad hanging onto the piling. He lost his grip on the piling and his footing on the boat and fell into the near freezing water of the bay.

He was a long way from shore and couldn't hang onto a piling as he didn't know when any of us might hear him calling, and he couldn't swim to the boat as it was floating faster and faster up the bay. The ladders that came down to the boats were too high to reach from the piling because the tide was out, so he set out swimming for shore as fast as he could go. They say that in the freezing waters of Alaska in the winter you might only be able to survive for 45 seconds, so he knew the danger and knew he had to swim fast.

He tells the story that he got to shore in record time, perhaps only a minute, and while wearing his boots, thick woolen trousers and his heavy wool jacket. He was only wet from the waist down, and on his arms, as he tried to swim more upright so as not to expose too much of his body to the cold water. With the tide going out, the shore was closer than if it had been high tide. Once ashore he came steaming (and I do mean steaming) up the stairs, and called to our mom and Jimmy to come help at once. They grabbed their coats and another hat for our dad and off they went to get a skiff and catch the *Ella June.* They had to stop and put an outboard motor on the skiff, then they hauled it down to the water and all three piled in as fast as they could.

They chased after the *Ella June*, which was now past the middle of the channel and heading for some rocks on the other shore. The tide was beginning to run fast and they had to catch that boat! When at last they caught up to the boat our mom held onto the side of the *Ella June* and our dad scrambled aboard. He tied the skiff to the back of the boat and climbed back into the skiff. Then our mom climbed aboard the boat and went into the wheel house to steer with the rudder. Our dad put a tire bumper between the bow of the skiff and the stern of the *Ella June* and turned the outboard motor up higher and higher. The little skiff would push the *Ella June* to safety.

It wasn't a very big motor, but soon the *Ella June* began to move and our mom carefully steered back to the dock. As they got near the dock Jimmy climbed up to the boat and with a rope in his hand he grabbed for a ladder as the boat got close to the dock. Jimmy tied the rope tight and then our dad turned off the outboard motor and finished tying the boat to the dock. He couldn't tie up at the float, as he still had to get the new engine into the boat and had no way to go from the float to get to the dock by the warehouse.

That was all the work that was done on the boat that day! I remember our dad sat in front of the little stove upstairs for several hours wrapped in a blanket with his feet bright red, while he drank big cups of coffee, and then finally he limped to the bed and slept and slept. We were very quiet, as we somehow understood that he was very ill from all this.

Our mom never explained things to us, and I'm sure that sometimes our imaginations made up things worse than the actual incident. Our dad hadn't had time to change out of the wet clothes before they set out in the skiff after the drifting boat and it was well below freezing that time of the winter, so he got very cold in his wet clothes, and his feet were almost numb from the cold.

A few days later he was out again, working on the boat. After he got the old engine out he had to put the ropes and chains around the new engine and lower it slowly into the boat. Jimmy stood on the deck of the boat and helped to guide the new engine into the boat. Jimmy then climbed up the ladder and our dad climbed down. He had to adjust the ropes very carefully to make the new engine come down just in the right place before he told Jimmy to let the ropes loose.

With the new engine settled in the boat our dad spent several days getting it all hooked up and ready to go. After it was all ready he started the engine and took the boat up the bay, but this time he had Jimmy with him, and the skiff was tied on behind the boat - just in case he needed some help.

10
DOGS, CATS AND SQUIRRELS

Someone left a dog with us, a golden retriever named Chi-Chi and that winter she entertained us with games of hide and seek. Often the snow was too deep to play outdoors. If the tide was out we could play on the beach, but it was a very cold winter that year so we spent many hours entertaining ourselves indoors. We had our lessons to do, of course, but we could do a week's lessons in a day or two so we didn't continually have lessons. Sometimes we would do lessons steady for two or three weeks during the heavy snows and freezes, and then have a month or more of no lessons.

If the weather was extremely cold we would not be allowed to play downstairs, it used too much heating oil to keep that big space warm, so we were all crowded together in the upstairs living quarters. With animals and people all together we did fill the space, and it was fun to have a break in our routine with a little fun.

Our dad would sit between two beds in our bedroom to play hide-and-seek with Chi-Chi. He would pull a big black woolen blanket over his head. We would then tell Chi-Chi to find him, and she would sniff all around the blanket, then look under the bed, sniff at the blanket again, then back to the beds or run to the kitchen, then sniff at the blanket, while we squealed in laughter, knowing that Chi-Chi knew where he was, but she played the game very well. After a short while Chi-Chi would pounce on our dad and we would cheer her for finding him. Then he would pull the blanket over himself again and it would start all over. We never tired of this game, and Chi-Chi never did either, but our dad had things to do, so it didn't last too long.

That winter I also learned to mend nets. Our dad was not a net fisherman, he used long poles and lines with lures or bait on them. He found some nets in the warehouse and decided that we would mend them. I wasn't sure if he was mending them for someone, or just because they needed mended. I learned the knots and the proper ways to add in more netting, and how to end it off. I liked the feeling of the nets and the satisfaction of making them whole again. We did this work in the downstairs as the nets were much too big to take upstairs, and too dirty too. Our mom would never have allowed something that dirty in her house!

If the weather was fair and warmer we might work on them in the warehouse, or drag them out to the wide boardwalk in front of our house, but mostly we worked in the old store space. After a while of knotting and cutting and fixing we would wash our hands and have a rousing game of pool, and then upstairs for lunch.

My brothers didn't care for net mending, although Jeff was too small to really do much work then, and he had that broken arm that slowed him down. Jimmy had other chores that kept him busy, he had to keep the area outside of the building clean, make sure there was no trash lying about and gather drift wood to burn in the stove upstairs. The stove would burn oil or wood, it had two heating sections, and the more wood we burned the better, as it was free. Jimmy would much rather be out on the beach picking up wood, or in the edges of the woods finding branches that had fallen in the storms than indoor mending nets.

In the empty fishing village at Kalinin Bay there were repairs that our dad was expected to take care of during the winter and Jimmy would help him with those too. They would take hammers, saws, nails and crowbars and go down the rows of cabins to fix doors, hinges, roofs or whatever needed to be done. I wasn't big enough to help with those chores so I got to spend a lot of time working on the nets.

Some days they would take me with them if there was sweeping or small chores to do in the cabins. I would walk behind them, lugging some piece of equipment, happy to be going along. There was also boat maintenance and chores to be taken care of in the off season. There seemed to always be something that needed to be painted or repaired, as the weather and the sea were harsh, and hard on a boat. Our dad had a big black blowtorch that he would use while working on the boat. One time I accidentally bumped my arm against it and even though it was turned off it was still horridly hot and I got a big blister on my arm, and I was much more careful after that!

We always had cats at Kalinin Bay. Where they came from I don't know. We had Andy and Pandora, and Patience, a big black cat who was not the least patient. Andy and Pandora were calico cats, with funny colored splotches all over them. Someone called them crazy quilt cats, but I didn't know what that meant.

Soon Patience and Pandora had kittens; one had three and the other had five. When the two mom cats wanted to go outside they would bring all the babies to Andy's box and leave them there for him to kittysit. When they came back from their adventures they would each take four kittens - and it wasn't always the same four - and go back to their boxes. This continued until one day our dad said he had to take care of all those kittens. We didn't know what "take care of" meant but we soon learned. Our dad got a big gunny sack and filled it with rocks and then with kittens, and I wanted to cry, for I knew what this meant. But as we were expected to be brave, I just stood as stiff and still as I could, hoping that I wouldn't move, for I knew the tears would fall out if I did, and then I'd be in trouble.

I spent the afternoon never once looking at the bay, and I was very surprised to see eight scraggly wet kittens coming up the boardwalk! How did this happen??? I was too frightened though, to be happy. I knew that our mom would NOT like this one bit, and sure enough, she didn't. Back into another sack went rocks, more and bigger this time, and then the poor kittens, and I ran up the beach and cried and cried. At first I didn't care if I wasn't brave, I was too sad for the kittens. Then I stayed away from home the rest of the afternoon, so ashamed of not being brave.

There were some ravens on the beach and I talked to them about how sad I was that the kittens were in the sack in the water. The ravens walked around and around on the beach, talking to themselves about this, and it made me feel a little better; they understood how sad I was. Then I heard our mom calling us for dinner and I knew better than to not answer or return home. I didn't dilly dally either; she was very strict about that!

And there, waiting on the corner of the boardwalk, were the eight kittens again! Oh! I could not believe it and wanted so to hide them, but then our dad came around the corner, looked at the kittens - and just shook his head. He muttered, "Well, well, guess you kittens are no match for me", and we were allowed to keep all of them for the rest of the time we lived there.

We simply named the kittens One, Two, Three, Four, Five, Six, Seven, and Otto, and they gave us many laughs as they explored and tumbled about on the docks and in the woods near our house. Pandora had gotten her name because she was so very curious, like Pandora in mythology, and if there was ever any box or cupboard that she came upon, she would try her best to open it. This sometimes got her in trouble, as she would fall inside of things and then not be able to get out, but one of the kittens would come running for us and take us to where Pandora was waiting patiently (<u>she</u> should have been named Patience!) for someone to get her out of another scrape.

Patience wasn't as curious, but she loved to swim, and would paddle about in the bay most afternoons except on the very coldest of winter days. Maybe that is where the kittens got their bravery to swim back to shore twice. When we finally moved away from Kalinin Bay, Patience jumped off the boat and swam ashore twice before she decided that it was ok to go with us on the boat. She was very particular about things, and after she had a swim she liked to have a snack. I thought this was funny, because when we still lived in California and would go swimming in the American River, I always had wanted soda crackers to eat after swimming. When Patience would come out of the water she would rub her fur on the rocks, perhaps to get the extra water off, then she would come to the house and meow until I would bring down something for her to eat.

One day I had a snack of crackers with me and teased her with it, telling her she should eat crackers after swimming, and she began to nibble my cracker, and always after that I would save her a cracker from my snack for her swimming treat.

Besides the food we brought from town, there were many good things to eat in Kalinin Bay. There were berries to pick: salmon berries, elder berries, blueberries and red huckleberries, as well as kelp to gather for pickles, crabs, clams and the fish our dad caught. After the *Mikey* burned, times were hard, as our dad had to spend his extra money to buy another boat, and we weren't able to get a shipment of meat for that winter. There were no berries left from the fall either. Someone gave us a one hundred pound bag of lima beans and we ate them for a long time.

I never have been fond of lima beans and this was almost unbearable to me, but I knew better than to protest. As the winter wore on our dad asked the game warden if he could shoot a deer to feed his family, and the game warden said that he could not hunt out of season, but if there was no evidence of a killed deer, no hide or bones, then he could not fine anyone for shooting a deer out of season.

Our dad must have been very careful, for we children never knew that he shot a deer for our meat that year, but heard the story many many years later. I just remember that we all of a sudden didn't have to eat only lima beans, and we would have a big roast for dinner. When Jimmy asked what kind of meat this was, our dad called it Roast Ghost.

Sometimes the wild things in Alaska were not as good as the berries and fresh fish. One would be the whale that was beached at the head of the bay. We walked up to see it one day, soon after it had swum up to the beach and got stuck there and died. We walked up close to it and we touched it, feeling the tough skin. It was interesting to stand beside a whale, as before this I had only seen them swimming. But it wasn't long before the whale began to smell awful. Fortunately we lived down the bay, and upwind of the whale, but occasionally we would catch a whiff and be glad that the whale was so far away, oh my, it did have an awful odor! I had smelled dead fish, and dead crabs and even once a dead eagle, but nothing had the awful smell of that dead whale.

I remember finding things to play with that were not really toys. There were all the store shelves behind the counter in the downstairs that I used for doll houses, so my paper dolls lived in style. The shelves were divided into small sections, like little rooms. The one problem was a squirrel that loved to come inside the store and run back and forth along the clotheslines our dad had strung, and sometimes the squirrel would jump down and chew on the paper doll's belongings that I had made for her.

We were not allowed to have toys upstairs in the living quarters so I made a deal with the squirrel. I told him that if he would not chew the paper doll's things that I would leave him a bit of food each day over in the other corner of the store, and so far as I could see, he lived up to his part of the bargain - except for one time when I couldn't get any food to him so he munched a little corner off a table I had made from cardboard. But that was alright; since I had not left him any food, he was still living up to his end of the bargain.

The squirrel would come in through a little flapping door our dad made for him up near the ceiling of the store and scamper about the room looking for something to eat. Our dad built a ferris wheel for him to jump into and if he ran and jumped hard enough, it would start going around. He could jump from one seat to another and keep the ferris wheel turning and that amused us. He would run back and forth at the window sometimes - just peeking inside to see what we were doing. The squirrel didn't like the cats and was careful to always look for them before scampering around in the downstairs.

11
FRIENDS

When summer came there were more people around as the fishing boats and the fish buying scow were often there. I met the lady who had given Jeff his sleeping pill when he fell off the dock. She had one leg that was about ten inches shorter than the other and she had a marvelous thing added on her shoe that made her legs almost the same length and I loved her. Her name was Jenny, and I was happy to check that name off my list. She kept their fish-buying scow spotless clean, at least the living quarters part, and had ruffled curtains and red checked window-seat cushions and baked the most wonderful gingerbread.

The windows on the scow were big and bright - she washed them every day. Sometimes she had curls in her hair that she got by winding her hair in rags at night. I thought she was so elegant. She had books and would read me grown up stories, not kid stories, and that made me happy. She read from books that she kept in her window seat - she would lift up the seat and under it was a wonderful storage bin full of books. She read me the titles of the books, and we picked a book together for her to read from.

As soon as I would see the fish-buyer's scow coming in the bay I would sit on the dock and wait (not patiently, for I have NEVER been patient) for her to call for me to come on board. We had many wonderful times and she told me stories about growing up in the north. Some days Jenny would get out her stitching and we would sit and have tea and stitch, like two ladies who were friends.

She taught me to embroider, to make fine small stitches and to take stitches out if they weren't to my liking. I embroidered some small napkins for my doll, with little forget-me-nots, all made with French knots, and Jenny wrote down the name for me and she spelled it 'Forget-Me-Knots', which made us both laugh. I had trouble getting the knots to sit close to the cloth, but Jenny patiently showed me over and over how to wind the thread and how to hold it with one hand while gently pulling the thread through with the other hand. I liked making the Forget-Me-Knots because they were Alaska's State Flower and grew in the edges of the woods near our house.

Our next stitch was the lazy daisy stitch, and although I didn't remember seeing a daisy before, I liked the stitch. After I learned the stem stitch I could make the whole Forget-Me-Knot flower, French knots in blue, stem stitch and lazy daisy in green for the stems and leaves. After our tea and stitching I would carry the tea things to the sink and Jenny would wash and I would dry the delicate flowery cups and saucers.

One day Jenny decided to send invitations to all the boats in the harbor for a tea party. Many of the wives off the boats came and I felt very important, for Jenny asked me to pass around the gingerbread.

Before the party Jenny wrote out the invitations on pretty paper and we put on our coats and scarves and went from boat to boat, delivering the invitations. Our mom wouldn't come, and at first she said I wasn't allowed to go, because it was just a silly idea, but she at last changed her mind - I was the happiest girl in the world as I put on my skirt and blouse and fine striped sweater.

We didn't wear our fancy clothes very often, but this was a very special occasion. I wished I had that pretty pink dress to wear that Aunt Herma had sent, but I was happy just to get to go to the party. It was a stormy day, so the ladies didn't have anything else to do that afternoon and they stayed a long time, drinking tea and eating gingerbread. I sat listening to their talk, about children and cooking and all sorts of wonderful things, and late in the afternoon I fell asleep on one end of the window seat cushions.

Jenny woke me when it was time to wash the dishes, for that was one of our private traditions. We put the sparkling cups and saucers back in their safe cupboard, with bits of fabric between each so they wouldn't get cracked or scratched in rough weather, and I set off up the dock for home. Our mom never asked me about the tea party. I wished that she would so I could tell her all about the wonderful day I had with Jenny.

Sometimes Jenny would invite me and my doll to tea and she would bring out her doll, which had a fur parka, mukluks and a nice corduroy dress. Her doll was very proud of the fur clothes and would have offered them to my doll to wear, but Sammy Sue was so much bigger they would never have fit.

The fish buyer was an important part of the life of the fishermen in Alaska. Many of the good fishing grounds were far from towns and a lot of time would have been wasted running back and forth between the fishing grounds and town to sell the catch. When our dad fished nearer to Sitka he would fill the hold of his boat with ice from a long chute from the ice plant on the dock. Then at the end of the day he would clean the fish and put them in the ice, filling the cleaned part of the fish with ice also. This way he could fish for several days without returning to port.

But when he fished farther away he had no access to the ice and would sell his catch each night to the fish buyer. The fish buyer boat or scow could hold tons of ice and fish and only had to go to town once every week or so. They would travel to where there were fishermen and everyone seemed to know where the fish buying scow was.

This one was often at Kalinin Bay and I was always happy to see them returning from their trips to town to sell the fish. If they arrived at Kalinin Bay before they had taken on any fish we would get fresh ice from them and make a freezer full of ice cream in the summer.

Another interesting lady was Diane (she pronounced it Dyyyyyyyy yan) who had a dog that would carry messages up and down the stairs to her from us kids in the downstairs store room. Her dog would carry the messages in her mouth, very carefully and Diane taught us to tell the dog to 'give' and the dog would release the note and then stand patiently waiting for us to read it and send a reply. We put important things in the notes, like what we had eaten for lunch, or what we were planning that afternoon, and Diane always took time to answer the notes.

She also knew how to knit and taught me and later I would knit scarves and hats and socks for my doll. I am left handed and our mom would not teach me to knit, as she felt that left handed people couldn't learn to knit, but Diane said to sit across from her, and when she knitted I was to follow exactly what she did, and it would be 'backwards' to her, but the correct way for a left handed person. And indeed it was. What a clever lady.

There is lots of maintenance on boats, and since Diane had taught me to knit I would go down and help sand the metal for painting on their boat when she needed help. Their boat, the White Light, was the nicest looking boat in the fleet; must have been all that sanding and painting.

There were frequent visitors in the summer. One couple stood out in my mind because he had only one leg as the other one had been cut mostly off from cancer. He got about on crutches and was constantly arguing with his wife, because she wanted him to have more surgery to stop the cancer from spreading to his other leg and he wouldn't do it. I never knew what became of him, but I certainly thought he was brave, which in our family was the best trait of all. He would get on and off their fishing boat and get around while on the boat, all on crutches, and it was a very small boat.

As summer came on, our dad spent more days fishing and we stayed in Kalinin Bay with the summer residents. There were not many kids my age that came to the houses there, and our mother said that we must keep to ourselves anyway, so I never got to meet any of them. They would go by our house on the way to the dock and I would watch out the upstairs window, wishing that they could stop and play with me.

12
THE NEXT MOVE

At the end of summer our dad announced that we would be moving away, he was no longer needed at Kalinin Bay and we would not be coming back. I didn't want to leave Jenny and the many nice friends there.

We packed the few things that belonged to us, our clothes and pans and what was left of our food, and of course our toys and school books and the three grown up cats. The kittens had been given away to other people that came to Kalinin Bay in the summer. We packed everything very carefully in the boat, making sure that all was secure and then we went back to the house to finish cleaning it up.

Our mom scrubbed everything upstairs and downstairs, and we hauled away any trash that was left. She washed all the store windows and took down the clotheslines in the store. She checked in the big wooden box, and in the store room where we had kept our food. She dusted the beds and fluffed up the mattresses. She cleaned out the inside of the window box and scrubbed the dishpan that we used for a sink. She said that the next people to live there would not have to clean the house before they moved in, like she had to do.

We ate our dinner on the boat that night and slept there too, and before the sun was up our dad woke us up and told us to get dressed so we could get under way. Our mom was cooking breakfast on the little black stove and it smelled so good! There was bacon and pancakes sitting on the back of the stove and a big blue pot of coffee boiling. There was always a pot of coffee on the stove - for fishermen drank lots of coffee. We got dressed quickly and Jimmy and I took our plates out on deck to eat. We looked at the buildings on the shore and watched as some of the last people were packing up for the winter and getting ready to leave, just as we were. We thought Kalinin Bay was a great place to live and wished that we could stay.

Our dad started the engine and Jimmy jumped to the float to cast off - and we were underway. I watched out the porthole for as long as I could see the buildings, then lay down in my bunk and thought about Kalinin Bay and our house and all the things we had done there.

When the boat first pulled away from the float, our cat Patience wiggled free and jumped into the water and swam ashore. She definitely didn't want to leave! The other cats meowed and put their feet up on the railings – they wanted her to come back, and they didn't swim, so they wouldn't jump in after her. Our dad pulled the boat back in to the float and Jimmy ran up and got Patience. She did this once again as the boat started away from the float and after Jimmy fetched her again or dad said the next time she would be left behind. I really hoped she would not jump overboard again so I took her below and petted her until we were a long ways from the float, and she didn't jump overboard again.

Late in the evening our boat slipped through a small channel between two islands and pulled up to a small float. The light on the rocks of the channel was so close to the boat it seemed we could reach out and touch it. Jimmy tied the boat to the float and we came up on deck to see our new home. The island we were going to be living one was small and was called Killisnoo. There were several big buildings, with a small building in front just across from the float.

There was no dock here, just a float and I didn't know how we would get to the land. We could see several big oil tanks like the ones that had blown over in Kalinin Bay, and two big long warehouses sticking out into the bay, built right over the water. Our mom said we would stay on the boat that night and then go ashore in the morning. I wanted to go and see the buildings, but there was no way to get there. We went to bed as soon as the dinner dishes were done. Our mom and dad stayed up on the deck, talking to some other fishermen who were tied up nearby. We could hear them talking for a long time, and from time to time one of them would come down and get some coffee from the big blue coffee pot.

Early the next morning we were up and eating breakfast before the sun was very high in the sky. Our mom made us some boat toast and oatmeal. Boat toast is made by putting thick slices of bread in the oven, right on the racks, and letting it stay there until it was brown on both sides. This would take a long time and the bread got very hard and crunchy. Then we spread margarine on it and it tasted delicious. If we were still at our house in Kalinin Bay we could have jam on the toast, but the jam was still packed in the hold. The oatmeal was hot and wonderful on a cool morning and as soon as our dad and Jimmy finished eating their breakfast they took the skiff down off the boom and started putting our things in it. Jimmy would row it ashore, unload it on the beach and then come back for more. One trip our mom went with him and she began to carry things up to the tallest house. Jeff and I had to stay below until everything was unloaded so we took turns looking out the porthole at what was going on. I wanted to help! I thought I was big enough to carry things to the new house, but our dad said to wait below, so we did.

By lunch time they had loaded everything into the skiff and taken it ashore, and the last trip Jimmy took Jeff and me to shore. We both sat on the back seat of the skiff and Jimmy sat in the middle to row. We liked riding in the skiff and wanted to ride around in the bay, but Jimmy still had things to do so we went straight to shore. Our mom had hauled almost everything up to the house except the big tins of flour and sugar. There was a wooden wagon there that she had used to make the trips back and forth and now our dad loaded the heavy tins onto the wagon, put Jeff on top and pulled the wagon up to the house. Jimmy helped by pushing on the back of the wagon and I walked along behind, with our three cats following and exploring along the way.

We walked past the small store building and up to the big, tall house. There was a porch all along the front of the house and it wasn't upstairs of a store. It was a house all by itself. We climbed the steps and Jeff ran back and forth on the porch, while the rest of us went inside.   There was a black stove like we had on the boat, and it was not much bigger, in the first room. There was nice wood on the walls and very tall windows.

The next room to the side was the kitchen and there was a kitchen table with a padded seat that went around three sides of the table, with two wooden chairs in front of the table. I remembered from California when we would go grocery shopping in Placerville that we would stop for lunch at Bob's Big Boy Restaurant. They had seats just like the one in our kitchen, soft and padded. In Placerville there were small juke boxes at each table to pick music to listen to and sometimes we would put a nickel in and listen to a song.   At Killisnoo there was no juke box, of course, but when I would eat my sandwich for lunch and I would be the last one at the table, I would kick my feet back and forth under the table and hum that 'Slowpoke' song to myself.

Also in the room that was the kitchen there was a long counter for fixing food and cupboards above it. At Kalinin Bay there were no cupboards in the kitchen, just a few shelves. There was no sink in the kitchen here at Killisnoo either; we would still have to use a dishpan for washing dishes.

We had nearer neighbors at Killisnoo, but none that lived on the same island as we did. There were old buildings nearby but no one lived in them. There were several families that lived across the channel, and the village of Angoon was just about an hour's walk from our house, after we rowed across the channel. At Kalinin Bay there had been no neighbors during the winter.

We arrived at Killisnoo in the fall, and set about cleaning up the house. It hadn't been lived in for a while so we had to sweep it clean, then scrub everything twice over. Our mom had brought buckets and mops and brooms. There was a large water tank on the front porch and Jimmy dipped pails of water out and put them on the stove to heat. Our mom tied a scarf around my hair so it wouldn't get dirty and I helped scrub the table and the counters in the kitchen.

Our mom scrubbed the black stove until it was shiny, inside and out. Jimmy swept the upstairs rooms and the stairs, while Jeff ran about, playing on the front porch. We still lived on the boat while we were cleaning, and each day as soon as we had breakfast and straightened up the boat we would go ashore in the skiff to the big house and clean. Jimmy would row our mom and dad across first and then come back for Jeff and me. I would stand close to Jeff to make sure that he didn't fall overboard into the water while we waited for Jimmy to come back for us.

We swept and dusted and nailed things back in place. We brushed the walls and scrubbed the steps and soon everything shone and we could move in. No one could clean like our mom, and our houses, no matter how old, always sparkled.

There was the store in the smaller building in front of our house and one day a big boat came with boxes and boxes of groceries. They had a big skiff with a motor on the back and they loaded it up and came ashore. The men from the big boat and Jimmy and our dad carried boxes into the store building. Our mom had scrubbed and cleaned the shelves and counters in the store too, so it was ready to be filled up.

They filled the shelves with cans and boxes and bags of good things to eat. There were many slabs of bacon that hung in the back room, and cartons of candy and cases of soda pop in short brown bottles. There were brooms and shovels, pike poles and peevies, gaff hooks and rubber boots - gloves, hats and rain coats, just about anything a fisherman could need. The men stacked everything in one corner of the store and then went up to our house to have coffee. They sat around our kitchen table and talked for a long time. Jimmy and I went back into the store and looked at all the supplies. Some of the boxes we couldn't see into so we tried to guess what was in them.

Our mom and dad came in later and we began to put things away where they belonged. Some of everything went on the shelves so the fishermen could see what the store had, and if there was too much to put on the shelves we would take it to the back room and put it on shelves there. All the shelves were behind the counters and there were windows along two sides of the store building to let in light. Our dad hung one slab of bacon from a hook in the ceiling and put a big knife and cutting board nearby so he could slice off the bacon to sell. I liked the smell of the store when there was bacon hanging there.

In the back room were many big hams, wrapped in cloth and also hanging from hooks. When a fisherman wanted some ham our dad would take one down and cut off a big piece. He would put it on a white scale on the counter and tell them how much it cost. I liked helping to get the store ready for business.

After the shelves were full and everything was put away the store was ready for business. Our mom would sell things to the fishermen in the evenings after they were done fishing.

Our dad was a fisherman but at the end of the day he was also the fish buyer. Tied up to the float was a smaller fish buying scow. It was full of ice and each night the fishermen would tie up alongside the scow to sell the fish they had caught that day. They would pitch their fish into huge hanging scales, which had a large scoop shaped bucket on a chain to hold the fish to be weighed. Sometimes one would slide out and Jimmy would get it and put it back in the scale. After the fish were weighed they were dumped from the scale into the hold of the scow and Jimmy would jump down into the hold and put the fish in the ice to freeze them until the big fish buying ship would come to Killisnoo.

When the huge fish buying ship would come to Killisnoo, Jimmy and a man from the ship would pile the frozen fish into large wooden boxes and then pile the wooden boxes onto big wooden platforms and the ship would lift the platforms up with a winch and dump the fish into the hold of the ship. Jimmy would have to shovel all the old ice out of the hold of the scow and scrub it with a wide broom and buckets of fresh water that he hauled out from the house.   Then the ship would send ice down a chute into the hold of the scow until it was half full of ice.

Each night our dad would write down the fisherman's name and how much their fish had weighed and then give them money. Sometimes they would not take money but would row ashore and pick things from the store to trade for their fish. I liked to watch the fishermen shop, trying to guess which things they would ask our mom for from the shelves behind the counters. She would take each item down off the shelf and put everything into wooden boxes. Then they would take the boxes, row out to their boats, unload their supplies, and bring the boxes back to the store so they could be used again. The boxes had hinges on the sides and you could flop the bottom of the box inside and then fold the box flat to put in the store room. That was my job - to take all the boxes from in front of the store where the fishermen left them, fold them flat and carry them to the store-room. I thought it was a very important job, and as soon as I saw them rowing back to their boats I would be ready to fold the boxes up.

13
ABOUT KILLISNOO

There had once been a town at Killisnoo, but now all that was left was the big house a ways behind the store building, and many old, rundown buildings, which gave us kids lots of places to play.

First Killisnoo had a whale oil factory and later processed cod and herring – for food, fertilizer and oil.

The whaling boats would bring the whales up to the warehouses. They were huge ships, because they had to haul a whale. When they got to the dock they would tie ropes around the whales and many people would begin to pull on the ropes and the whales would slowly slide up a ramp and into the warehouse.

Workers would then begin to slice the blubber off the whales. Blubber is the fat under the skin of the whale that was used to make whale oil for burning in lamps before there was electricity. It would be chopped into smaller pieces for processing and melting.

The head of the whale was important because it had a different kind of special oil in it. Oil was needed to keep machines running smoothly and this oil was obtained from the head and jaws of whales with teeth. It was a thick oil that never got completely hard, even in the coldest weather, so could be used on machinery to keep everything running smoothly. It was often called train oil because it was used on the wheels of the big trains to make them turn smoothly. It was even used on things as small as watches.

First the oil was taken out of the head of the whale, and then the blubber was cut up and put into gigantic kettles hanging over fires out behind the warehouses. The oil that came to the top was skimmed off and put into barrels to be sold. This type of whale oil would become solid when cooled and was used for lamps and for making candles. The oil burned brightly, without a bad smell or smoke so it was very popular for home lighting. But it was expensive and so was used only by those with enough money to buy it. Others used tallow from cows and sheep to make their candles, and they also made oil from the seeds of kale, called kolza oil. It burned badly and smelled even worse - but was all they could afford.

Baleen was another product of some whales. It is the big plates attached to the upper jaws of baleen whales instead of teeth. The whales use baleen to filter plankton from the water. This is how they feed, filtering hundreds of gallons of sea water through the baleen filters. The baleen is very flexible and can be separated into thin strips that will bend and not break, so they were used in women's corsets, hairbrushes, buggy whips, collar stays and hoop skirts, making the skirts stand out in a full circle. All these products were obtained from the whales that were brought to the warehouses at Killisnoo.

The plant burned in 1928. Later it was a refugee camp during WWII for the people from the Aleutian Islands when they were invaded during the war, and the people were told that they were taken to Killisnoo for their safety. But what they wanted were people that they could make to work for the government at a cheap price. The living conditions were terrible on Killisnoo and often the people had to build shacks to live in. There was enough food for the people on Killisnoo because they could eat the fish they caught. There were guards at Killisnoo and no one was ever allowed to leave the island for many years. Some of the people would get lonely for their homes and try to get off the island in small boats, but the guards had bigger, faster boats and they always made them come back to Killisnoo.

After the war most of the people there were at last allowed to leave. Later new warehouses were built to be used for boat and net repairs for fishermen.

The building of most interest to me was a tiny cottage just to the right of the house. It no longer had glass in the windows but did have some furniture, the most interesting piece being what we thought was an apple press. It had two flat metal surfaces, one on top of the other, that you could screw down tight, by turning a big steering-wheel like thing at the top. We pressed all sorts of things: leaves, acorns, shells, kelp, berries, bear's teeth - whatever we could find - and found it interesting to see how flat this apple press would make things. It was only later that I found out that what we actually had was a book press, used to flatten books after they are first bound, or to reflatten books that had been wet.

We set up the little cottage with whatever we could find to furnish it. We had stumps for chairs and small tables, a rickety table with pencils and paper held down by rocks, as the wind was free to come in and blow things about. We hung vines over the windows for curtains but had to replace them often, as they soon wilted. I had learned in the encyclopedia about making twig brooms so we had a nice assortment of twig brooms, one for any occasion.

We would gather very thin twigs and bundle them together. According to the encyclopedia we should bind them with thin leather strips, but as we had none, we would find bits of twine or some rope that we could unravel and use that to twist around the twigs to attach them to a bigger twig for a handle. We found a lot of twigs on a little hill that rose right behind our house, so we piled them up and sorted them according to size for our brooms. We had tiny brooms for sweeping out the window sills, medium size brooms for sweeping off the furniture and one or two bigger brooms for the floor and the steps outside. When a broom was no longer useful we would press it flat in our apple press and hang it on the outside of the cottage as a souvenir. We thought this was a clever way to hang things, as we had learned in school about tanning hides and hanging them on the outside walls of the houses.

We would hunt around the old buildings on the rest of the island and bring back things that we could carry for the cottage. I liked to do my math problems in the cottage but didn't have a blackboard, and wanted to save my bits of paper for lists, so I would mark out three inch square spaces on boards and do the math there. We had learned in our correspondence school lessons to draw accurate three inch squares on our paper, one for each problem, and so that is how I did it in the cottage. One time our dad was making a cupboard and found math problems all over the lumber he wanted to use - that was the end of writing on lumber for me! I did, however, learn to use sandpaper on wood at that time.

The house was big, with two bedrooms upstairs and a kitchen, living room, one bedroom and a storage room downstairs. The stairs up to our bedrooms turned a corner part way up and there was a landing there, then eight more steps and a second landing in a little hallway between the two very large bedrooms. The brick chimney from the cook stove in the living room ran up through one side of the landing and there was space enough next to the chimney for snuggling down with a book or a piece of paper and a pencil. We were not allowed many books while growing up - they were considered a big waste of time - and if caught reading one we were told to get up and do something useful.

There was a small window opposite the chimney, on the top landing, and through it you could see the hill behind the house. There was also a window at the bottom of the stairs. When you opened this window you could reach out your hand and touch that hillside, it was that close.

Both bedrooms upstairs were very large. Mine had a big bed and my brothers' had three smaller beds. There were plenty of windows and no curtains, since there were no neighbors. We could lie in our beds at night and see the stars or see the rain running down the windows. I found a copy of Lorna Doone in one of the old buildings and brought it back to my room, and each night I would try to read a little of it. On cold rainy days I would sit next to the chimney in the hallway and read. It is not appropriate reading for a third grader! But it was the only extra book I had. When we got our school books from Calvert Correspondence I would read all the way through each book, as we were allowed school books without restriction. I didn't find the math very interesting reading, but at least it was a book. I managed to get all the way through Lorna Doone that year, although I did not understand most of what I read.

Sometimes I would volunteer to straighten the food storage room, for there is much good reading on the backs of packages and cans, but I had to read fast or our mom would get suspicious and think I was wasting time.

My brothers' room had big, free-standing cupboards with doors, and we would play hospital up there, the cupboards being the place we stored our "medicines". We had no way to know what medicines should be called, so we labeled and named the medicines after animals. Jimmy knew more than we did about hospitals so he told us what kind of medicines to make. When we lived in California he had the chicken pox one year and had to have the doctor come out for several visits, so he was the authority. I don't remember the doctor coming when I was sick, so I believed anything Jimmy told me. We had Bear Salve for burns, Otter Water for sick tummies, Seal Soup for when we were hungry and not ill, and on and on. All these 'medicines' were stored in little metal containers we had discovered in an old store building, and all medicines were made of rocks or bits of shells found on the beach. We sorted rocks and shells by the hour to make sure we had only one color in each container. There was a beach full of small pebbles, and we hauled them up in pans to sort in the cottage, then fill our medicine tins and deliver them to the upstairs cupboards.

We also kept a supply of sticks for splints, in case we had to fix broken bones in our hospital and scraps of fabric for wrapping injuries.

When we were working in the medicine cabinets I would put my scraps of paper in there, but I always went back and took them out, as we didn't have much paper to write on. We never did actually do any 'doctoring' in all this, just sorted and kept our supplies ready. We must have seemed like a family of packrats. The cupboards of 'medicines and supplies' were kept very neat, we had learned that from our mom, and if we left a mess she would have thrown everything out.

My room was 'L' shaped and the short leg of the 'L' I made into a dollhouse, complete with small log table and chairs and a doll bed. I always wanted some dishes for the dollhouse and that next summer our Grandpa Deke (pronounced Dee Kee) came from California to visit us and brought me a child's Blue Willow tea set. I was sick when he arrived and was lying on a mat in my doll house, playing with my doll. He set out the tea set for me and I was delighted, as was Sammy Sue. Now we could have real tea parties, and on such fancy china.

There were not only teacups and teapot, but sugar and creamer, a soup tureen with a lid, a big platter and dinner plates. Our Grandpa Deke had also brought a small wooden salad set, with a big salad bowl and small individual bowls, just the right size for dolls. I was setting up the dishes for a tea party next to the mat and I put my elbow down and broke one of the saucers the first day. I was in awful trouble with our mom for being careless. But it was so grand to have a tea set for Sammy Sue and me, and I thought I must be the luckiest girl in the world.

Jenny and her husband would sometimes come to Killisnoo and I was proud to show her my very own tea set and we would set up our tea parties on the big wide front porch that ran all the way across the front of the house, and drink tea and discuss important things, like which kind of cake was the very best, and who we would invite to our tea parties if we could invite anyone at all. I could only think that I would invite my two cousins, Cookie with the red hair and her wonderful sister Cathy, and one very special uncle from California. But Jenny knew of many people, kings and poets and scientists and she would tell me all about them. In my child's mind I thought that Jenny knew all these people, and learned later that she had read of them in books. I was learning poetry in my school lessons that year and Jenny and I would quote our favorite poems at the tea parties also.

My favorite poems were small ones, but Jenny knew some very long ones and I loved to sit on the porch and listen to her recite them. She said poetry was like singing, without the tune.

I Meant To Do My Work Today
by Richard LeGallienne

I meant to do my work today,
But a brown bird sang in the apple tree,
And a butterfly flitted across the field,
And all the leaves were calling me.
And the wind went sighing over the land,
Tossing the grasses to and fro,
And a rainbow held out its shining hand,
So what could I do but laugh and go?

Fog
by Carl Sandburg

The fog comes
on little cat feet.
It sits looking
over harbor and city
on silent haunches
and then moves on.

All Things Bright and Beautiful
by Cecil Frances Alexander

All things bright and beautiful,
All creatures great and small,
All things wise and wonderful,
The Lord God made them all.

Each little flower that opens,
Each little bird that sings,
He made their glowing colors,
He made their tiny wings.

The purple-headed mountain,
The river running by,
The sunset, and the morning,
That brightens up the sky;

The cold wind in the winter,
The pleasant summer sun,
The ripe fruits in the garden,
He made them every one.

He gave us eyes to see them,
And lips that we might tell,
How great is God Almighty,
Who has made all things well.

(Cecil was a lady poet)

At the Seaside
by Robert Louis Stevenson

When I was down beside the sea
A wooden spade they gave to me
To dig the sandy shore.
My holes were empty like a cup,
In every hole the sea came up,
Till it could come no more.

Bed in Summer
by Robert Louis Stevenson

In Winter I get up at night
And dress by yellow candle light.

In Summer, quite the other way,
I have to go to bed by day.

I have to go to bed and see
The birds still hopping on the tree,
Or hear the grown-up people's feet
Still going past me in the street.

And does it not seem hard to you,
When all the sky is clear and blue,
And I should like so much to play,
To have to go to bed by day?

The Cow
by Robert Louis Stevenson

The friendly cow, all red and white,
I love with all my heart:
She gives me cream with all her might,
To eat with apple tart.

She wanders lowing here and there,
And yet she cannot stray,
All in the pleasant open air,
The pleasant light of day;

And blown by all the winds that pass
And wet with all the showers,
She walks among the meadow grass
And eats the meadow flowers.

Good Night and Good Morning
~Richard Monckton Milnes, Lord Houghton

A fair little girl sat under a tree,
Sewing as long as her eyes could see;

Then smoothed her work, and folded it right,
And said, "Dear work, good night! good night!"

Such a number of rooks came over her head,
Crying, "Caw! Caw!" on their way to bed;
She said, as she watched their curious flight,
"Little black things, good night! good night!"

The horses neighed, and the oxen lowed,
The sheep's "Bleat! bleat!" came over the road;
All seeming to say, with a quiet delight,
"Good little girl, good night! good night!"

She did not say to the sun, "Good night!"
Though she saw him there like a ball of light,
For she knew he had God's time to keep
All over the world, and never could sleep.

The tall pink foxglove bowed his head,
The violets curtsied and went to bed;
And good little Lucy tied up her hair,
And said on her knees her favorite prayer.

And while on her pillow she softly lay,
She knew nothing more till again it was day;
And all things said to the beautiful sun,
"Good morning! good morning! our work is begun!

Mary's Lamb
~Sarah Josepha Hale

Mary had a little lamb,
Its fleece was white as snow,
And everywhere that Mary went
The lamb was sure to go;
He followed her to school one day-
That was against the rule,

It made the children laugh and play
To see a lamb at school.

And so the teacher turned him out,
But still he lingered near,
And waited patiently about,
Till Mary did appear.
And then he ran to her and laid
His head upon her arm,
As if he said, "I'm not afraid-
You'll shield me from all harm."

"What makes the lamb love Mary so?"
The little children cry;
"Oh, Mary loves the lamb, you know,"
The teacher did reply,
"And, you, each gentle animal
In confidence may bind,
And make it follow at your call,
If you are always kind."

Nonsenses
~Edward Lear

There was an Old Man with a beard,
Who said, "It is just as I feared!-
Two owls and a hen,
Four larks and a wren,
Have all built their nests in my beard!"
The Rainbow
~Christina Rossetti

Boats sail on the rivers,
And ships sail on the seas;
But clouds that sail across the sky
Are prettier than these.

There are bridges on the rivers,
As pretty as you please;
But the bow that bridges heaven,
And overtops the trees,
And builds a road from earth to sky,
Is prettier far than these.

The Star
~Jane Taylor

Twinkle, twinkle, little star,
How I wonder what you are!
Up above the world so high,
Like a diamond in the sky.

When the blazing sun is gone,
When he nothing shines upon,
Then you show your little light,
Twinkle, twinkle, all the night.

Then the traveler in the dark,
Thanks you for your tiny spark,
He could not see which way to go,
If you did not twinkle so.

In the dark blue sky you keep,
And often through my curtains peep,
For you never shut your eye,
Till the sun is in the sky.
As your bright and tiny spark,
Lights the traveler in the dark-
Though I know not what you are,
Twinkle, twinkle, little star.

Topsy Turvy World
~Albert Midlane

If the butterfly courted the bee,
And the owl the porcupine;
If the churches were built in the sea,
And three times one was nine;
If the pony rode his master,
If the buttercups ate the cows,
If the cat had the dire disaster
To be worried, sir, by the mouse;
If mamma, sir, sold the baby
To a gypsy for half-a-crown;
If a gentleman, sir, was a lady-
The world would be Upside Down!
If any or all of these wonders
Should ever come about,
I should not consider them blunders,
For I should be Inside Out!

Little Things
~Julia A. Carney

Little drops of water,
Little grains of sand,
Make the mighty ocean
And the beauteous land.

And the little moments,
Humble though they be,
Make the mighty ages
Of eternity.

Little deeds of kindness,
Little words of love,
Make our earth an Eden,
Like the heaven above.

Some of the poems that Jenny quoted were long, but she helped me to learn them, and sometimes at night I would say the poems for Sammy Sue after we had gone to bed. Our mom didn't really approve of these tea parties, but Jenny seemed to have a way of getting our mom to let me do things with her - perhaps because then I wasn't a bother to our mom if I was with Jenny. Jenny had another name, she said it was her earth name, but I have not been able to remember it at all.

Grandpa Deke also brought us a five gallon can of honey that summer. I remember him walking up from the boat carrying a big, square gold colored can. He was a small man and the can seemed very big for him. He had bow-legs and walked sort of sideways carrying that big load. We did not have such a treat usually, and we were allowed honey on just about anything.

Our mom had a big black waffle maker that she put on the black stove to heat. When it was hot she would pour the waffle batter into it, filling it just over half full and then close the lid. After a few minutes she would turn the waffle maker over by lifting it up and swiveling it around on the hinge at the back. Then the other side would cook to a nice brown color and she would lift it out of the waffle maker with a fork. She would keep making waffles until there was a big stack of them on a plate on the back of the stove. She put the platter full of bacon, sausage and waffles on the table and we each put waffles on our hot plates. We spread margarine on the waffles, filling the holes full and then drizzled honey all over the waffles until it ran down on the plate. Our dad didn't like to put the honey right on his waffles. He had a small bowl that he poured honey into, and then dipped each bite of waffle in the honey.

We put honey on biscuits, pancakes, fresh hot bread and in our milk, although honey in canned milk is not a very good tasting concoction. We enjoyed that honey to the last drop. Jeff tried it on his mashed potatoes, but even he didn't like that.

We bought our food for a year at a time, and had to store it in the small room downstairs where there was no heat. That way the food would not spoil. We all carried boxes and boxes up to the storage room when the food order arrived and our dad brought it out in our boat from Sitka. The story is that I carried the margarine to the house and lost it somehow, and we had no margarine for the rest of the year. I don't know that I actually did carry it, or lose it, but that is what was told. I don't know how a case of margarine could be lost in such a small room, and there weren't any other places to put it. I often thought that it wasn't ever ordered, or at least not received, but the family story still is that I lost the margarine.

We had to be clever then, as to how to serve foods that needed margarine! Jeff again preferred jam on his mashed potatoes, as he didn't care for gravy (or honey) and we used peanut butter on our toast and pancakes, with honey or jam, and that is still a favorite of mine. Our mom had Crisco to bake cookies, pies and cakes with so we still had desserts.

I don't know how our mom managed to bake all that she did, as her stove was very small and had to be stoked with wood to keep the temperature up. She would start bread dough at night, mixing it in a big yellow bowl, and in the morning she would begin forming loaves of bread and then as they rose she would mix more dough and bake one loaf after another all day long, and sell loaves to the fishermen when they would come in to sell their fish at night.

She did this day after day, along with her regular house chores and raising three children and teaching them their lessons, and she ran the store too. Sometimes a fisherman would stay and eat dinner with us, and one I remember the most was Cracker Box Mack, whose boat was the *Flicka*. He loved the mashed potatoes and biscuits best and would always say, 'These are so light you'd better get the butterfly net!'. I didn't know what a butterfly net was, but it made everyone laugh when he said it. Later when I learned what one was I would laugh to think of biscuits or mashed potatoes with butterfly wings.

Mack was called Cracker Box because his boat was rickety and put together strangely. He had built most of it himself with odds and ends of wood scraps and it was painted several colors, whatever he happened to have at the time he needed to paint.

I liked to watch our mom make the bread. She put some hot water in the bowl, and added some sugar, salt and yeast. The yeast was in a cake and had to be broken up with a fork before she added it and I was sometimes allowed to break up the yeast in a small bowl. Then she would stir that up and add a little flour. As she added more and more flour the dough began to get stiffer and stiffer, until finally she turned it all out onto a big board on the kitchen table. She sprinkled on more flour and began to work the dough back and forth with her hands, twisting and turning it until all the flour was in the dough and it was smooth and soft.

She took a small scoop of Crisco and rubbed it all over the dough, then put it in a clean bowl. She turned it over once in the bowl and then set it near the stove to rise, with a clean dish towel over the bowl. I would watch to see when the dough would be taller than the bowl and then our mom would push it down with her fist so all the air was out and it was flat in the bottom of the bowl. Next she would cut the dough into sections and put each one into a bread pan. She had four bread pans and filled all of them.

Two she set on the counter in the kitchen, far from the stove, another she set on the table, a little closer to the stove, and one she set on a small table next to the stove. The closest loaf would rise fastest and when it was ready to go in the oven she would move the bread pan from the kitchen table over to the table by the stove. One of the loaves on the counter would move to the kitchen table. As soon as the first loaf of that batch was in the oven she got out the big yellow bowl and started another batch of bread. By the time the last loaf of the first batch was baked she would again fill the bread pans and put them on the counter, the kitchen table and the small table by the stove.

This way she could make bread for most of a day and always have one loaf ready to go in the oven. When a loaf was done she would open the door of the oven, thump the browned bread with her finger and pull it out of the oven. There was a towel on the kitchen table for turning the fresh bread out to cool. I loved the smell of the freshly baked bread and if it came out of the oven near lunch time our mom would cut big slices and put margarine and jam on it for our lunch. When we didn't have any margarine left, she would spread peanut butter and jam on the hot bread.

We had many more visitors at Killisnoo, as it was much easier to get to than Kalinin Bay. Our dear Aunt Norma came to visit one summer – she was our dad's little sister. One day she went with us in a large skiff to fetch water. We loaded big wooden barrels into a bigger skiff that our dad had built after we moved to Killisnoo and started across the bay, squished in the boat beside the barrels. We went a little ways up the creek that flowed into the bay, because at the mouth of the creek the salt and fresh water mixed and we couldn't drink that. Most of the water we used on Killisnoo had to be hauled across the bay. There were also big barrels at the ends of the house that were used to catch the rain water off the roof for things like bathing and washing clothes.

Aunt Norma laughed and had such a good time while we were getting the water. Our dad, Jimmy and Aunt Norma would carry buckets to the creek, dip into a deep spot and carry the buckets to the skiff and dump the water in the big barrels. I couldn't lift the heavy buckets so I stayed out of the way while they were carrying water. I built little houses of sticks and leaves, leaving them there for the little people in the woods to live in after we left. Sometimes I would go down to the beach and get some pebbles and shells and make tables and chairs for the houses.

After the barrels were full of water, we had to get back in the skiff. The barrels of water were very heavy and Jimmy had pushed the skiff out a little ways from the shore where it could stay afloat, so to get to the skiff we would have to wade in the water. First our dad waded in and climbed into the skiff, then Jimmy, who pushed the skiff a little farther out so it would stay afloat. And last came Aunt Norma, carrying me.

She stood beside the skiff and put me in, then she climbed aboard, with her soaking boots and pants. We were all wet, but we had a good time and didn't care. Jimmy pushed the skiff out into deeper water with an oar; our dad let the outboard motor down into the water and started it by pulling a long rope that wound around and around a pulley. Even with the motor going full speed we still went slowly across the bay because the water barrels were so heavy.

When we got close to the shore we all would lean towards the back of the skiff and our dad drove it as far onto the beach as he could. We jumped out of the boat into the water and waded ashore, then he and Jimmy pulled on the rope in the bow of the skiff to get it farther onto the beach. Then began the job of hauling the water up to the house and pouring it into the big barrels that sat beside the front porch. I didn't help with that - but walked back and forth with everyone as they carried water and listened to them talk.

It was a good day when we had full water barrels again. Our mom had stayed home with Jeff and she had cooked a big pan of fried chicken, mashed potatoes, canned carrots and beets, biscuits and gravy. One of the fishermen had brought out a chicken from the store in Sitka so we could have some fresh meat that wasn't fish! We washed our hands and sat down to one of the most delicious meals we had ever tasted. After all that fresh air and walking and carrying we were very hungry.

I wished that our Aunt Norma would stay with us forever. Many times when I was sad I would recall the sound of her laughter. She soon left and went to northern Alaska as a nurse, and we didn't see her again for several years.

Also across the bay from Killisnoo there were other families. Billy Somato and his wife lived right by the little float where we left our skiff when we rowed across to walk to Angoon.   They had a small garden and when we walked up from the float on their side of the bay we would stop and talk to them while they worked in the garden. We would take bags of carrots, lettuce and other fresh things home with us to cook for dinner. Billy's wife would make rhubarb wine and after drinking it would be blind for several days, and then she would do it all over again. Someone had to follow her around and make sure she didn't fall into the bay until she could see again. Billy often came over to our house to help our dad with building projects.

Farther down the bay lived a very small Japanese man name Asakitchi Ioto (the spelling is mine, since I never saw his name written). I don't know why he was there, or what he did. He was very old and had a small dog, that he named Dog. His nickname was "Itch" and he would put the dog in a skiff and row across to our store to buy a few things. It wasn't all that long after WWII had ended and we had heard stories of the Japanese and the fighting, and so one day we were watching Itch row across the bay, we crouched in the grass and shouted 'The Japs are coming, the Japs are coming', as we had often heard them called. We were punished severely and told never to call anyone by such a name again, and I never forgot that. I felt sorry that I had called Itch a bad name, although at first I didn't know it was a bad name, since I had heard it in our home many times.

Itch and his small dog were always together and he would tell us stories of the funny antics of Dog. He said that sometimes Dog would pace back and forth in their little house.   Itch said that Dog would "walk around, walk around, alla time walk around", and apparently Dog was upset because there was a bear outside. I thought Dog was very brave, but knew that little creatures would not be safe outside with a bear around and always hoped Itch would not let him outside.

Many times I watched Itch rowing across the bay, with the strong currents pushing against his little skiff, but he always made it, though it seemed to take a long time. He only had one full arm and a small part of the other arm, and he stood up and rowed his boat. He would put one oar in his good hand and hold the other tight under his other part of an arm, pressing it against his side to hold onto it.

He would stand in the store and talk for hours and hours with whoever was there, our mom and dad, or customers at the store, or fishermen from the boats. He loved to tell stories of bears.

We found many interesting things in the buildings on Killisnoo. There was an older store a little ways down the beach that was a treasure chest of wonderful things. The second story floor was missing and we would climb the rickety stairs and then walk across the ceiling beams, balancing like high wire walkers. It was a long ways to the floor below, but we never once slipped. Downstairs in the store section there were old boxes of spices and the cloves, though old, still smelled good.

Outside that old store there was a barrel of blue crystals; our mom told us they were poison and we were not to touch them. We understood what poison meant, but we played with the pretty bright blue crystals just the same. We would pile them high in bowls and boxes and use them for our jewels. I don't have any idea what they were, or why they were there, but we found them interesting, and we never got sick from touching them.

Farther away from our house were old cottages that were overgrown with berry bushes and tall stands of stinging nettles and fireweed. I imagine these must have been the houses the workers lived in when there was a whale processing plant on Killisnoo. There were giant plants with long spiky thorns on them, called Devil's Club. We had to be very careful to not touch them because the thorns would catch in your skin and make big blisters. The thorns were hard to pull out and stayed sore for a long time, so we were careful.

We looked around at all the cabins and opened the doors when we could. We would go inside if there was something interesting to look at and in one of the cabins and we found some chairs and a small box that we took back to our cottage for furniture. Mostly we made mazes in the bushes and grasses around the other cottages, and played store in the old building, buying and selling the spices to each other. We also mixed some fine concoctions of all the contents of the spices. We had wanted to take the spices to our "hospital" but weren't allowed to; no food upstairs. It wouldn't have done any good to argue that we were taking medicine up there, so we didn't.

Going the other direction from the house were the long, long warehouses, and now they were empty so we could run and play in them on rainy days. Our dad hung a long rope swing in one warehouse and we could swing there even on the coldest days. Pumping to make the swing go higher would keep us plenty warm.

On the outside of the warehouse there was a pipeline of some sort, on a rather narrow wooden ledge that ran along the side of the building. The pipe was about nine inches across and the ledge only about an inch or two wider, and we would carefully balance as we walked along the pipe, far out over the water. Halfway out on the pipeline was an outhouse with several "seats"; I suppose this had been for the workers that used to be in the warehouses. I don't know if they had an easier route there or if they too had to inch along the pipe to get to the outhouse like we did!

We would like to go out along the treacherous route and through the outhouse - it had a door on each side so you could enter and exit along the pipeline - and on to the end of the pipeline at the far end of the warehouse. I suppose that this was the line that carried oil to and from the big refinery-sized tanks that sat back from the beach, behind the warehouse.

Every town we went to in Alaska had these big tanks. At Killisnoo they were empty and one had no top, so we could climb up the ladder built onto the side and then down an inside ladder to the bottom. There was a thick gooey layer of oil or tar, about 6 inches deep and we would gather tar balls on sticks and take them out of the tank, always being careful not to step into the tar. I don't remember what we did with them, but they were interesting to form with two sticks by rolling the tar balls around and around. We had to be careful not to get any tar on our hands or clothes.

We slung a rope over the top edge of the tank and attached a bucket for hauling the tar balls up to the top, then one of us would carry the bucket down the outside ladder - usually Jimmy as he was the strongest. We were afraid that if Jeff went into the tanks he might not be careful and would fall into the tar, so we never let him come with us when we were going in the tanks. And he would have told our mom what we were doing if he knew.

The tanks sat in a big field and it was one of our favorite spots to play. We made our first snowman in Alaska in that field, Jeff and I did. Jimmy was older than me and he had begun to do other things than play all the time with the little kids. The winter before we left California we had a very rare snowstorm and built a snowman in our front yard. The snow was much more plentiful in Alaska and we had many snowmen.

Later the next summer we were playing tag and I was running through the same field and tripped and fell down. I hopped up and ran on, not wanting to get tagged and be "it". After a few minutes I reached down to scratch what I thought was a bug on my leg, and I had blood all over my hand. I ran to the house to show our mom, and after searching the field they found that when I fell I had pierced my leg quite deeply on a broken off small tree stump.

Our mom cleaned off the blood and made a bandage from some gauze and tape that she wound around my leg to hold it in place. Every morning she would take the bandage off, clean the sore and put on a fresh bandage. I was not allowed to go in the water on the beach because she didn't want me to get the sore wet. I had that big bandage on my leg for a long long time. Different medicines were used on the sore, some that stung and some that didn't, and it just wouldn't heal over.

About six months later we went to Baranof Warm Springs, on the other side of the island from Sitka. We traveled all day in the boat, and arrived there just about time for dinner. Wayne Short came down to the float and helped us tie up the boat, and said that his mother had just cooked dinner and we were all to come up and eat with them. We settled the boat in for the night and walked up the ramp to the boardwalk that ran in front of all the houses at Warm Springs.

After dinner we kids would play on the beach and run up and down the board walk. We would go back to our boat to sleep that night and the next day, after breakfast was finished and dishes were done we went to the bath house at the warm springs. I was left in a room with a gigantic wooden tub full of strange smelling, steamy water. I was told to bathe in it, but it looked so deep and I was not at all brave, even though I was expected to be. I was very small, so I sat up on the ledge at the back of the tub and sort of splashed water on myself from the deep, dark steaming water.

I couldn't see the bottom of the tub and I didn't know if I could get out once I got in. No one told me that the tub was no deeper than to the floor! After what I thought was enough time to take a proper bath I dressed and went back to the boat, never telling our mom I had not taken a bath at all. But in just two days the scab on my leg dried up and the sore was completely healed! It was all because of the minerals in the water of that warm springs bath, even though I had only splashed the water on my legs. I was happy to have my leg back to normal, although the spot would hurt for a long long time.

The beaches at Killisnoo were marvelous, and one, up at the head of the channel running between the two islands, was covered with seashells. We could spend hours and hours there, picking out different shells; swirly ones, striped ones, cones, snail shells, clam and mussel shells, as well as sea urchins and sand dollars. The currents must have been just right to deposit all this treasure there for us. Killisnoo is the first time I remember being allowed to go off and play without supervision. I suppose because I was eight now, and didn't need as much watching as when I was younger. We could wander up and down the beach, play in the warehouses and explore all sorts of places all by ourselves. If we went we had to take Jeff with us, and watch him carefully, but we didn't mind and had many adventures together.

When we got to the seashell beach Jimmy and I would sit Jeff down in the best spot and tell him to find only the biggest and prettiest shells. That kept him busy for a long time! If he got tired of that we would take him up to the tall grass just beyond the beach and tell him to hide in the grass. He would tell us he was too big to hide in the grass and we told him to lie down. Before long he was fast asleep and Jimmy and I could hunt for shells and pretty driftwood until we heard our mom calling us to come home. Then we would wake Jeff up, pretending to 'find' him in the game of hide and seek, and we'd all set off for home with our buckets of shells.

At the seashell beach the channel narrowed and there was a small lighthouse there to keep the boats from running ashore. When the tide was low the channel was not wide enough for our dad's fishing boat to get through, so he had to make sure to come home early or leave for fishing on the high tides. Because the channel was so narrow it still was a bit dangerous to come through even at high tide, because of the strong currents. When we rowed across the channel to walk to Angoon we had to be careful also to go across at times when the current was not as strong. It was like a bathtub drain there, with the water swirling through past the rocks and it would carry the skiff far down the channel if we got caught in it.

One day while walking on the beach, Jimmy found a dead bald eagle. Our mom took a photo of him holding it, with its wings stretched out as far as Jimmy could reach, the wings were still not fully extended. We didn't know how the eagle died; it didn't seem to have been shot.

Me and Jeff with snowman in rare
California snow storm

Birthday Party in California

Me, Melissa Ferris, Jeff, back row –
Susan Fenske, unknown

Me in California

Summer in California

Our dog Gizmo, Jeff, Cousin
Mike, Wayne Fenske, Jimmy

Birthday in California

All the cousins and our
grandparents and our dad,
far right back

Cousins in California – front
to back, left to right, Cathy,
Jeff, me, ?, Linda, Jimmy

Birthday at Grandparents' house

Linda with her doll, me with Bunny, Jimmy and Cathy in back

Our grandparents

Neal and Hazel Dunlap

Cathy, front, Linda and me, back

Me and Jimmy with Bunny

Jeff and Jimmy on oil barrel horse

Cathy on oil barrel horse

Me, with Linda hiding
behind

Our mom's birthday party at Kalinin Bay

Jenny, Me, unknown girl, Jeff with cast and black eye, Jimmy behind Jeff, Edna Barr , our mom, our dad

Me and Jeff with snowman on Killisnoo

Vicky Jacobson with skunk cabbage leaf in Angoon

Dinner at the new house in Sitka

Grandma, Grandpa, our dad, Perry the Parrot (on the table), our mom, Jeff, Margery and Dennis Forrester

Sammy Sue

My very own angel
ornaments

Blue Willow tea set I received when
we lived on Killisnoo

Donkey and cart, made in
ceramics class when we first
moved to town.

My art – third grade – Calvert
Correspondence School

14
A TRIP TO ANGOON

Angoon was a small fishing village but it was different from Kalinin Bay or Killisnoo; people lived there year round. Peg and Jake Jacobson were friends of our dad's. They were the ones that took care of him when he first went to Alaska and had the mumps, and they helped him find his first boat to buy.

They lived in a very large house outside the village, about a twenty minute walk away. They had three children, Hunter, Christine and Vickie, who were just a bit younger than we were. They were fine playmates, and I liked the days when our dad had an errand in Angoon and we could go along. We always had to have our lessons done if we were to be allowed to go anywhere and I learned very early to do my work first and play later, just in case a trip to Angoon would come up unexpectedly. I always wanted to do lessons though, even in the summer, but there were only so many lessons to do and then we sent them to the headquarters to be graded.

The Jacobson children were very wild, according to our mom, and I loved them. At their house we made forts in the bushes, ran up and down the big stairs that led down to the boat harbor, picked berries, read books as long as we pleased and on rainy days we would go into the big study that overlooked the bay and play "Surveyor". One of us was always named 'Jim' (say that with a deep voice, and very quickly). It seemed to us kids that whenever there were survey teams in Alaska they were always headed up by a man named "Jim".

Sometimes we would all want to be "Jim" so we had to have "Jim 1", "Jim 2", etc. Of course Jimmy got first choice at the name since his name was already "Jim", but he didn't often play this with us so we all got a turn at being "Jim". As surveyors we knew we had to write things down and I usually got to be in charge of surveyor lists. We didn't know what they put on their lists, or what exactly they were doing, so I was free to put anything I wanted on the lists. We could have as much paper as we wanted at Peg and Jake's, and so I listed all the many books in the study, carefully copying the words on the backs of the books, which took many days of playing surveyor to finally accomplish, and then listed names of animals we had spotted on our survey trips. You might be interested to know that we had on our list, antelope, elephants, anteaters and koalas, as well as the regular bears, squirrels and fish that we might encounter in Alaska. We were, after all, a very thorough survey party.

The boys would leave for surveying and we girls would be in the office. Vickie and Christine would tire of making survey lists and wander off, but I would stay in the office and read the books from the shelves there. Our mom was always busy someplace else on these trips to Angoon and when I read books in Angoon she never made me stop.

I had never seen so many books in one spot before. There were shelves all along three sides of the room, from ceiling to floor, with windows taking up the fourth wall. The windows looked down the hill to the bay, and when you looked out you saw tops of tall trees below and the bay beyond. On summer days sometimes the window would be opened and you could hear the bay and seagulls below, and boats coming in and out of the small harbor. On very still days you could hear the roar of a waterfall that was across the bay and in the woods on the side of a hill. Often the foam would be floating out into the bay from where the waterfall crashed down the hillside.

Jake must have brought the books with him from the east coast when they moved there. He was from a wealthy family and his family had wanted him to become a doctor. It was not the life he wanted, and he moved his young family to Alaska, along with all the wonderful things he had brought from Massachusetts. He was not only the store owner, but also the mayor, the magistrate, the coroner and the undertaker. He was loved by everyone in Angoon and they would often come to him for help with their problems.

Jake would work hard all day as a commercial fisherman, run the store and tend to village business and in the evenings play music on the record player from an opera or ballet that he liked. I especially liked the books! There were science books and books of photographs, books in languages I didn't understand and children's books. There were books that were very old and some that were very new. This was my favorite room in their house.

Hunter Jacobson had a nice skiff and we would row about the bay for hours at a time. One time we decided to row to the head of the bay and explore an old barge that was grounded there. No one else wanted to go with us so we set off alone. We tied the skiff securely to the end of the barge that was still in the water, and we scrambled up the barge and jumped down to the beach to explore. We found many things to explore: a little creek bubbling up out of the mossy ground, seashells on the beach to carry in our pockets, sticks to toss into the small waves on the beach and watch them float back to shore, and the wild huckleberries nearby for a snack.

We were back up on the barge and getting ready to leave when we spotted the big brown bear not far from the barge. We knew the dangers of bears, and had heard only recently of a bear eating a man, so we knew it was time for quick action. Hunter was quicker than I, and was in the skiff, had it untied and was rowing off while I was still scampering down the barge. I knew that I had only one hope. I had to jump to the skiff or the bear would eat me.

I yelled for Hunter to come back - but he didn't stop rowing. Not being brave at all I ran as fast as my little legs would go and jumped with all my might. It seemed that I flew through the air for a long time before landing with a clunk in the skiff! Hunter was indeed rowing the skiff away from the barge so I had to jump some distance, and the force of landing in the skiff knocked the wind out of me and tipped the skiff dangerously so we took on water.

I sat gasping in the skiff for a long time, until I could breathe again. But I was safe in the skiff and Hunter continued to row until we were far down the bay. The big brown bear just stood up on his back legs and watched us go, probably glad to get rid of the two pests that were eating his berries.

I bailed the water out of the skiff and we rowed around the bay for a while longer, taking turns rowing and watching for the bear - always checking the shore for that bear, thinking that perhaps he had followed us down the bay. We even talked about what we would do if the bear had followed us and was waiting for us on the float. We never saw a sign of him again all that morning and finally hunger brought us back to the float. We tied up the boat and put our oars away, folded the life jackets and checked to see that everything was as it should be with the skiff before going up to lunch.

The walk back to their house from the boat float was along a narrow path, with the beach on one side and thick undergrowth of bushes right close on the other side. Each creak and crackle in the bushes made us jump, as we were sure the bear was walking along beside us, just waiting for the right time to jump out and eat us. We hurried up the long steps, sure that the bear would not be far behind. We washed our hands and ate our lunch; we were starved. For the rest of the day we were happy to stay in the study and play surveyors, although this time we played surveyors who needed a nap, and slept the afternoon away, until the smell of the surveyors' mothers cooking dinner woke us.

Food at the Jacobsons was a big event. Peg loved to cook and since they ran a grocery store out of a huge room on the side of their house, they had access to just about anything they could want. Peg made salads from the vegetables they grew in their garden. I remembered fresh lettuce from California and loved to eat salad. She made one special salad which I adored. She piled spinach leaves in a big bowl, then cooked some bacon until it was crispy and crumbly. She had hard cooked eggs that she chopped into the spinach, sprinkled on the crumbled bacon and then made a dressing of the bacon grease and other tasty things and poured it over all, while the dressing was still hot. What a wonderful treat that was! Later, when I would visit their family by myself she would always make me a big bowl of that salad.

The garden at their house was great fun for me too. I remembered a big garden in California, with corn and tomatoes and melons of all sorts, but I had not been allowed in the garden, for it seemed I stepped on plants and that upset our mom.

Early in the mornings, as soon as the sun was coming over the hills Peg and Jake would go out to the garden to work before breakfast. As soon as I heard them moving about I would rush to get dressed and go quietly down the stairs to the garden. They showed me how to weed, and how to carefully pull the soil up against the roots of the plants, how to mulch things to keep the soil moist and how to build a compost pile. I learned to plant new rows of lettuce and green onions so there would be fresh ones all summer long.

I loved the feeling of my hands in the soil, loved the quiet talk as we worked up and down the rows of the garden, the sound of the birds and watching them hop about in the garden, not afraid of us as we worked. I was only eight, and I was eager to learn as many new things as possible. I wanted to know the names of the birds, especially the big blue ones that squawked and shouted as we dug in the garden. Peg told me they were blue jays, but I misunderstood and thought she called them "Blue Jakes", after her husband Jake, since it was, after all, his garden. I loved the name Blue Jakes.

The ravens and crows walked neatly among the rows of the garden and picked at bugs and tasty things they could find. Peg taught me that if you want the birds to not eat all your crops you must plant some for the birds, and some for the bugs, and some for the gardener. She said that leaving tasty bits of food on a platform for the birds would also give them something else to think about.

Peg had grown up in Boston and knew any number of interesting things. I didn't know where Boston was, but was glad she had come to Alaska. While we gardened she would tell me of the winters in Boston, the fancy cars and the stylish gowns she had worn to dances. She told me of grand parties, where ladies would wear jewels in their hair, and the men would wear fancy suits. Once I asked her if she missed these things and she said that she didn't, that she found the world to be mighty fancy wherever she was, and that was what made her happy. Even though I was just eight I thought that was a good thing to do, though I did think it would be nice to have a fancy dress and jewels in my hair instead of my flannel lined denim pants and my big heavy sweater.

In their house Peg and Jake had a record player and lots of records. They loved the ballet and the opera and the first music I was exposed to was "Porgy and Bess" one rainy day while waiting for our mom and dad to come back from a trip to Sitka. I loved the pictures on the album cover and could imagine those fine people dancing to the wonderful songs. I listened to the record over and over and Peg never once got impatient or told me to play something else, or to turn off the record player.

They had a power plant that Jake would fill with gasoline early so we could listen to music and have plenty of light for reading. He knew exactly how much fuel to put in the generator to last just one day. Near bed time the generator would give a little blink as the fuel was about to run out, and we knew that we must scamper up the stairs to bed before the last of the fuel was gone and the lights went out! It was a fun game to get all ready for bed and then wait for the generator to blink once, telling us the day was over. When we later moved to town, I was surprised to find that our electricity didn't go off at ten each night!

We were allowed to talk in bed at Peg and Jake's house, and there would be soft murmuring between the rooms when our mom wasn't there. We would talk softly until we fell asleep, or listen for owls and wild animal noises, trying to correctly identify them to each other, or to be the first to hear them. I often tried so hard to listen that I fell asleep before all the others.

There were other houses on the road into Angoon, and we got acquainted with the families that lived there. Harry and Kyra Garnes lived in the next house; it was neat and had a fancy yard. The lawn was kept mowed and all sorts of flowers grew along the borders of the walk. The house was painted dark red with windows all along the front, with sofas and comfy chairs lined up looking out the windows. In the kitchen there was a gigantic (at least to an eight year old) wood burning stove that Kyra kept polished and it seemed always to be warm and toasty. It was many times bigger than the small stoves we had in our houses and on the boat.

She baked their bread also, but could bake three loaves at one time, unlike our mom who could only fit one loaf at a time in our small oven. On the wood stove was a very big teakettle that gurgled and sang and Kyra used the hot water to make us huge mugs of the most wonderful hot cocoa. I don't think that Harry and Kyra had any children, but they did have a nice toy box next to the stove; it was full of toys that Harry had made. He carved cars and trucks, trees and houses out of blocks of wood and it was fun to make towns with them. He also sanded big blocks smooth and we stacked them into castles and canneries, or mountains for our houses to sit next to.

Sometimes Kyra would paint little designs on the wood blocks, fish or birds or flowers. Those were my favorites. I would sit on the kitchen floor and play with the blocks and listen to the soft sounds of the adults talking in the other room, or move the blocks to the back of the kitchen when it was time for a meal to be prepared and I would get so hungry smelling all the good food cooking on that stove.

Kyra had the biggest pots I had ever seen. She would peel mounds of potatoes and chop them into a big pot, add onions and I don't know what all, and out would come the most wonderful soup you had ever tasted. If there were freshly dug clams she would chop them into the soup and we would have clam chowder. She had some big bowls with a handle on one side and she would fill them with the chowder and call, "Come and get it; it ain't gonna come and get you!" Everyone would gather round the table to eat soup and talk about the catch that day, or of plans for the next day.

Kyra went to the store at Jake's house and bought most of her food, and when she wanted something that Jake didn't have, she would make a list for the pilot of the small planes that came and went. The next time that pilot came back he would have a box full of wonderful things from the grocery stores in Sitka or Juneau.

One day Kyra showed me where they had gotten the potatoes. I thought they got them from the storage room, like we did, but she took a small shovel and dug into a mound in her back yard, and there were piles of potatoes there, under the dirt! She picked up a few of them that were strangely shaped, or dark in spots and tossed them into the brush on one side of the yard. She said she fed them to the deer over there so they would leave her garden alone. I had a funny vision of deer coming in with their shovels and hoes and working in her garden, and Kyra chasing them out so she could do the work. I didn't realize that she meant she was keeping them away from her garden so they wouldn't eat it!

Outside their windows was a wonderful view of the bay and a float where small sea planes could land. When anyone flew into Angoon this is where they landed and Harry and Kyra were the first people they met. The surveyors flew in and out from here, and although I never knew what or why they were surveying, they spent a lot of time doing it. If it was a chilly day Kyra would have hot mugs of coffee waiting at the float for the passengers and if there was time, they would be invited to her house for slabs of hot rhubarb pie, or gooseberry pie, or brownies, whatever she had baked that day. She had a very large patch of rhubarb and seemed always to be baking a pie.

She had a big, heavy rolling pin and would whip around her kitchen and turn out a table full of pies in no time at all. She set the pie pans on the edge of the counter, took her rolling pin to the big table and rolled out five or six pie crusts. Then she put the crusts in the pie pans, rolled out the same number of top crusts and made the fillings. She had an apple tree in the yard and we would sometimes pick apples to bring into the kitchen for pies. Kyra wore a big white apron and she would hold up the corners of the apron to fill it with apples. I asked her for an apron and she put one of hers on me and folded it up so it didn't drag on the ground. I filled my apron with apples and was careful not to drop any and bruise them, or she would have to cut the bruise out before making the pies.

Kyra would then fill the pie crusts with all the good fillings that she had mixed up. She would cover the fillings with the top crusts, pinch the edges together in a pretty design and spread some milk over the top of the crust with her fingers. Next came the big sugar shaker, shaking sugar all

115

over the top of the pie. She could bake two or three pies at a time in her big oven, while she washed the dishes that we got dirty while baking.

Kyra had water in her kitchen in faucets. They had a big tank of water up the hill that filled from a spring farther up the hill and the water ran down the pipe into the tank and then into their house. Her stove had a special compartment in it to hold water. The water ran into the stove and got very hot from the fire and then out the faucet in her sink. She never had to heat water for dishes or baths!

Her house smelled of pies no matter when you went there. And no matter how much baking she was doing, or how many people were in her house, it was always shiny clean.

Out in the yard were several outbuildings and one of them was used for canning fish. We would get to help with the canning sometimes. I liked to see the big boxes of shiny new cans and the little flat boxes with the lids in them. Our dad would bring salmon up from his boat and the others would clean it and cut it in chunks. We kids would push the chunks of fish down into the cans, making sure there were no air spaces left. I had to have a special low table as I was too short to reach the high work bench.   Harry fixed a table that was just for me and called it the Little Fish Table. He said it in such an important way that I am sure it was spelled with capital letters, and he called me the Little Fish. We would work all day, putting the fish into the cans, then cleaning the outside of the cans with a rag dipped in hot water and putting on the lids.

There was a small machine that secured the lids to the cans. You put the can of fish on a platform in the machine, laid a lid blank over the top of the can and lowered the lever that held the lid in place. Then a crank was turned and the lid was stuck to the can.   The cans were put in in a big kettle out in the yard over a fire and cooked for a long time, until Kyra came out of the canning shed and checked them to make sure that they were done.   The cans were lifted out of the big kettle with a special tool that took three cans at once, and set on a table in the yard to cool. Later Kyra would write the name of the fish and the date it was canned, on the cans, so when she wanted a certain kind of fish she could pick the right one.   That night we would have salmon patties with creamed peas, fresh from Kyra's garden -my favorite meal.

Besides her vegetables Kyra grew sweet peas and other pretty flowers, and with her mowed lawn it was a wonderful yard.   There was a clothesline in the yard and I thought it funny, since our clothesline had been inside the store building at Kalinin Bay and on the porch at Killisnoo. I liked the feel of being in their yard. It was surrounded by trees and had nice little corners and secret places for sitting and reading. You could see the bay and the mountains from most parts of the yard, and hear when the planes were coming in. When we would hear a plane coming we would jump up and run to the float to see what interesting cargo or people were coming. We always hoped that there would be a package for us.

It was here that I learned that when you fly in a plane at dusk, or even just after dark, the light from the sky is reflected off the water and you can see a lot more from the plane than you can see from the ground. We would sometimes get to go up in the plane if a pilot was going only a short way and coming back quickly and it was the most fun in the evening.

We would climb into the plane, stepping from the float to the pontoons and then up the little step into the plane. I was braver now and bigger, so I didn't have to be lifted into the plane anymore. The pilot would close and lock the door and off we would go. It would seem very dark at first as we taxied out into the bay but as the plane gained speed and rose in the air you could begin to see the houses near the shore and the small islands and all the water. The flights we got to go on were short. The plane slipped quickly back down to the water and the pilot opened the door and passed the packages to people waiting on their floats and we were soon back in the air, and back at Kyra's before it was too dark to see anymore.

Another activity when we went to Angoon was to gather the long bullwhip kelp in the bay. It grows attached to rocks on the bottom of the bay. Bullwhip kelp has a round, hollow bulb at one end, with ribbons at the top of the bulb. The air inside the bulb keeps that section afloat, while the long tail, up to 120 feet long, attaches itself to the rocks underwater. In the spring, when the new kelp is still tender, we would row out in the skiff, reach over the edge of the skiff , pull up on a piece of kelp, and cut off a piece about 6 or 7 feet long. We would cut the ribbons off the top of the kelp and gather a good supply for our dad to make kelp pickles. He would cut the kelp up into pieces about 1" x 2" and make the pickles. They are like watermelon rind pickles, and are very sticky sweet. We always had a lot of jars of them on hand. Sometimes our dad would add green food coloring to the pickles because they were naturally a dull brown and not very pretty.

After we had gathered all the kelp for the pickles, then we would gather a few older bulbs of the kelp to make rattles out of. We would cut the tail to about a foot long and rinsed out the bulb. We left the ribbons on the end of the bulb for decorations. Then we filled it completely with sand from the beach, to make the bulb hold its shape while it dried. Otherwise it would get flat as it dried out. We would cut a second piece of kelp to make a funnel to pour the sand into the one we were making into a rattle.

After the kelp bulb was very dry we would shake the sand out, tapping the bulb to make sure it was empty – then we put in a few small stones from the beach, making sure they were dry, plug up the end of the handle with moss, stuffed in very tightly, and we had a wonderful rattle. We sometimes attached a stick to the handle and lashed it on with twine to make the handle stronger.

Kelp has a lot of other uses. It was used to store whale oil and deer suet and some people used it instead of carrots in cake, as well as the kelp pickles and pickle relish, but we only used it for kelp pickles and rattles.

Between the Jacobson's house and the Garnes' house were a lot of shrubs, just perfect for playing in. I don't know what the shrubs were, but they grew a little taller than our heads and had lost a lot of the leaves and branches inside, so they were hollow. There were thick leaves on the tops of the bushes so it was like a secret hideout. We would make channels and tunnels, forts and palaces inside of the brush. We eventually could go almost all the way from Jacobson's to Garnes' without ever walking on the path; we just followed our maze of tunnels in the brush.

Sometimes we could hear it starting to rain and we wouldn't feel the drops for some time if we got into one of the deeper forts that had a lot of growth at the top. We fixed up tables and chairs with logs that we rolled in from the tunnel entrance and kept many secret things in the castles - things such as bits of rope, or shells that we found, and one time we found bits of bird egg shell and we made a special little nest of pine needles for the shells. The eggs were brown and tan speckled and I don't know what kind of bird they were from.

There were many swampy areas nearby and we picked the gigantic leaves of the skunk cabbage and used them for fans, or umbrellas or table clothes, whatever suited our fancy. We have a photo of Vickie when she was about 6, holding a skunk cabbage leaf up and it was almost as tall as she was. The skunk cabbage was the first plant up in the bogs in the spring and their scent carried a long distance. I didn't know that we were supposed to think they smelled awful, and I rather enjoyed the scent of a skunk from a distance, while others were holding their noses and making faces. I've seen skunk cabbage growing in other places and they seem like miniatures compared to the huge plants that grew in Alaska!

Also near Peg and Jake's house was the house of Paul and Gerry. He was a tall thin man, and she was short and he called her a dumpling. I had no idea what a dumpling was, but it sounded sweet. Paul had a fishing boat, but he didn't go out every day anymore to fish. Their house was built into the side of a hill and was very new. There was a big hill behind their house and it was a perfect spot for picking huckleberries.

Most of the trees had been cut down off that hill, and some had been used to build the house. I would take a big bucket up the hill and sit on a tree stump and pick just the berries I could reach from there, and would soon have a large bucket completely filled. We would make jam and jelly and pies from them. Gerry had a gooseberry bush in the corner of her yard and she made gooseberry tarts that were so delicious. It was fun to be a kid and be allowed to have your own whole pie to eat, even if it was a small one.

Gerry knitted like a whiz. She would order the kits from Mary Maxim Catalog and knit big jacket sweaters, with a warm flannel lining and a zipper down the front. The sweaters were of very heavy yarn and had a special picture knitted into them.

A lot of her friends had these sweaters, all knit by Gerry. There were eagles, whales, wolves or deer on the sweaters, along with trees and fancy designs on the sleeves. I was intrigued because she could knit without looking at her work and her stitches were perfect. She taught Christine to knit those big heavy sweaters too. I stuck to just knitting my small things with my little needles.

The town of Angoon was about a twenty minute walk from these houses and we often walked to town. It was a fishing village, with a post office, school and church, plus houses. After a while, Peg and Jake moved the store from their house to a big building in the town of Angoon. We would then play in the old store section of their house, making forts and towns, or whatever we could think up. It was always good to have indoor spots to play in Alaska as it rained a lot there and was cold and snowy in the winter. But we did have our slickers and rain hats and stout boots, so we often went out to play in the rain, as if it were not even there. You can't stay inside all the time it rains, or you would rarely be outdoors.

Playing outside in the rain brought special fun. There were different things to listen to, and the rain would ran our hats onto our slickers. Sometimes we would tilt our head forward and the rain would run off the front of the hat and we would try and catch it in our mouths, but usually succeeded only in getting our faces wet. Rain on the bay made a special whispering sound, like someone talking far away. On very still days you could hear each drop as it fell and it sounded a little like bacon sizzling in the big black skillet.

Those first summers that we lived in Alaska were strange to us because of the long twilight. It stays light there until well after 10 p.m. and we always had a strict bedtime of 7:30 p.m., while the sun is still high in the sky. Our mom would put the heavy black woolen blankets over our windows to darken the room and we went to bed at our regular bed-time. Later, when we moved to town, we were allowed to stay up until 8 p.m., and after that first summer we learned to go to sleep without the blankets on the window. When we weren't at home we would get to stay up later and that was great fun, to be able to be outside in the sunshine until the sun started to go behind the trees very late in the evening.

15
AND HOOD BAY

When we had been at Killisnoo a little while we met another family from Hood Bay, about an hour or so away by boat, the opposite direction from Angoon. Wade and Mary Forester had two children, Margie and Dennis, who were a little older than we were and they too did their schooling with Calvert Correspondence Course. Sometimes we would go to visit them, but first, in order to have time off to do this, we would have to finish up a week or two of lessons. It isn't as hard to do lessons ahead when you are the only one in your grade.

Our mom would set our work out for us on a long bench-like table and we would know how much we had to accomplish before we could have a holiday. I would do all the lessons in math first, to get them out of the way, and then the science. I saved history, geography, English and art for last as they were my favorites, although I really did enjoy every part of school, I just liked some subjects a little better than others. As we watched the piles of lessons go down we knew our holiday was nearer. I would always finish first and wished that I could help my brothers so that we could leave earlier.

Jimmy didn't like to do lessons as much as I did and Jeff was very slow at them - he seemed to find more reasons to do something else than to do his lessons - but we couldn't leave until all the lessons were finished and in their envelopes to go out to the teacher so she could give us our grade. There was much excitement as we loaded our clothes and food into the boat, and a few playthings if we could manage it. We made sure that the fire was out in the stove in the house and pulled the door shut behind us as we set out with our last load to take to the boat.

Margie's dad was the watchman at Hood Bay during the winter months, like our dad had been at Kalinin Bay, and there were no other people there in the winter except their family. In the summer there were the families of fishermen there and the town bustled with people, boats and dogs. Their house was big and white and Mary Forester was a wonderful cook. She would make us big slabs of toast and mugs of cocoa and we would sit in the den and dip our toast in the cocoa, something we were NEVER allowed to do at home. The toast was not boat toast, but made in a big silver toaster that toasted first on one side and then the other after you flipped the toast around. At our house dunking was not for ladies and gentlemen, but we would pretend we were kings and queens and declare it a dunking day, and so we could dunk all we wanted and still be proper ladies and gentlemen, and Mary never minded.

I remembered our house in California. It had been painted white and had electricity all day and night; we had a telephone and hot water in the faucets and a nice tub for bathing, and I hadn't thought any of those things were out of the ordinary. We had none of those things in our two houses so far in Alaska, but Mary's house was more like the one we had in California. They had pretty dishes with blue flowers on them in the cupboards, nice silverware that was shiny and matched and a tablecloth on the table all the time.

There was soft furniture for sitting on after dinner and a warm bath without heating water on the stove and pouring it in a big wash tub. They had soft beds with pretty covers on them. Most of the houses in Hood Bay were not like this; they were more like the ones that we lived in at Killisnoo and Kalinin Bay. I liked to walk up to their house along a boardwalk, with a railing along the side, and up the steps to their porch. Their house sat a little above the others and above the bustling docks.

At Hood Bay there was also a big warehouse that we played in during winter visits, and they had a swing that was even bigger than ours. One time I was swinging and didn't see Dennis coming up near the swing and my foot kicked his face and one of his teeth fell out! Without doctors nearby the moms had to take care of things, like broken teeth. Mary Forester gave Dennis a warm cloth to bite down on so the bleeding would stop - then she wrapped a warm towel around the sides of his head and under his chin and he sat in a soft chair and looked at a book until he felt like going back out to play. His mother never got mad at him or me.

We had a fort in the woods in Hood Bay, and it was our club. Since there were only five of us, we all were members of the club, and spent a lot of time writing letters back and forth between our boat and their house about the rules and membership and other things about the club. Since I loved to write I got to do most of the letters. When others lost interest in the club I kept up a correspondence with myself, writing and answering all letters.

We had a box rigged up with a lid and the letters were placed inside the box, to wait for the answer. I still continued to have fun looking to see if I had left myself a letter and was always surprised to find when I had. Then I would sit down and write an answer to myself and place it in the box, to wait for me to discover it later on.

We often would take the skiffs out on the bay to fish or just to explore. We took turns rowing and fishing, or being explorers. We would hook some kelp and drag it to the float, pretending we were bringing in whales. There were a lot of things to entertain us there. Growing next to the wooden walkway to their house were choke cherries, growing in little clusters. We tasted them and didn't like them, but they made great pretend food for our adventures, we packed little tins full of them to carry with us for provisions.

Jimmy and Dennis would put the tins in the big pockets of their jackets when we went out in the skiff. We would open a tin every now and then and toss some of the choke cherries over the side of the skiff, to feed the fish. We never saw a fish come up to eat them, but we thought it was fun. Sometimes we would drop a few choke cherries in the water every so often like a trail, pretending that we were leaving markings so we could find our way back to the dock. We rowed the skiff under the dock, among the pilings and pretend we were exploring new lands.

Margie and Dennis had a tire swing tied to a tree limb near their house and I remember swinging in it by the hour. One day I heard Dean Martin on the radio singing, "That's Amore", and Margie's mom was singing along, it was fun to be swinging and listen to the happy sound of her voice. I don't think she knew I was there, but maybe she did.

The Forresters had a big power plant on the dock that ran all day, Mary ironed with an electric iron, something I didn't remember from California and I thought it was a marvel, since our mom had to iron with a big heavy metal iron that was heated on the wood stove.

I liked to help with the dishes there, because you would turn on the faucet and out would come nice warm water! It drained right down the sink; we didn't have to carry the water outside and dump it on the beach. I liked this modern house, and the Jacobson's too, with all the fancy things that electricity could bring. I never minded living in our house at Killisnoo, with outdoor facilities and water that had to be lugged over from across the channel in big barrels in the skiff, or lanterns and the wood stove for cooking on, but it must have been hard for our mom to see these fancy things and then go back to the harder way of doing things. Many more people lived the way we did and it didn't seem different to me.

In the summers when we visited Hood Bay the store was open and Margie and I would help behind the counter, handing down food that the customers would pick out, and then adding the bill for them. I could only reach the low shelves or things that leaned against the wall, but Margie could reach the higher shelves or climb a small ladder if she couldn't reach something. All the food in the stores in Alaska that I had seen was stored on tall shelves behind the counter. People would come in and give the storekeeper a list, or pick out things and point to them and the storekeeper would pile them on the counter. There were all sorts of things in the store: canned foods, slabs of bacon, tools and repair items for the boats, rope, sometimes fabric for sewing clothes, clothespins and writing paper. Just about anything you could want or need was there on those big shelves.

Sometimes the people would come into the store just to chat or see who was around. They would stand around the big stove if it was a chilly day and warm their hands and talk. In our store at Killisnoo there was a bench on one side and often there were one or two fishermen sitting there discussing the weather or the fishing, or telling stories of where they came from.

One time I had a wart on my left hand and one of the fishermen saw it. He told me that if I would rub the wart with a special penny every day it would go away. He pulled one of these "special" pennies out of his pocket and rubbed the wart, round and round. Then he told me to keep the penny in my pocket and a couple times a day to take it out and rub the wart. Well I was very careful to do it, and within a few weeks the wart was gone. I was sure the penny was magic.

Sometimes Margie and I would earn a little money from working in the store, and off we would go to the other end of the village, to where we found the man who sold candy to the kids. He had a big tray of candy that he carried in front of himself, with a big leather strap around his neck. He had tootsie rolls, lollipops, Seven-up bars, Baby Ruth, gumballs, root beer barrels, Necco wafers and all sorts of wonderful candies. We would each buy several different candies and then go to the end of the dock and watch Margie's dad sell fuel to the fishing boats as we munched on our treats.

Long gas hoses were lowered over the side of the dock and they would pump their gas and then Wade would make notes in a book as to which boat bought the gas. Loving to make notes and lists, I convinced him that even though I was only eight, almost nine in my head, I could keep the lists for him, and he let me. He gave me a cap to wear that had the company name on it (I think Standard Oil) and I felt important wearing my hat and marking down the boats and their fuel. My cap would slide over on my face but I didn't mind; it was my "job" hat.

I would stay there as long as there were boats fueling up; then we would hang up our hats on nails in the office and go up to the house for lunch. At first there was only one nail, but Wade said that if I was going to be working there I needed a nail for my hat too. It was a very important job. Mary would have lunch waiting for us and I would eat whatever Wade did; since we had done the same work all morning it seemed right that we have the same lunch. I liked to sit in the big white chairs in their kitchen and listen to the adults talk. Wade and Mary would include us in the talk and listen carefully to our answers when they asked us something. I felt very grown up having a job and helping with the fueling lists.

When we would go to Hood Bay we always went back to our boat at night to sleep. Sometimes Jimmy would take Jeff and me down to the boat at bedtime and help us get ready for bed. Margie and Dennis would go to bed in their own bedroom and the adults would stay up playing card games and drinking coffee.

Sometimes Margie and Dennis would come to visit us at Killisnoo, but when they did, their mom and dad never came, so they stayed in the house with us. Margie and I slept in my big bed and stayed awake to talk in whispers. One night we needed to use the outhouse, and even though we had cans under the bed for emergencies, we knew that it had better be an emergency before we used them. So down the stairs we crept in the dark of the night, everyone else was fast asleep. The outhouse wasn't too far from the front of our house, and we opened the door and stepped out onto the porch.

We were not very brave and took small steps, listening for anything that might be out there. Holding hands, we inched nearer the steps, and as we got to the first step we heard a bear growling!! Up the stairs in record time, but without a sound, as that was not allowed! By now we knew we really had to go back and get to the outhouse, so we started our trek again. And again, as we got to the first step we heard the bear growling. Shaking in fear, we hurried back inside and tried four or five more times to get off the porch and to the outhouse, but each time we got to the first step that bear growled and we knew that if we went down the steps he would bite our legs. We got back upstairs and pulled the can out from under the bed - surely this was considered a real emergency!

At last we fell asleep, but in my dreams there were bears everywhere that night, some of them carrying cans and laughing. In the morning we were up early to see if we could still find that bear to show our brothers. But then as we stepped out on the porch and heard the surf roaring on the beach and we both knew just what our "bear" had been the night before. But when you are a little girl and it is very dark outside it is not hard to imagine that there is a bear out there waiting to eat you.

People told us there were no bears on Killisnoo, but in our adventures we came upon a big tree at the edge of the woods, and digging around at the base of the tree we discovered some bear's teeth. They were big and scary looking, and Jimmy liked to drill holes in the wide end of the teeth and string them together. I didn't understand at first what we had found, and thought it was sad that the bear's teeth had fallen out. Later we went back to the tree with a shovel and found several bear skulls and other bones. Someone told us that it was a bear cemetery, that the bears would come there to die. I'm not sure if that was the truth, but I did know that if there were dead bears on Killisnoo there could be live ones and I watched very carefully for them.

The brown bears are very large and one morning I awoke in my bed to see one looking in my bedroom window! That was about all the scaring I needed for a long time! He was standing on his hind legs and could see in my upstairs window. I don't know what he was looking for, but from then on I slept with my head under the blankets. I thought that if the bear couldn't see my face he wouldn't know I was in the bed. Well, it made me feel a little safer anyway.

16
WORK AND PLAY

Doing laundry at Killisnoo was a hard job - our mom had to wash the clothes by hand on a scrub board and iron with an iron called a sad iron, heated on the wood stove. She would take the washtub out on the wide front porch and fill it with hot water from the teakettles on the wood stove. It took a lot of kettles of water to fill the tub. She would sprinkle some soap in the water and swish it about until it was mixed in, then she would take a big bar of soap, place a shirt on the wrinkles of the washboard and scrub back and forth with the bar of soap against the washboard until the shirt was sparkling clean.

She would wash all the clothes this way, piling them into a second tub and then she would add water to the second tub and rinse the clothes, dipping them up and down until they were free of suds. Sometimes it would take two rinse waters to get them all rinsed properly. I was too small to help with the scrubbing or rinsing, but I would stand and hand the clothes to our mom as she hung them on the long lines on the porch, where they would dry, even on a rainy day.

After she was finished with the wash water she would tip the tub and spill the water out on the porch, take up the broom and scrub the porch clean with it. Then the rinse water was poured out on the porch and the boards given another good brushing with the broom. This kept the porch nice and clean, and free of splinters, for they were brushed off with the broom.

After our mom finished her washing she would always go inside and bake a cake. Sometimes it was a chocolate cake and sometimes a lemon cake, both with mounds of seven-minute frosting, which I never cared for, so I would eat the cake and give the frosting to my brothers. The seven minute frosting was hard to make because our mom had to beat it stiff without an electric mixer, and she could only make it when she had fresh eggs brought out from town. She would whip and whip it until it stood in high shiny peaks. Wash day always was cake day.

The next day she would take the laundry down from the lines, fold it and take it to our rooms and put it on our shelves, except for the things she would iron that day. She had a pop bottle with a little metal sprinkler attached to it. It was silver colored and had small holes on the end that the water sprinkled out of, onto the clothes to be ironed. She rolled the clothes up in a tight little bundle and put them all in a basket. When everything was damp she heated the iron on the top of the hot cookstove and spent the afternoon ironing and hanging the clothes on wire hangers to go in the big closet downstairs. I often heard her say that just because we lived in the country didn't mean we had to look like tramps.

In the storeroom in the back of the store there were cases and cases of brown bottles, full of pop. There was root beer and cream soda, orange and strawberry too. I liked the orange and the root beer and Jimmy always picked cream soda. I thought that he must be smarter, since he was older, and so I would try the cream soda, but never liked it that much. A bottle of pop was a real treat and sometimes we would get a small packet of peanuts with it.

Once I climbed up a ladder that led to the shed roof on the front of the store to drink my pop and eat my peanuts. Our mom and dad had gone to Angoon for the day and Jimmy was in charge. He thought it was fun to tease me and he took the ladder down. I didn't mind being up on the roof; I could see a long ways, and it was interesting to see things from a different view. Jimmy had thought I would be scared up there because it was too far to jump down, but I just waited until our mom and dad were coming back across the channel later that day, and then Jimmy had to put the ladder up to let me climb down or he would have been in trouble. It was nice to be on the roof, for no one could tease me up there. It hadn't been as much fun for Jimmy as he had wanted it to be, but I had a good time.

There was an outhouse was high above the beach, on the side of the big warehouse, next to the store. We liked to go out along the narrow board to the outhouse, to paly. We had to be very careful not to fall into the water when we were making our way along the wide pipe that led out to the outhouse. We had to place our feet sideways as we inched along out to the outhouse, which was about 25 feet out from the shore. Sometimes we would carefully ease ourselves down to sit on the pipe, being so careful not to wiggle too much and fall the long distance to the beach, or the water if the tide was in. When we sat on the pipe we would always sing and kick our feet back and forth, making a nice banging drum sound on the pipe.

One time we decided to hoard our stash of treats that our mom or dad would give us from the store; we had several packs of gum saved up, some candy bars and some peanuts. When we received them as a treat we took them out to the outhouse on the side of the old warehouse and put them up on a ledge to save them. I don't remember just what it was we were saving them for, but we never went back to get them, and much later when moving again we all thought of them up on the ledge and it was too late to go back and look for them. I suppose that mice probably had gotten to them, but we were sorry that we hadn't eaten them when we had the chance.

That outhouse out over the water was a place of amusement for us, and we never used it for its intended purpose. The holes - there were two or three - were sometimes used as portholes in our submarine and we would put our faces in the holes and look down at the water when the tide was in. We could often see fish or star fish, or just driftwood going by. I don't think our mom knew we did this, or she would have put an end to it!

Sometimes we would find interesting things to drop into the ocean from the outhouse. One of us would drop things and the other two would be on the other side of the warehouse, on the beach. When the two on the beach spied something coming under the dock that warehouse sat on they would yell what it was, and if it was what had been dropped, and not something that just happened to be floating then the one who guessed right got to go and drop something out of the outhouse.

We made little boats of pieces of wood, with wood or leaf sails, to drop down. Sometimes we would have a piece of cardboard from the store, although I never dropped my cardboard down because I wanted to write on it. Candy didn't float long enough to work for this game so we quit wasting that right away. The candy wrapper would float nicely, but sometimes the wind would blow it up on the beach before it traveled under the warehouse. So we had to pick carefully something that would float well and last until it got to the other side, or if we wanted to have a longer turn, we would throw down light things that might end up on the shore under the warehouse.

Sometimes our mom and dad would invite friends over for a party at Killisnoo. The friends from Angoon would come, and also some of the fishermen. We kids had to go to bed early, as usual, even when we wanted to stay up and see the fun. We found a hole in one of the boards in the hallway between our bedrooms and we would lie on the floor and put our eye close to the hole and we could watch the party in the living room below. The adults got silly, something we were not used to, and they got very loud sometimes. One time one lady had to use the outhouse and she came running back inside in just a little while. She couldn't find the outhouse, but she had found a patch of tall plants and used that instead. But to her dismay she had found stinging nettles and was very unhappy for the rest of the night! When she came inside crying about it we started to giggle and our mom said if there was any more noise upstairs we would be in big trouble. We knew what that meant and so we didn't giggle any more that night, at least not loudly. These parties weren't very frequent but they were sure funny.

At New Year's we would always go to Peg and Jake's for their party. They invited all the school teachers, the fishermen, all their neighbors, the postmaster, a man named Mr. Hamburg, and other friends. They had a very big house and would fix a Scandinavian Smorgasbord with all the fancy foods you could imagine, ordering special food from town for the party. People would start coming early in the afternoon and there would be several new kids to play with. The upstairs bedrooms were fixed up for all the kids to sleep in that night, and we were allowed to stay up past 10 o'clock, which was a rare treat for us.

There was also a special table set up out in the old store room for kids only. We had party hats and all kinds of delicious food to eat and bottles of pop to drink. Someone usually made a very big cake and a smaller cake just for the kids. I always wanted to stay up until midnight to see just what it was they did, but being used to a 7:30 bedtime, I was almost always the first to fall asleep. Then in the morning when I woke up there would be lots of people sleeping downstairs, all the kids upstairs, and Peg would be in the kitchen washing up the dishes and making breakfast for everyone. She would make big pans of cinnamon rolls and bowls full of scrambled eggs, plus pots of coffee.

Coffee was a funny thing in Alaska. There were different ways to make it, but it was always there, no matter how you made it. There was boat coffee, which was made in a big enamelware coffee pot with a wire handle with a wooden bar in the middle of the handle for holding the pot. The water was poured in the pot and brought to a boil on the boat stove, then a cup full of coffee grounds was poured into the boiling water and it continued to boil for a while. When it was time to drink the coffee, a raw egg was put into the pot, if you had an egg, and it was supposed to collect all the grounds at the bottom of the pot, but I've seen our dad's cup and it usually had a big glob of grounds in the bottom, which he tossed overboard before pouring another cup. The coffee would sit on the back of the stove most of the day and would get stronger and stronger. As our dad was pouring the coffee he would say, 'Get the scissors and cut off what you want.'

Our dad would bring home fresh fish just about every day for our dinner. We only ate salmon and halibut, never any cod or red snapper, our mom considered them scrap fish. We ate fresh crabs in season, and clams when we could dig them on the beach. It was hard to learn how to capture a clam. We practiced walking up very quietly, then waiting for a clam to squirt water up through the sand, then we would dig fast, because the clam can move through the sand at an incredible speed! We had a special clam digger, it looked like a very big fork, with thin tines and a long wooden handle. When our buckets were full of clams we would head back to the house for a feast of fried clams or steaming bowls of clam chowder.

One of our favorite dinners was when the herring were running and we would stand on the dock and jig for herring. We would fill our buckets with herring and lug the buckets up the dock to our house, and then our mom would fry them up nice and crisp for dinner. This was one of the times when we were allowed to stay up late, to wait for the tide to turn and the herring to run so we could catch enough for a meal. To catch a herring you get a long line with lots of hooks attached up and down the line. You don't catch the herring like you catch a bigger fish, by having it bite the hook, but you swiftly jerk the line up and down (jigging) and the line snags into the sides of the herring. When there are schools of herring the fish swim very close to each other and it is easy to snag them. Before long you haul up your line, flip the fish off into the bucket and lower the line off the dock again. Hot fried herring, a big cold canned tomato in a small bowl and Pilot Bread for dinner; there isn't much that tastes better.

17
WE MOVE TO TOWN

After Jimmy finished 8th grade our mom decided that it was time for us to move to town so we could attend regular schools. She said that she had to stay up nights to study the lessons so she could teach them the next day. I had only gone to public school for the first grade and I wasn't sure what the schools in Alaska would be like.

First grade was spent in a one room school in Lotus, California. Our family lived just down the hill from the school, and I had been sent to kindergarten there. When we were waiting for the teacher to arrive on the first day of school, some big kids had given me a key and told me to put it in the door and open the door for them. When I did, the key broke and it scared me so that I couldn't stop crying. I didn't know that I had not hurt anything - it was a rusty old key and wasn't any good, and the teacher used a key to the other door to get into the school. But that didn't matter, I was sent home and the teacher told our mom I was too young to come to school because I cried. I didn't mind, as I hadn't wanted to go to school because I had heard that the teacher was mean and never let you look up from your desk. She would whack you on the head if you moved your eyes off your work and I certainly didn't want to be whacked on the head! Jimmy would often come home from school and say that he had been whacked on the head, but our mom didn't seem to care. I always told him I was sorry he got whacked on the head.

When I went to first grade the next year we had a new teacher, and she had a daughter named Melissa who was also in the first grade. There were no kindergarten students that year. I don't remember learning much in first grade, but I must have learned something. I think the teacher was busy with the older kids and their harder lessons.

Melissa and I would get to clean our big round table. We would wash it with a sponge, then we would take off our shoes and climb up on the table, stand on paper towels and slide around to dry it off. Then we would go to the blackboard and write our letters. This is where I learned to write the word LOOK with big fancy eyes for the Os.

We had singing classes and while we were standing around the piano singing the big kids taught me to put pins in the tips of my fingers, just under the skin and I thought that was funny. I would put four or five pins in each finger, as would Melissa. There was a small pincushion that sat on the piano, and I never knew what else was done with it except to use the pins to make our prickly fingers with.

When it came time for Christmas we had a tree brought in by one of the fathers and we set about to decorate it. Melissa and I made big red circles of construction paper, cut them out and decorated them with paste and glitter. All the kids got to help with stringing the popcorn for the tree. The first day we barely got any popcorn strung because we liked to eat it, but the second day one of the mothers who was helping sprinkled Ajax all over the bowls of popcorn and it no longer tasted good so we got it strung fast!

Melissa's mother popped us some bowls of popcorn for eating and we were careful not to put the Ajax popcorn in our mouth. That was about all I remembered about going to public school, and I had been two years now in home schooling, which we called correspondence school.

It was about time to move to Sitka, so we set about cleaning the house on Killisnoo. As usual, our mom cleaned until there was not one speck of dirt or dust anyplace. She scrubbed the big porch one more time and as she walked backwards down the steps she scrubbed each step so there would be no footprints on them.

Then Jimmy rowed us across the bay and our mom, Jeff and I walked over to Angoon to Peg and Jake's house to wait for our dad and Jimmy to bring the boat over the next day. That night the weather turned stormy and we didn't know if they would get the boat through the storm, but they did, and I remember our dad saying it was one of the worst storms he had been through. He and Jimmy had finished packing all our belongings into our boat, except for my doll, Sammy Sue, which I had carried to Peg's house. I wanted her to be with me, for I still remembered having to leave Bunny behind, and I couldn't bear the thought of Sammy Sue not being with me. She was a big doll, and heavy, but I carried her all the way, without one complaint and without asking to stop and rest, for I knew what would happen if I complained - our mom would have tossed my doll in the bushes and left her there.

Early the next morning our dad and Jimmy went down to the boat to get it ready for the trip to town. When our dad would start the boat he would send Jimmy below so he would not be in the way on deck. That morning he told Jimmy to finish winding the ropes on the stern of the boat, and he went in to start the boat. There were other fishermen in the boat harbor and they said that the minute the boat started, a huge fireball lifted the cabin off the boat and blew everything inside the boat out into the water, where it burned until the water put it out. Jimmy was knocked overboard off the stern of the boat when it exploded and our dad was blown many feet away from the burning boat into the water.

The other fishermen rushed to get them out of the water, but had to be careful, as the boat was completely on fire and was drifting. They pulled Jimmy into a skiff and were able to get our dad onto another boat that was nearby. When the explosion happened our dad had tried to shield himself and had closed his eyes. The only place on his body that wasn't burned was under his arms, the bottoms of his feet and in the creases of his eyelids. Jimmy was not burned at all, just wet, so he only had to change his clothes.

Peg Jacobson was a nurse and one of the fishermen ran to get her. She rushed down to the float where our dad was lying on a blanket. She quickly had them move him to a piece of canvas because the blanket was getting lint in the burns. Our dad's clothes were badly burned and ragged but Peg left them like they were, so he would be a little protected until he got to the hospital. Someone called on their radio from their boat and a plane was sent out from Sitka to pick up our dad. Someone else called for the doctor in Sitka and he said to find something smooth, like a plastic sheet, to wrap around our dad for the plane ride.

The doctor said that the plastic sheet would keep him from getting any dirt in the burns and would keep him warm, which is important after a person is badly burned. By now Jeff and I and the Jacobson kids had walked down to the float after hearing the explosion. We watched in fear as Peg and the fishermen worked to save our dad. We didn't know what was going to happen and everyone was too busy to talk to us. Our mom saw us standing on the float and ordered us to get back up to the house – and fast, and we took off running.

Just at the same time Gerry came down from their house on the hill above the float and gathered all of us kids around her and took us up to her house, where she fixed us all some hot cocoa and cookies and sat with us, telling us that everyone was doing all they could to help our dad. I would go to the big windows and look down at the float, but I could only see people scurrying about and our dad lying on the float, wrapped up in plastic and with blankets over him.

Sometimes I could hear our dad cry out in pain and it made me cry – and Gerry didn't get mad at me for crying, she came over to where I was at the window and put her arms around me and gave me a hug. I covered my ears and closed my eyes so I didn't have to hear our dad, or see what was going on. Gerry took me into her bedroom and let me sit on her bed.

At last we heard the plane coming, it had seemed like an awfully long time since the fisherman had called for the plane. Several of the fishermen found some boards that they nailed together for a stretcher and our dad was lifted carefully onto the boards and tied on with some long rags so he wouldn't slip off. The plane was bigger than the one we had come to Angoon in and there was a space in the back behind the pilot where the fishermen could slip the boards in with our dad on them.

After our dad was in the plane our mom climbed in the front seat next to the pilot. She got on her knees and reached over the seat so she could help our dad if he called out during the plane ride. Jimmy wanted to go too, but there was not room in the plane. Our mom told him to find me and Jeff and take care of us until she could come back for us. Jimmy said our mom was crying when she got in the plane and we had never seen that before.

The pilot rushed our dad and our mom off to Sitka, leaving us kids behind. I thought we were going to have to walk back to Killisnoo and stay with Jimmy, but Peg told us to come up to their house and stay until our mom could come back. She told us that the doctors would have to work hard for our dad, but that the doctors knew just what to do for him to help him get better. That night when we were in bed we could hear Peg and Jake talking and they were saying that they didn't think the doctors could save our dad because he was burned so badly. It scared Jimmy and me, and we looked to make sure that Jeff was asleep so he wouldn't hear.

Our dad was taken to the Veteran's Hospital on Mt. Edgecumbe, across the channel from Sitka, where he was to spend several months. That first day when they got to the hospital our mom had to sit with him for hours and hours, talking to him to keep him awake - the doctors said that at first, when they were trying to bandage the burns that he must not sleep. All the burns were not really serious, but they were still burns and he was covered in bandages from his head to his feet.

We were very scared and didn't know what was going to happen, but Peg and Jake were understanding and told us all they could so we wouldn't be so frightened. We didn't tell them that we had heard them talking the night before. Jimmy had not been burned at all, but it was a good thing he was on deck and not below when the explosion happened.

There was much studying of the parts of the burned out boat, but the fishermen knew right away what had happened. In the storm the day before, a connection in the gas line had gotten wiggled loose and gasoline had been leaking out all night. When our dad started the boat in the morning, the fumes and the gasoline in the bilge had exploded. This sometimes happened to boats that had gasoline engines. From then on our dad would have diesel engines in his boats. Even though they were more expensive, he never had a gasoline engine again.

Our mom came back after several weeks to get us kids and fly us to Sitka, where she had found an apartment for us to live in while our dad was in the hospital. It was summer and so we didn't have to be in school yet. We lived in a downstairs apartment behind Pete Hogan's hardware store, just across the dock from the ANB (Alaska Native Brotherhood) boat harbor. We didn't have anything at all except what we were wearing, some clothes that people had given to us after the fire and Sammy Sue. I was so happy that I had taken her with me that day, and thought that if I hadn't had to leave Bunny behind in California I might have put Bunny and Sammy Sue on the boat and they would have been exploded in the fire, so Bunny was safe in California and Sammy Sue was safe with me in Sitka.

Everything else we owned had been on the boat, except for one or two boxes of things that were still at Peg and Jake's house because there wasn't enough room for them in the boat, including my school papers from the correspondence school, our mom's fancy crocheted lace tablecloth and our dishes.

Our apartment was small, but it didn't matter because we didn't have many things to put in it. People were very good to us and brought us blankets and mats to sleep on. There was one bed for our mom to sleep on and a stove, table and two chairs in the kitchen. There was one big soft squishy chair in the main room, and when you sat down in it you almost disappeared.

Someone brought us some comic books to read. I had never seen them before and enjoyed reading them over and over. I found out that if you had a comic book that your friend didn't, you could trade with them for one you hadn't read. So began the life of children trading comic books, a fun activity which was carried out in a very serious way. One thick comic book could get you two regular ones, so you always had to make sure you came out even. We met a girl who had the biggest stack of comics I had ever seen. Her name was Janice and she would sometimes share with us, without the required trading. So I had a nice pile of comic books to read. This was the first time I was allowed unlimited reading time, because our mom was not home during the day, and she didn't consider comic books to be real books, which she wouldn't allow in our home.

In the apartment in town, when we first came to Sitka, I discovered all sorts of things that we hadn't had when out in the villages. There was that wonderful running water in the kitchen and bathroom, and warm baths in a big white tub, and lights on day and night, - just flip a switch! The people in the apartment upstairs had their own telephone and our mom was able to use it when she needed to. Not living in town for almost three years, I had not seen a lot of things that were now available, or had not remembered them from California.

There were stores to shop in with aisles you walked down and picked out your own items. There were lots of cars, I think about 15 when we moved there, which seemed like a lot to me, churches, four schools and all sorts of things to see and do. It was like going ahead in time about 10 years, as we had lived with the barest necessities when in the villages.

In the upstairs apartment there were two sisters and their mother. I had never met a family that didn't have a dad before and I thought they were quite interesting. They had fancy flowered skirts and curled their hair. Jancee was older than me, and Laura Lee was maybe a little younger. Since they lived upstairs they could climb out onto the roof of our apartment by going out their window. We would sit out there and watch the fishing boats go by. They had a clothesline out on the roof and let our mom bring our clothes to hang out to dry. Our mom carried our clothes down to Gert's apartment, a few buildings away, and used Gert's washing machine when our clothes were all dirty. I remember her carrying a big basket up the stairs and out the window to hang up the clothes. The window we went out was very big and was more like going out a door.

For their meals, our upstairs neighbors cooked whatever they wanted, sometimes having pancakes for dinner or sandwiches for breakfast. Each of them got to choose what they wanted to eat; their mother almost never cooked the same thing for everyone at a meal.

I was constantly surprised at the things I saw in town. We had lived in the country in California and I was only six when we left there, and then living in the villages in Alaska we had gone back in time, now I was nine and here were all sorts of things to discover. When we had made trips to Sitka on our boat we usually stayed on the boat while our mom and dad did their errands; we never went into the stores, except when we would go into Jack and Mikey's store for ice cream.

Things in Alaska were still way behind the states, it was still a territory at that time and more primitive than the states, but the things I saw were new and curious to me. I was now old enough to do things on my own without waiting for our mom and dad to go with me, so I was free to explore. Our mom spent many hours in the hospital with our dad so Jimmy and I could do whatever we wanted while she was gone, as long as we got our chores done first.

My chores were to wash the dishes and put them away, sweep the floors and make up the beds. I had to do an extra good job, or I would not be allowed to go outdoors the next day, and I didn't want that. I would get up early and begin getting everything in order, read some of the comic books and then set out on my day of exploring. I liked to walk along the street in town and look at all the store windows. There was a barber shop, so our dad and brothers could go in and get their hair cut, no more haircuts by our mom.

There was a hotel with a fancy lobby with roses on their dark pink carpet. Each Sunday we would go to the hotel to get a newspaper from Seattle. These were flown in on an airplane each week and if the weather was bad there would be no newspaper until Monday or Tuesday. Later our dad would let me take the dollar into the hotel and ask for our newspaper. I think that whoever wanted a newspaper each week put their name on the list and the paper was saved for them. I felt important carrying the big newspaper, and I was happy to have something that I was allowed to read.

I didn't understand all the things that I saw in Sitka, so I tried to find out as much about them as I could. I figured that all the other kids in town had grown up with all these things and had already inspected them to see what was going on. I felt I was a long way behind them, so I studied everything very carefully, but was cautious about asking my mom questions, because I was afraid she would make me stop going in the stores.

I would go to the barber shop and ask if I could sit in the chair. The barber asked if I wanted my hair cut and I said that I didn't, that I just needed to see what it was like to sit in the big tall chair. He put a little board across the arms of the chair and said that the smaller boys would sit on a board like this so he could reach them. Then he showed me the fine bottles and interesting smelling potions on the shelf behind the chair, also his little broom and fancy dustpan with a long handle that he used to sweep up the hair.

There was some hair on the floor from his last haircut and he let me sweep it up while he held the dustpan. I was a very good sweeper, even though the broom was quite big for me. I thought the barber shop was interesting and the barber would wave at me each time I went by after that. If there was no one getting a haircut he would ask me if I wanted to sit in the barber chair. I would climb up and he would talk to me about haircuts and boats and many interesting things.

There was a store with fabrics and sewing supplies. All the time we lived in Sitka we just called it the Little Old Ladies' Store. There were two sisters who seemed very old to me, who ran the store. They had a few bolts of fabric on the shelves behind the counter, a book you could pick a pattern from, and threads, buttons, snaps and trims for sewing. They had other things in the store, but the only thing I was interested in was the sewing supplies. I would think of all the things I could stitch if I had some fabric.

I hadn't seen a sewing machine before and there were several in the store. They were black and shiny and wonderful and I couldn't wait until we could have one! One of the sisters in the store showed me how the sewing machine worked one afternoon. I had always stitched all my doll clothes by hand and could see that you could do a lot more with a machine, and much faster. I wanted to have patterns and fabrics and all the fancy threads, and especially one of those little black sewing machines.

I would sit on the little chairs by the pattern book and read all the information about sewing and look at each pattern carefully. I had sewed all the clothes for Sammy Sue without patterns and so I could look at them and then go home and make her something new to wear. The sisters had a big stove in the middle of the store and it was always toasty warm, and their cat sat by the fire and let me pet him. Sometimes he would eat his fish and then sleep right next to the stove. Other times he would walk very carefully among the fabrics and pick a nice cozy spot to have a nap, or sleep in the window display and people would stop and look at him there.

There was a store with men's clothes and on one side of that store there was a yarn shop, with every color and size of yarn you could ever wish for. I would sweep the floors or do other chores for Cecelia, the owner, and she paid me in yarn. I loved the fine yarn and wanted to knit a sweater of angora yarn but never was able to do enough chores there to earn enough for a whole sweater. I could make mittens and scarves with the yarn I earned and I loved to sit and talk with Cecelia about things she was knitting.

She showed me how to unravel a sweater and reuse the yarn. We would carefully pulled out the rows of knitting, separating the colors if there was more than one, and wind the yard loosely about a revolving wooden wheel that had hooks hold the yarn. After it was all wound we would tie it into a bundle, placing the ties about every three inches; then she would dip it in water and lay it out to dry, or hung it over a wooden rod, and all the kinks would come out of the yarn. In a few days we would wind the yarn carefully into balls so it would be ready to knit again.

Cecelia also showed me how to make balls of yarn that would unwind from the inside. She would take the cardboard core from a roll of bathroom tissue and start winding the yarn around it, leaving a tail sticking up through the hollow middle. She wound around and around the core, making even circles that swirled up and down along the core until the yarn was all wound. Then she would slip the cardboard core out of the ball and there would be a nice plump ball of yarn with the beginning end sticking out of the middle, so when you knit with it, your ball of yarn wouldn't roll all over the place or get tangled with the other balls of yarn in the basket.

She would show me how to wind very softly, not pulling the yarn tight, or it would have no stretch left in it when you began to knit. Cecelia would give me bits of yarn that were not enough to make a complete item out of, and I would knit small squares with them. I kept the squares in a box and after a while had enough to begin sewing them together with yarn into an afghan. I would arrange the squares on the floor in different designs and finally decided on putting all of one color together, fade to the next color like a rainbow, until they were all used. I didn't like the way the squares looked when they were stitched together so Cecelia then taught me to crochet and I put a pretty edge around each square and crocheted them all together. It made a fine looking afghan that was very warm. I kept it folded on the end of my bed after it was finished, but that wasn't for several years.

On some days there would be some old ladies sitting on the sidewalks in town, wearing clothes that looked different than ours. They wrapped themselves in fancy blankets with woven designs in them and sat right on the sidewalk, without a chair. They had leather boots that they told me were called mukluks and kept their feet warm. Next to each old lady was a wagon or a box to hold the pretty things they had made and were trying to sell to people that walked up and down the streets.

Sometimes there would be six or seven of these ladies and when they talked to each other I couldn't understand them. When they talked to the people that were buying their products I could understand fine. I liked to look at all the things in each wagon and sometimes the ladies would let me sit by them while they sold things. They would talk to each other and pat me on the head and laugh, and it made me feel good, even though I didn't know what they were saying.

They had the most interesting things for sale. Tiny purses, little boxes, mukluks for babies and adults, little seals made of real seal skin, toys and many fine things lined each wagon, all made from the hides of animals. There were fancy designs on everything done in beads of all colors. Some of the designs were eagles, or flowers or just pretty designs.

When it was about dinner time they would gather up their fancy items, fill the wagon full and go off towards their homes. They all lived down the street past our apartment and I would walk with them, sometimes being allowed to pull a wagon for one of the ladies. They walked in a row, with their blankets still around their shoulders and I wished I had a blanket to wear, but I only had my brown jacket and my scarf.

When we got to our apartment they would all wave to me and then continue up the street to their houses. I would watch them go until I couldn't see them anymore then I would go inside and get ready for dinner. It was often my job to start cooking dinner and I always had to have the table set for dinner before our mom got back from the hospital where she was helping to take care of our dad.

I would wash my hands very carefully and then set the table, making it as pretty as I could. Our dishes didn't match and our silverware was old and scratched but I would put it out carefully and set the glasses at the correct place. Our mom had taught me to set the table properly and I knew where each piece went. One night I was starting to cook some soup from a packet, it was chicken noodle soup and the instructions said to put the soup mix and the water on to boil, so I did. Then our mom came home and she saw what I was cooking and asked if I had put salt in the water. I said I hadn't and so she added some salt.

When the soup was done and we sat down to eat we were very surprised when we tasted the soup, it was too salty. Our mom asked if I was sure I hadn't put salt in already and I said that I hadn't. So she got out the soup package and read the instructions and saw that it didn't say to add salt, but she had added it and now our soup was too salty to eat. We started to laugh about salty soup and laughed and laughed. It was a funny night, eating salty chicken noodle soup and laughing and when we finished dinner we went for a walk along the dock and looked at all the boats. Sometimes our mom would say 'wasn't that the saltiest soup?' and we would laugh again. It was one of my favorite times, because our mom was laughing.

Of the many places I had seen in Sitka, I really liked the hotel, but had never been in one. I wanted to know what went on there and would sometimes go in and watch everything. I saw the lady who cleaned the rooms; she would let me stand outside the doors and watch her. She showed me her cleaning supplies and how to make a bed with tight sheets. She would dust and clean and make everything fresh for the next people who would stay there and sometimes she let me help her. I was very good at cleaning.

She told me that people stayed in hotels when they were traveling, or when they had to wait for their house to be ready for them. I wished that we could have stayed in the hotel instead of our apartment, but I didn't understand that it cost more money. After that, when I would make the bed our mom slept in I would try to get the sheets as tight and neat as the ones in the hotel. The mattress was old and lumpy so I never got the sheets as tight or neat, but I tried very hard. The cleaning lady would tell me stories of when her children were babies, she had nine of them, which I thought would be a fine number of children to have, and decided that was how many I would have when I was a mom. I wanted lots of babies to play with and love.

In the lobby of the hotel, near the big tall desk where you could buy the newspaper, were some nice leather chairs and a leather sofa. I had never sat in such fine chairs before so one day I decided that I would try them out. I sat in the first one and it was very comfortable. Then I sat in the next, and was going quietly from chair to chair, trying them all, when the desk clerk noticed me and asked 'What do you suppose you are doing there?' and I replied, "I am sitting in the chairs." I thought it was pretty obvious what I was doing, but I was not a child to be rude when spoken to by an adult. He said "OK" and I continued to try the chairs until I had sat for a little while in each one, and on the sofa too. Then I saw all the magazines on the small table, but decided that I would come back another day to see what all was in them. It was nearly time for our mom to come home and I must be home before she was; she didn't like us running around town being a nuisance.

Many days it was rainy in Sitka, and I would put on my jeans, roll up the cuffs a little bit, put on a heavy flannel shirt, my boots, jacket and a scarf for my hair and I would set out to explore the town. I was careful to be quiet while exploring and never touched anything, unless someone in the store invited me to. I would hold my hands together behind my back and look at everything there was to see, and I learned a lot of things that summer. I was determined to see everything I could before school started so I would know as much about the town as the kids that lived there.

The boats had gotten their fuel from the docks at the other places we had lived in Alaska, with long hoses that ran over the side of the dock down to the boat. The boat captain would lock the big hose onto a pipe on the boat and fill the tanks, then the hose would be drug back up to the dock. Now I would see cars drive up to the gas station and get gas from the little pump. I liked to stand across the street from the gas station and watch the different kinds of cars that came to the gas station, and listen to the talk there. A car didn't come every day, but I waited long enough to see several cars get gas during the week.

At that time we didn't have our car yet, but I hoped we would get one so we too could go to the gas station. Before we had a car we would sometimes ride in the taxi. There was a small building downtown for the taxi, just big enough for one person to sit on a stool at a high desk, with a phone and a list of people who wanted a ride. When someone called for a ride the taxi would come quickly and you would pay the 50 cents for the ride anywhere in town. Sometimes there would be someone else in the taxi and you would get to go to their stop first and then to yours.

We didn't ride in the taxi often, but it was fun when we did. If we had a lot of groceries to carry home and it was raining hard we would call for the taxi and it would take us and our packages right to the apartment. The driver would help carry the packages into the kitchen for us. The grocery stores would also deliver your food to you, but our mom liked to pick her things out and not just send a list for them to choose from. Sometimes we would have the delivery man come with the food we had ordered, but most often we would go to the store and shop for ourselves. And sometimes we would go to the store and pick out our groceries and then the delivery man would bring the packages later. Our mom would pick out the groceries at the store and then instead of giving money to the clerk she would sign a paper, and every time the clerk would say, "Now don't you worry about a thing Mrs. Dunlap; you can pay this when your husband is out of the hospital and working again." I didn't understand what the clerk meant, but she said it every time we went shopping. Our mom always had a quarter to give to the delivery man when he would carry our groceries home for us.

Another store was Neal Anderson's; it was called a drug store and had everything you could possibly want. There were racks of magazines to pick from and a record shop in the back of the store where the older kids would ask to have a record played so they could decide if they wanted to buy it. I would sit on a stool and the big kids would show me the records they wanted to buy. I had never seen such a place before and loved to watch them pick their favorite records and then play them. Sometimes they would ask me if I wanted to pick a record, but I didn't know what was on them, so I always told them no thank you, and would just sit on the stool and listen.

In this store there was also jewelry in shiny glass cases, radios and toasters and irons and such, and regular drugstore things like Band-Aids and pills. On one side was a soda fountain with a mirror behind the counter, rows of shiny glasses and ice cream dishes and a rack for candy bars. I spent many days walking up and down the aisles of Neil Anderson's, seeing what was there. The clerks would sometimes ask me if I needed any help or if I was looking for anything special but I told them I was just looking at everything. It was just a marvel, since we hadn't shopped in stores like this in California, at least not that I remembered. There had been a gap, from when I was 6 until I was 9 when we didn't see all the fast advancements that life was making in the states. People were getting automatic washers and fancy cars, televisions and new houses; it was a time of prosperity that Sitka wasn't seeing. As a nine year old I was happy to investigate all the new things that were there in town, and didn't know that Sitka was still way behind the states. They were certainly ahead of Kalinin Bay and Killisnoo!

There was a bowling alley and I liked to go there to watch the bowlers. In the afternoons, after I had gone home for lunch I would walk all the way back through town, to the bowling alley, to see the ladies do their bowling. I liked the sound of the balls swooshing down the alleys, the clunks and clanks of the pins as they fell down, and the happy people who were bowling. I found out that they would get shoes from the man in the little office and wanted to get some and try bowling, but I was shy and wouldn't ask for any shoes, and besides I didn't have any money and thought that you would have to pay for the shoes to use them. Since I didn't know how to bowl I thought it would be hard to learn and I just knew that I couldn't lift those heavy bowling balls.

Some of the ladies showed me how to keep score and would let me mark down their points and I liked how it would show up on the little screen overhead. When I went to the hospital one day to visit our dad I told him that I had gone to watch the bowling and he said that sometimes people would drop a bowling ball on their foot, and that I should be very careful in there. He said that there was a place in town with a pool table, but he didn't know where it was. I was interested in finding that, since I already knew how to play pool, but I didn't find it, and I didn't have my little box with me so I knew I couldn't reach the pool table anyway.

The shoreboat was another thing that was great fun, but I was not allowed to ride it by myself unless I had something important to do. Sitka is on a big island, and across the harbor was a smaller island with the BIA (Bureau of Indian Affairs) boarding school and the Veterans' Hospital. You would get on the shoreboat, a small passenger ferry, at the float in Sitka and ride across, about five to seven minutes, to the other island, called Mt. Edgecumbe. After you got off the boat you would walk up the ramp and then to wherever you were going.

There was a waiting room on the Sitka side, which was just an open ended covered building with rough benches along the sides, just enough to keep the rain off, unless you were at either end, and then the rain might blow in on you. Sometimes, in the busy part of the day the building would be full of people. The shore boats ran every half hour most of the day, and every 15 minutes during busy times when people were going to work, the kids were going to school or when there was a basketball game between the two schools, Mt. Edgecumbe High and Sitka High.

The shoreboats started running around six in the morning and stopped around 11 o'clock at night. If you were on the wrong side and missed the last shoreboat you might have to find a private boat that would take you across to the other side. On nights when there were basketball games the shoreboats ran until everyone was back home.

There were five different shoreboats, the *Teddy, Dorothy, Diane, Donna* and the *Arrowhead*. Some had covered cabins to ride in and others were open to the weather, while still others had a combination. Each boat held between 35 and 60 passengers. The captains would stand at the top of the ramp and count people as they loaded on the boat, putting their arm out after the last person allowed on that trip.

Sometimes you would get cut off from your family or friends and then had to decide if you would wait for the next shoreboat, which would be along in half an hour, or you if would go across and then wait on the other side for them.

On the Mt. Edgecumbe side there were outdoor benches under a covered dock and also a heated waiting room, which was nice if you had just missed a boat and had to wait the half hour for the next one. It was free to ride the shoreboat from Sitka to Mt. Edgecumbe, but cost a dime to go the other direction. There was an interesting little pot on a post that you slid your dime into and it disappeared down a funnel shape in the middle of the pot. If you worked at the school or the hospital and lived in Sitka you would get a card that allowed you to ride the shoreboat all you wanted for each month, and you didn't have to put in a dime each time. There was no pot for dimes on the Sitka side, just on the Mt. Edgecumbe side.

On stormy days the captain would help the ladies off the shoreboat, warning them to be careful where they stepped. The captains were always friendly people and some would tell stories as they piloted the boats back and forth all day. The harbor could get very rough during storms, but was peaceful and smooth most of the time, and it was always fun to ride the shoreboat. Some of the shoreboats were bigger than our dad's first fishing boat. They would always run the bigger boats at the busier times of the day.

There was a large post office building in Sitka, you had to walk up two flights of steps to get to it. I don't know what was in the basement, but the post office boxes and the window for buying stamps or sending and receiving packages were up those two flights of steps. There were steps on each side of the door, one set going up from the left and one set going up from the right, and they met at the big double doors going into the post office.

Inside you would find the rows and rows of post office boxes, for there was no home delivery of mail in Sitka then. Everyone would come to the post office to get their mail, at first not every day because mail didn't arrive that often. Once a week there would be a mail plane and we couldn't wait for the mail to get sorted so we could see if there was anything there for us. When the freight barge would come in every two weeks there might be packages from Sears that we had ordered over a month ago or there would sometimes be packages from relatives in the states.

I liked to go into the post office and watch the people go in and out. Sometimes they would stop and chat with each other or with the postmaster, and sometimes they would hurry in and right back out.

For those that had cars there were a few parking spots in front of the post office, so everyone with a car would have to turn around to park, as they came down the other side of the street when approaching the post office. There was a driveway that led to the back of the post office and the drivers would pull up into the driveway, then back out to turn around to get to a parking spot. Then usually someone would jump out of the car, run up the steps and fetch the mail, then run back down and into the car and off you'd go, for there was usually someone else waiting for one of those few parking spots. It got more crowded there after more people started buying cars.

One of my favorite places to visit was the Photo Shop, a small shop with racks and racks of old black-and-white photographs of Sitka in the "olden days" Two sisters ran the shop and they had a curtain across the back room, so you never knew what they were doing back there. They developed the rolls of film that people would bring in, so that must have been what was going on back there, but they rarely let anyone go in the back.

They were aunts of the Dangels, for Katie and Jimmy Dangel would be there in the shop sometimes. The sisters would show me old photographs and talk about all the things that had gone on in Sitka.

A few years later when a fire destroyed a large portion of downtown the Photo Shop was spared. It was right next to buildings that burned, but the fire stopped before it got to the Photo Shop. I don't know what happened to all of those photos. We didn't have a camera then because it had burned up on the boat, and we never took film in to be developed, but I would visit there and learned many things about Sitka.

There were about ten steps up to the entrance, they were wide steps and I would often just sit there, over to one side and watch the people going past. By this time I had met a lot of the store owners and people in town and they would wave at me while I sat there, and some of the store owners would ask me if I was coming to look at their store any time soon. They would ask me how our dad was feeling and I was surprised to think that they already knew who he was. I thought everyone there was very friendly and nice.

Sometimes I would peek in the door of the big Russian church that sat in the middle of the street. The cars had to drive around the church. We had gone to Sunday School when we lived in California, but it was in a small white church building. Jimmy would walk with Jeff and me to Sunday School and we would sit in the back and listen to stories and sing songs, then walk home again. The Russian Church in Sitka was much larger, had no seats in it and was filled with beautiful pictures and statues. One day the bishop was coming up the steps and he let me come inside with him and he explained a lot of the things that were in the church.

He said that all of the pretty things in there were to show that the people thought God was very important. I didn't know who God was, but I was sure he was very important from the looks of things. The bishop told me that whenever I wanted to come inside I could, as long as I stood quietly and didn't bother anyone that was in there. I told him I might come back some time and bring our mom so she could see the pretty things, and as I was leaving he said that he hoped our dad would feel better soon. Again I was surprised to think that someone in town would know who our dad was, since he was still in the hospital.

There was a very tall building next to the Russian Church; I counted seven layers of windows in it. I wanted to know what was going on in such a tall building, so I would sit in one of the chairs just inside the door and watch the people come in and go out. They would sometimes have packages like they had been shopping; sometimes groceries in bags, and one day I saw the delivery man coming with groceries and I figured out that people were living in this building. They would often stand before a big flat door, push a button and then wait for the door to open. Then they would walk into the tiny little room and the door would close. The next time the door opened they had disappeared, and I could not figure that out.

So I sat myself down in a chair just opposite the big flat door and decided to watch what went on there. I would see them push the button, then walk inside and the door would close. Then I saw something else happen, the big flat door would open and out would walk someone that I had not seen walk into the tiny room Well, that really confused me and I watched and watched for several days to see if I could figure it out. I was not brave enough to go inside the little room, although I did check to see if I could reach the button to make the door open, and I could. But I didn't want to go in, because I never could figure out what happened to those people once they got inside that little room. They all seemed happy enough to be getting inside so I didn't think it was scary to them, but I didn't want to try it.

After several days I kept seeing the same people going in and out of the little room, and one lady asked me if I'd like a ride up. I did not have any idea what that meant and so I said no thank you, that I would just watch to see what was going on. She must have figured out that I didn't know what that little room was, so she sat beside me and told me a story I didn't really believe at first. She said that the little room was not actually a room, but an elevator, a little car that would take people up to the other floors of the building and let them off on the right place where their apartment was. She said the elevator was pulled up and down by some big cables on pulleys. Well I knew what apartments were, but I had only climbed up stairs to get to an apartment before. She showed me where the stairs were and said that most people did not use the stairs, but went on the elevator.

She asked again if I wanted a ride up, but I was still a little frightened of it so I said no thank you again. She said that she was going to walk up the stairs and I was welcome to walk up with her to see where her apartment was. I decided that stairs were safe enough, so up we started. We went up some long stairs and came out into another big area that was like a big hallway, with several doors, and another big flat door in it. We talked as we walked up the stairs and she told me interesting things about where she had lived before, and about her brother who raised sheep on a ranch far away. She told me about her job - she was a secretary to an important man at a mill, and she liked to write things just like I did.

Then we went through another door and up another set of steps, and then another. She lived on the fourth floor of the building and she let me look out the window at the end of the long hallway there. My, it was high up, I could look down on the church and I could see the little people below walking and cars driving on the streets. That was about as exciting a thing as I had seen so far. Then she opened another door and said this was her apartment and she put her package inside and came back out. She said we could walk back down the stairs or we could ride the elevator. Still I didn't want to get in that little room that made people disappear and so she said she would get in, after she showed me where the stairs were. I waved goodbye to her and started down the stairs, they seemed much bigger when I was by myself.

I came out the door after going down one flight of stairs and there she was, standing in the door of the elevator! I was relieved to see that she had made it that far, but still did not want to get in that little room. Again I walked down the stairs while she rode the elevator, and there she was again, at the end of the second set of stairs. She asked again if I wanted to ride down with her, so I decided that I might try the elevator, as long as she went with me. My legs had gotten tired from so much going up and down the stairs.

We both went in, and she smiled and said she was happy to be able to show me how the elevator worked. The big door slid shut and she showed me the line of buttons on the side of the wall. She said I should push the '1' button, so that we would go to the first floor where I had been sitting in the chair. She said if we wanted to go to her apartment we would push the '4' button.

I pushed the '1' button and then the little room make a funny jerk and my tummy felt a little strange. There was a railing to hang onto and I did hang on. We stopped in just a short time and the door opened and there we were, at the place where I had been sitting watching that little room take people away and bring them back. I was happy to be there and not so frightened now. The nice lady asked if I wanted a ride to the top of the building but I thought that she meant we would be going out on top of the whole building and I didn't want to try that; I had had enough adventure for one day, so I told her I had to get home and help start dinner. I walked slowly home and was still thinking of riding the elevator that evening when I went to bed. I didn't know how it worked and I decided that one day I would try and ride in the elevator again, maybe even by myself.

Not too far from our apartment was a big building that looked a lot like a hospital to me. It had many windows and a big yard around it. Jimmy told me it was called the Pioneer's Home and that people would go to live there when they got old. I liked to walk around in the grass there and often the people that were out for walks would stop and talk to me. They all seemed to be old like our Grandma and Grandpa and they were very nice.

Sometimes they would ask me to sit on the benches with them and we would have a nice chat. There were lovely flowers in the gardens and lots of trees. All around the big lawn was a rock wall, and along the top of the rock wall was a flat cement slab that was wide enough to walk on. In some places the wall was just a little higher than the regular sidewalk and in other places it was very high and scary to walk on. I would get on the wall at the end nearest our apartment and walk along until I began to feel that the wall was too high and scary, then I would walk back a little ways and jump down to walk along the sidewalk instead. The wall didn't seem tall compared to the adults that walked by it, but it seemed very tall to me.

I made plans that someday I would be brave enough to walk all the way along the wall, clear from one end to the other but it took me a long time to get that brave. I never did it that summer, even when I would see other kids walking all the way along it. Sometimes boys would be walking along the top of the wall, and when they would see someone coming they would begin to run - and then they would get careless and lose their balance and fall to the sidewalk. They never got hurt, and I was careful to not laugh at them, although they looked very silly showing off; I knew it wasn't fun to have anyone laugh at you.

Across the street from the Pioneers Home was a big grassy square with a tall totem pole in the middle. There were sidewalks that went from the corners of the square, past the totem pole and out to the other corners. You could walk around and around the sidewalks. Many people walked here because it was the way to get to the shore boat.

Some days, if I had done my before dinner chores and was finished early, I would walk back down to the square and watch the shoreboats come in until I saw our mom get off. Most days she took Jeff with her to the hospital where she helped with our dad, and I would see the two of them coming up the dock and run to meet them. Then we would all walk home together and sometimes I would tell Jeff of things I had seen. I was careful not to tell him too many things or our mom might not let me go out the next day if she thought I was being a pest. I wanted to show him how to walk on the wall around the Pioneers home, but we always walked home on the other side of the street so I didn't get to.

Just before you got to our apartment there was a big white school, with long windows and rows of desks inside. I was hoping that when it was time to start school that I would go to that school. It looked very interesting and some days there would be men there working on the rooms. They would be cleaning or repairing things and I would stop and watch them. When they would stop working and have their snack they would offer me something to eat, sometimes a cookie or a few bites of pie. One man always asked if I wanted coffee and then he laughed and laughed when I said no thank you. I said that children weren't allowed coffee to drink but he laughed and said it would make my hair curly. I didn't believe him so I never had any to drink; besides, I already had curly hair.

I asked them if I could go to that school when it was time and they said they thought that would be all right with them. I wanted to go to school and learn more and have more books to read. I didn't know how long it was until school started in town, but we had always started our classes after fishing season ended. Now I had no way to know when fishing season ended because our dad didn't have a boat anymore, he wasn't fishing, he was sick in the hospital.

So every day I would look to see if other children were starting to go to school there, but all summer long I didn't see anyone going into the school except the workmen. I watched very carefully each day to see if there were any teachers going into the school, for if I saw one I could ask them if I could go to that school, but I never saw anyone but the workers all summer long.

18
CARS AND HOUSES

Our dad didn't come home from the hospital for a very long time, several months, and when he finally did come home we didn't recognize him. I knew that our mom was going to get him from the hospital and the only way I knew it was him was she had a hold of his hand as they walked up the boardwalk, helping him to walk. He was still wound in bandages on most of his face, his arms, his hands and chest. He was like that for a few more weeks and he told stories of how the nurses would come in to change his bandages and some of the nurses would rip the bandage off. Our dad had lots of hair on his arms and chest and so when it began to grow in again as he was healing it would pull something awful when they would change the bandages. But he was very brave and never cried.

When he first came home from the hospital we still lived in that little apartment and it was very crowded. After he was well enough to start doing things, we moved into a house out on Halibut Point Road, across from Mark and Abey Rigling, and got a small car. It was a black and white Ford, from about 1940, which he bought from Mark, who was the car dealer in Sitka. Now a car dealer in small towns in Alaska in those days was different than a car dealer in the states. There were no car lots full of cars, no salesmen going about telling you all the wonders of the latest car, or the joys of the used car. There was no fancy showroom with the latest and shiniest car of 1955 for you to sit in and wish to buy. Mark had only one car for sale; it sat inside a dark room with two big glass windows. I only remember seeing a black car in that room. If you wanted any other car Mark would either order it from the States or tell you of someone who was leaving Sitka, or wanting to sell their old car and you would both go out to talk to them and make a deal.

I suppose that Mark must have gotten some money for this sale, but I was too young to want to pay attention to that part. I just knew that we had a car, after several years of not having one. For the people that wanted a new car, and in those years most people did not buy a new car in Sitka, they would have to order it from Seattle and it would come up in a month or two on the barge.

I remembered the cars we had in California, one was shaped like a big upside down bathtub; it was big and black. Sometimes we would go to visit friends and when it was time for us kids to go to sleep our dad would fold the back seat down into the trunk and there would be a big bed for the three of us to sleep on. We would cover up with blankets our mom kept in the trunk and go to sleep, and when it was time to go home we would not even know that the car was moving. Our dad would carry us inside to our beds, although I would think that Jimmy walked, as he was older.

We would take long drives in California and go to our Grandma's house, which always smelled of baked ham. She had cookies in a jar on the table and would give us a cookie before dinner. Our mom didn't want us eating cookies before dinner, and one day, on the way down the driveway to Grandma's house our dad gave us instructions. He said that if we took the cookie that Grandma offered us before dinner then :God help you when you get home." He was very stern and we knew better than to eat a cookie before dinner.

But Grandma offered us one, not knowing what our dad had said, and Jimmy looked at her and said, "Grandma, we can't have cookies before dinner anymore, or God will help us when we get home." Well, Grandma knew what that meant, even though we didn't and she was so upset she went to her bedroom and wouldn't come out the rest of the day. We ate our ham dinner, but it wasn't as much fun without Grandma there. After that we got our cookies after dinner.

Sometimes in California we would go for Sunday drives, finding new and interesting places that we hadn't seen before, driving around on all the roads near Lotus, sometimes going into Folsom and getting an ice cream cone for a treat. Everyone had a car in California and driving was common, but in Sitka, when we arrived, there were very few cars, probably not 15 in all.

We walked everywhere in Sitka, as the town was small, and we didn't need a car until we moved those several miles out of town. But still we walked most places, just using the car when our mom and dad went grocery shopping or had to haul things. There were trucks and school buses and other cars, but only 14 miles of road in the whole town, and Sitka is on an island so there were no connecting roads to any other towns.

It was near the end of that summer we moved to our house on Halibut Point Road and my exploration of downtown stopped. It was too far for me to be allowed to walk into town by myself. I was sad that I couldn't walk to town and continue exploring, but I found a lot of interesting things to do at our new house. Our house was small, but had some different things in it that I had never seen before. One of those was a mechanical toilet. There was a little water involved, but a lot of noise as blades that you could see would grind things up.

Well, it didn't take the three of us kids very long to try and see just what the toilet would grind up, besides what it was intended to. When our mom and dad were gone to town we tried a lot of different things, starting, of course with soft things, like bread and a foam curler, a sock (that kind of had us worried because it got a little twisted) and then another sock because we didn't know how we would explain losing one sock. We made sure it was a white sock, as I had several pairs of those and we hoped one pair wouldn't be missed. But our mom soon after asked where my other pair of white socks were. When we didn't say anything, she made me sit on a chair the rest of the day and think about losing socks. I sat on the chair, and I thought about socks, but mostly I thought about how funny it was to see those socks going into the mechanical toilet, getting all tangled on the blades and then flying apart and disappearing.

There was a small shed next to our house and we made it into a playhouse. There was no glass in the windows, so we had to be careful not to leave anything where the rain would get it. There was a small attic in the playhouse and it had an open window frame in it and the rain would pour in through it and leak into the room below. One day Jimmy decided that he would take a piece of plywood up there and nail it over the opening to keep the wind from blowing the rain in. He got up on the ladder with his piece of wood and asked me to hand him the hammer. I turned to get it and when I did he lost his grip on the plywood and it flew down and the corner of the plywood smacked into the top of my head! It knocked me to the ground and Jimmy rushed down the ladder to see if I was ok. There was a little blood, but not like at Kalinin Bay when I had fallen on the rocks. We asked our mom to look at it and she said it was just a small dent in my head. I had a great headache for many days after that but finally it went away. I could still feel the dent in my head though, and it was very tender if I would bump it. Seems my head got a lot of pounding in Alaska.

Down the road from us lived the LaCours. They had a son my age and a daughter that was a little younger. In their garage they had set up a ceramics shop and that year our mom let me go there and take lessons with some other kids that lived on the same road. The first thing we made was a leaf dish. We picked a nice big leaf and dried it off carefully. Mrs. LaCour gave us each a small piece of clay and a jar - which was our rolling pin. We rolled the clay out very carefully until it was thin and bigger than our leaf. We put our leaf on top of the clay, making sure that the clay stuck out all around the leaf, and with a pointed stick we pressed down into the clay all around the leaf, to cut out the exact shape of the leaf. We pulled the extra clay away from the leaf and then picked up our clay leaf and put it on a special table, turned it over and wrote our name on the back with the pointed stick. We turned the leaf carefully back over and drew the veins on the front of it, looking at our real leaf to see how to do it.

We then took a small piece of the extra clay and made a long rope of it by rolling it on the table with our fingers. We decided how long we wanted the clay rope to be and clipped it off, then stuck it to the top of our leaf, like a stem, twisted it around and stuck it down again a little ways from where we attached the first end, forming a loop for a handle. We could bend the edges of the leaf up a little bit if we wanted, to form a bowl. That was all for the first day, and the next week we came back and our clay was dry. Then we put a glaze on it, it was not green when we painted it on, but after the clay was fired it was a very pretty green.

My next project was a bunny mug; one ear of the bunny was looped down and formed a handle for the cup. These were already formed and we just had to paint them. I painted my bunny with a little brown shading and pink inside her ears, blue eyes and a black nose. We would paint one week and come back the next week to glaze the bunnies.

I liked the classes and after we finished one project I looked at all the things there were to paint and decided that my next project would be a little donkey with a cart. I painted a special glaze on that had little lumps in it; when it was fired the lumps melted and made tiny specks of darker brown on the tan donkey. The cart was painted the same shade and I cut out teeny tiny hearts and put them on the corners of the cart.

Jimmy had a bicycle when we lived in California, an English racing bike. One day he was riding down the long driveway to our house and the brakes wouldn't work and he went through a barbed wire fence, scratching himself up and badly bending the bike. Since moving to Alaska we hadn't had a bike, until someone in Sitka gave us a great big, old, orange bike. I had never ridden a bike before and I wanted to learn, but this bike was so big I couldn't figure how to get on it. It was a boy's bike and had a big tank sort of thing between the seat and the handlebars, so it was hard for me to get my leg over to ride it.

I would watch Jimmy ride it up and down the road and wanted so badly to ride it. When he tired of riding it I would get the bike and prop it up against a big stump near the road, climb on the stump and then lower myself to the bike. To get started I would push with one foot on the stump and fling myself into the road, hoping to stay upright until I could get my feet on the pedals. After many attempts and some scratches on my knees and elbows I would get the pedals going and stay upright for a few feet. I practiced and practiced, over and over, until I could make it a little ways down the road.

Then I had to practice turning around and getting back to the stump, as I could not reach the ground to steady myself if I stopped. It is a good thing that there wasn't much traffic on our road, as I spent most of my afternoons practicing to stay upright on that bike. After a week or so I could ride a ways down the road, turn around and get back to the stump without mishap. If I fell on the way I would have to push the bike back to the stump and start over again.

Jimmy later showed me how to get one foot on the peddle and push with the opposite foot to get a little speed, then to fling my pushing foot over the seat and off I'd go. It was hard for me to balance and get my foot over the seat, so I mostly would get on the big stump, shove off and fly down the road. I loved the feeling of the wind in my hair and the fun of riding along looking at the scenery, birds and animals that I might see. I had to concentrate very hard on keeping the bike upright and keeping it moving, so I couldn't wave or stop and chat if I met anyone, but I could sure ride, and that was the best part.

Later that year there was a drawing at Neal Anderson's Drug Store for a new bicycle. Each time that you bought anything at the stores in town you got a ticket to put in the big jar. Each merchant gave out tickets and the bicycle was hanging in the window of Neal Anderson's. When we would walk to town I would look at the bike and hope that we would get it with our tickets. We kept the tickets in a box on the dresser in the living room and finally the day came for the drawing. Everyone in town came in to see who would win the bicycle, and when they picked the winning number, I could not believe that we had won it!

Our mom said it was Jimmy's bicycle, so he always got to ride it and I was given the big old orange bicycle. But that was fine with me, because now I could ride my orange bicycle any time I wanted, without waiting for Jimmy to be done with his turn. I got very good at riding the bicycle and tried to teach Jeff to ride it but he was too small and wasn't very interested at that time.

Sometimes Jimmy and I would trade bikes because he wanted me to have a chance to ride the nice new red bike. It wasn't quite as big as the orange bike and I really preferred the orange one, but when he would offer I would always take a ride on the new bike. I was always happy to get my giant orange bike back.

19
SCHOOL AT LAST

When we started school that fall we rode the big yellow bus into town and I thought that was great fun. I had never seen, or didn't remember, school buses from California and I liked how all the kids would load up on the bus and we would talk and laugh on the way to town, nice and dry instead of walking in the rain. We would stand across the road from our house each morning and wait for the bus to come. We would see it from our house when it was going out to the end of the road and we knew we had about 10 minutes to finish getting ready and get across the road before the bus got to the end of the road and turned around to come back and pick us up.

We would put our school books in our bags, get our rain coats and boots on and wait on the side of the road. We were nearly the last ones to get on the bus and when we walked up the inside steps all our friends would greet us and we would settle in for the drive to town. In the afternoons, when school let out at 4 p.m. we would board the bus and ride home. We wanted to ride to the end of the road and get off on the way back into town, but we had to get off most days at our house on the first trip past. Once in a while we would get to ride all the way to the end and back to our house; that was a great treat.

A few days before school started, our mom had to go into town and have a meeting with the principal about what classes we were to be in. She put on her nicest dress and borrowed a hat from Abey, and walked into town in the afternoon. I had finished third grade before we moved to town, but the principal told my mom since we had correspondence school and because we were fisherman's children we would have to be put back a year. Our mom wouldn't stand for that, so they put us in the D class. At that time you had A, B, etc., for classes, the smartest kids were put in the A classes. So the first day I went to school and found the room for the D class.

My teacher was Mrs. Shelton; she was a sweet lady who wore red lipstick. I thought that was the fanciest thing. The first day she had each of us read from a book while she listened carefully. I was proud that I could read without any mistakes. I remembered the book from my second grade in correspondence school, even though this was fourth grade. There were lots of new kids that I hadn't met before and I wrote down all their names when Mrs. Shelton was busy with some of the other kids, so I could mark them off my list of names I had at home.

Each day I would finish with my lessons early and was allowed to pick a book from the shelf to read while the others finished up.

Then one day Mrs. Shelton said it was going to be library day the next day, and we had to fill out a little card with our name and phone number on it so we could go to the library. I didn't know what a library was and we didn't have a phone. I wanted to cry; because even though I didn't know what a library was, I was sure I wanted to go with the other kids. Trying to be brave I walked to the front of the class and threw my card in the waste basket. Mrs. Shelton took it out and asked why I would throw it away. I said, in my bravest voice, "We don't have a phone in our house so I can't go with you." She smiled at me and said that it was all right if I didn't have a phone, I could just put my name on the card without a phone number. I was relieved and that night I told my brothers I was going to the library.

Jimmy asked me if I knew what it was and I had to say that I didn't know, but that everyone else was going. He told me it was a big room with nothing but books and a few tables in it; he had been in a library before because he was older. I was so excited I could hardly sleep - imagine, a whole room full of books! And Jimmy told me that you were allowed to take a book home from the library to read at your house. Now I was excited. Books in our house! That was going to be so much fun!

In the morning I was up before our mom called us and dressed and did my chores extra well and very fast. I could hardly eat my Cream-of-Wheat and drink my milk, I was so excited to get to school. The canned milk diluted half with water didn't even taste funny to me that morning. My dad asked what was the excitement all about and I told him that today we would be going to the library to get a book.

Then my little world crashed down. Our mom said that she would not have us bringing home any books except the ones that the school assigned us to read; no foolish time would be spent reading library books. I didn't cry, I knew better, but I wanted to. When we got on the bus I was so disappointed and asked Jimmy what I should do, for I thought now that I would be expected to take a book from the library, if that is what everyone was doing. He said to take the book to my classroom and read it when I had extra time, but never to tell our mom that I had a library book.

I was a little happier, but still sad because I had hoped to have books to read at home. I so loved books and wanted to read all I could. At school I didn't know what time it was that we were going to the library; each time we changed subjects I hoped it was time to go and see the library. Lunch time came and we still hadn't been to the library. As we all walked to the lunch room to eat our bags of lunch I tried to look into each room to see if I could find the library. I ate my lunch, but only wanted to go to the library and see the books.

After lunch Mrs. Shelton said that we should take out our crayons and get a big sheet of paper off the table at the back of the room, and take our library cards with our names on them, for we were going to the library. We lined up with our cards, crayons and paper, then marched quietly down the hallway to the very end, turned the corner and down another long hallway.

I walked very quietly like I was told to, but inside I was jumping and skipping because at last I would see the room of books. We stepped into the library and it was grander than I had ever imagined. Books almost to the ceiling, books on tables, books on shelves, tables with nice chairs for sitting and reading, big windows on one side of the room and a lady who stood at a counter who spoke to us as we came in.

The other children had all been to the library before but I had never seen one. I just couldn't stop staring at all the books, and I was a little overwhelmed thinking that perhaps we were supposed to read all the books there, and it would be hard for me to do that without being able to take some home to read. The lady at the counter talked to us about always washing our hands before looking at books, about being careful with the library books because lots of others would read the books after us, about never marking in a book or tearing the pages. There were pretty posters on the wall and she explained to us that when we picked a book today we would have time to read a little of it and then we could draw a poster about our book and what we had read. We were instructed to always be quiet in a library so we wouldn't disturb the others that were reading.

She showed us the sections of books that were for our grade and then she said that we could go quietly to find a book, pick one out and take it to a table to begin reading. I didn't know where to start, so I went to the first book of the first section she had said was for our grade, and took that first book. Mrs. Shelton asked me what kinds of books I liked to read and I said I had read "Lorna Doone" the summer before. She looked at me strangely and asked if I was sure that was the name of the book. I said it was, and told her a little of the story. She just said "Oh my, that is a big book for such a small girl." I was rather proud that I had read such a big book, even if I hadn't understood most of it.

The book I picked had poems in it and I remembered learning poems in our Calvert lessons and was excited when I found some of the same poems in the library book. I read several poems and then took out my crayons and paper and drew a picture of a poem about a boy and his boat.

On the bus going home I told Jimmy about my book and he said to be very careful to not tell our mom that I was reading poems, for she disliked books of poems even more than she disliked books of stories. It didn't matter though, for she never asked what I had gotten from the library. Each day at school, when I had time, I would read in my book of poems, but I finished it in just a few days and so decided to learn the poems in the book. I still can quote some of them.

It wasn't long into the school year that I was told I was going to change classes. I didn't want to leave Mrs. Shelton, she had been so kind to me.

Mrs. Shelton told me I could stop and see her before classes started if I wanted to, but that she thought I would learn more by being in Miss Campbell's class, the A class. I was proud to be moving up to the A class, because the other kids said it was the best class, but still a little sad to be leaving my friends and Mrs. Shelton in the D class. I wished that we could all be together in one big class.

I walked into Miss Campbell's class and all the other boys and girls said hi to me. Miss Campbell gave me a seat near the back of the room. The room looked about the same as Mrs. Shelton's and I knew some of the kids from the bus and from the time we had lived in town when our dad was in the hospital. The first thing we did that day was an art project.

Miss Campbell read to us from a book about Alaska history, telling us about totem poles and what they meant. She said that they were carved from wood to tell stories and the animals and birds on the totems had meant something special to the carver. After the story we were each given a fat candle and some small tools to make our own totem pole. Miss Campbell said to try and carve things into the totem that would make a story about our life. I thought that the first thing I wanted to carve on the totem was Bunny, my doll that was still in California. I wanted her to be on the very top because she was the most important thing in my life. I started at the bottom of the candle and put a whale, then a raven, for the ravens that had walked around on the beach the day in Killisnoo when the kittens had swum ashore.

Next came a big fish like the kind our dad had caught on his fishing boat. I made the big fish stand up on its tail like it was walking. I put some flowers on the totem too, little forget-me-nots here and there. I made a bird that was supposed to look like a sea gull, but it didn't look exactly like one. I liked it, and then I put a kitten, and a dog for Chi-Chi who had spent a winter with us. I didn't know how to make a dolls face very well, so I made an eagle at the top and put a faint face on its tummy to be Bunny. One of the boys in the class had told me I couldn't put a doll on the totem, but I wanted Bunny to be on it.

The next week in art class we got some paints and painted the designs that we had carved. I used a lot of red on my totem because that is my favorite color. We had big sheets of paper on our desk to set our project on and we painted for a long time; it seemed that we got to paint all afternoon. After our totems were finished we took turns showing them to the others in our class and telling what they meant to us. I was very shy and didn't want to speak in front of the class, but Miss Campbell said that we each had to, so I did. I liked hearing the other stories about why each student had put certain items on their totem. One boy had put a kangaroo because he had seen one in a zoo one time. That was the most interesting animal on the totems that I remember.

Then the very next week Miss Campbell told us that we would be going on an outing to see real totems. After lunch on that Friday - we always had art on Fridays - we put on our coats and boots and formed a line. We followed Miss Campbell down the hall and to the sidewalk. We walked a long ways, along the bay, past big houses and Sheldon Jackson college, and into some woods. When we were passing Sheldon Jackson College we saw a gigantic rock that had a sign on it.

There was a small tree growing right beside the rock and a couple of the boys ran very fast at the rock and right up the front of it. They stood at the top and reached up to try and touch the top of the little tree. I thought I would like to try that, but didn't want to in front of the other students. I knew we lived too far away to be able to walk down here to the rock so I decided I wouldn't get to see what it was like to run up the front of such a big rock, one that was much taller than any grown up I knew. It did look like fun.

At the beginning of the woods were two very tall totem poles, with whales, birds and masks carved on them. Miss Campbell told us what the different things meant on the totems and we walked along a wooded path with many more totems along the way. This was called Totem Park and we saw where there had been a fort that the Natives had lived in before the Russians came to Alaska, and where the Indians had fought a war to try and keep their land. There were just some logs put in the ground like a fence, so they couldn't very well protect themselves against boats with cannons.

It was the first time that I understood about war and I thought it unfair that one group could come and take what had already belonged to another. I thought of the children that must have been there and how afraid they must have been, and I thought that there should never be wars. Even at nine years old I hoped that there would not be any more wars in the world, even though I had not heard of any other wars when I was nine.

We walked to the end of the park, where there was a small river. We sat down on logs and Miss Campbell asked us questions about what we had seen. Then she passed around cookies and milk that she had brought from the cafeteria. It had been raining a little when we started out but it was sunny and clear by the time we stopped for our snack. We walked back through the park and to the school, where we picked up our totem poles to take home, and then it was time for the bus.

I carried my totem very carefully on the bus; I didn't want it to crack. I showed it to Jimmy and Jeff and they thought it was a good totem pole, although Jeff asked why I didn't put a cow on it. I didn't know why I hadn't, so I couldn't tell him why. Cows didn't seem very important to me I guess.

When we got home there was a big surprise waiting for us: our Aunt Norma had come back for a visit. She had been away to the far northern part of Alaska, where she was a nurse. She was ill now and had come to stay with us until she was better. I was so glad to see her; I remembered the fun we had when she had visited us at Killisnoo. She asked how our day had been at school, and I was happy to tell her of the walk to Totem Park and to show her my very own totem pole.

Our mom never asked us about school and I liked it when Aunt Norma did. She has the sweetest laugh and I went to bed that night very happy that I could hear her laugh again, and I fell asleep listening to her talking to our dad and laughing about things they had done as children. It was fun to imagine them as children, but in my imagination I just thought of them with their same grown up faces on smaller bodies. It was a night of silly dreams.

Aunt Norma stayed with us for a few months and soon she was well enough to go back to her job as a nurse. She had lived in Northern Alaska, where it was very cold and she showed us her parka. It was made of white rabbit skins all sewn together and had wolf fur trimming about the hood. One day she let me put it on and said that someday the parka would be mine. It hung to the floor on me and was very heavy, but I liked the feel of it, and it smelled like Aunt Norma, which I liked too. She had mukluks and mittens to go with the parka and told us of how the ladies in the village had carefully stitched all the beads to them to make the fancy designs. She said that sometimes the designs told stories and sometimes they were just fancy and pretty.

Another thing she showed us were Eskimo yo-yos. She gave each of us kids a set as a gift. They were a toy that the children played with in Alaska. I had never played with them before, but had seen them on the boxes and in the wagons of the ladies who sold things along the sidewalks in town, and I found them quite interesting. There were made of seal skin and shaped like a small pot with a lid on it, but no handle. There were two of these 'pots' about 1" tall. The sides of the yo-yos had the fur on them from the seals, but the tops were smooth leather and had pretty bead designs on them. Mine had a little ring of soft blue bead forget-me-nots.

The two yo-yos were joined together with a long twine made of very thin strips of braided seal skin. Each yo-yo had a long twine coming out of the top of it and these were held together at the other ends of the twine with a small piece of black bone, about 1 inch long and less than 1 inch wide. You held onto the piece of bone with one hand, and one of the yo-yos in the other, and tossed it so it would go in a circle around your hand, and you began to gently move your hand up and down to keep the yo-yo circling. Then you would take the other yo-yo that hung down and toss it in the opposite direction. The twine to each yo-yo was a different length, you tossed the longest one first.

By moving your hand gently up and down at the wrist you were to try and keep the two yo-yos from smacking into each other as you spun them in opposite directions. It took some practice, but eventually I got good at it and could keep them going for a long time. Aunt Norma was patient and showed me over and over the correct way to do it.

One night our Aunt Norma said she would be moving over to Mt. Edgecumbe, where she would work at the hospital. We were all happy that she was going to be so close, although I would have rather had her stay living with us. She said her apartment was ready to move into and she would be taking her things over on the shoreboat the next day. I watched her pack up that night, folding all her clothes neatly back into her suitcase. I was sad to see her go because it was such fun to come home and tell her all about my day at school.

Our dad took her and her suitcase in the car to the shoreboat. I asked if I could ride along but our mom said kids would just get in the way. I waved to her as they drove off down the road and she waved back. In a couple weeks we all went over to her apartment to see where she was living. She had a nice big room with a small kitchen in one corner and a sofa, chair and radio in the other. Through one door was her bedroom and through another was her bathroom, with a fancy bathtub and a sink that had a towel bar on one side. She said she liked living there, but she would come to our house for Thanksgiving and Christmas dinner. She came over other times, usually on Saturday night if she wasn't working. I was always glad to see her come to visit.

20
A VERY BIG HOUSE

Not many days after Aunt Norma moved out, our mom told us that we would be packing up our things into some boxes and moving into town. They had bought a big house in town. I would miss our little house but I thought living in town would be fun too, since I had so much fun that summer before when I went exploring.

We put everything in the boxes and cleaned up the little house, then a friend came to our house and we put everything in his dump truck. I watched as they drove off with our dad and Jeff riding inside the truck, and with Jimmy sitting on top of the boxes in the back of the truck.

Jimmy was going to help unload all the things at the new house. Our mom closed the door to the little house and we walked into town to see the new house. It was much bigger and I was to have my own room. There was a very big yard in front of the house, with a tall tree. At the back of the house was a porch that connected the house to a shed, where my dad and Jimmy unloaded all the boxes. They took our furniture inside the house and put it in all the rooms.

My bedroom was a small one and I was happy to have a place without having to share with brothers. Jimmy got a small bedroom at the back of the house that had a little door that went outside. Sometimes I would go and knock on his door and he would let me in, we would talk or draw or read comics, or he would play his clarinet for me.

We had a living room and dining room and next to Jimmy's bedroom was a small entry room that had a refrigerator in it. I didn't remember refrigerators from California and this one seemed so wonderful! Our dad told us that a truck had brought it from the store just that day. It was white and shiny and very cold inside. We would be able to have very cold food all year long. I didn't realize that almost everyone else already had a refrigerator, so when I told some kids at school about it they laughed and said we were just fishermen and didn't know any better.

I didn't understand what they meant, but I knew it was unkind, so I wouldn't talk to those kids anymore. I loved that refrigerator and we would take everything out of it once a week and washed it with warm soapy water so it would stay clean and fresh.

Next to the refrigerator was a washing machine, one that had a wringer to put your clothes through instead of wringing them by hand. Our mom must have been excited to have such a new washing machine, as she had been doing all our clothes by hand since we moved to Alaska.

It was 1955 and there were more modern washing machines around, but it was the newest one we had ever had and I thought it was great. I learned right away how to do laundry. I would fill the tub of the washing machine with hot, hot water from the faucet using the little hose, then carefully I would shave some soap from the bar into the water and turn on the agitator so it would swish the soap and make a big mound of suds. After sorting the clothes into piles of different colors, I would fill the tub with clothes and poke the clothes down with a smooth wooden stick.

The lid then went on the washing machine and we pushed a lever to one side on the outside of the tub that started the agitator inside the tub to let the clothes wash for a while. The lid had a handy little hook on it and would hang right on the side of the washing machine when it was time to take the clothes out. Behind the washing machine, up against the wall, were two big cement laundry tubs that were filled up with water; hot water in the first one, and cold water in the second one.

I would stand on my box, the same one I would stand on to play pool, and lift the steaming hot clothes from the washing machine with that smooth stick. The water was still very hot in the first tub, and so I would have to work fast to get the clothes into the wringer at the back of the washer before I burned my fingers.

There was a little tray under the wringer and it would drain the water back into the washer, but it moved up and down, so we had to be careful that it was pointed in the right direction so the soapy water wouldn't drain into the rinse water. The clothes would squeeze through the rollers into the rinse water and then I would put in the next load of clothes. We used the wash water over three times. The first load would be white clothes, which weren't very soiled, then colored clothes and finally the heavy trousers and jeans.

While the second tub of clothes was washing I would swing the wringer around so it sat between the two rinse tubs and wring the clothes from the first rinse into the second rinse, then swing the wringer one more time to the edge of the second laundry tub and wring the clothes into the laundry basket to take outdoors. If I wasn't careful, the smooth round stick that I used for dipping the clothes out of the water would get caught in the wringer and it would go shooting through the wringer and out the other side, banging into the wall with a loud noise. Also when wringing out clothes that had buttons I had to be careful to fold the buttons under some of the cloth and make sure they were flat as they went through the wringer, or they would pop off and have to be sewn back on after the clothes were dry.

If the bundle of cloth going through the wringer got too thick, especially if it was sheets or towels, the wringer would pop open so you could pull the clothes out and start again. Soon the clothes were all washed and hung on the line to dry. Wash day was much easier now.

We had long clotheslines out in our yard and I could stand on my box now and hang up the clothes. It was good that I could help with these chores, because our mom started working in an office when we moved into town. She would leave just before we left for school and get home after we got home, so there were more chores for us kids to take care of now.

We no longer rode the bus to school, because we lived right next door to Baranof Elementary School. We could leave home right before time for school to start and we no longer packed our lunches each morning, but walked home to eat and then back to school after cleaning up our lunch dishes. If I hadn't gotten all my chores done before school I could finish them up after lunch and still have time to get back to school. I liked living by the school because we could go there after school and swing on the swings or meet our fiends there and have a good time.

Walking all the way across the playground we would come to the Market Center, a nice grocery store where we did most of our shopping. If our mom needed something from the store she would send one of us over there to get it. Our dad smoked cigarettes and he would send us over with a note to buy cigarettes for him too. On shopping days we all walked over to the store and carried home the big bags of groceries. It was certainly different than when we had ordered our food for a year when we were at Killisnoo.

There were shopping carts - again, something new to me - in the Market Center and we pushed them around the store and picked out whatever was on our list. This must have been the way we shopped when we lived in California, but I didn't remember the stores from there.

We now could have ice cream any time as there was a freezer in the top part of our refrigerator, and if there was one thing our dad loved, it was ice cream. He would serve up huge bowls of it to our company and they would be so shocked at how much he had served. He used the big soup bowls for ice cream. We often were sent to the store to buy more ice cream if company came over. We loved the big bowls of ice cream.

We still would make ice cream in our big hand cranked ice cream freezer from time to time, especially if we were going to go on a picnic, but we didn't have to wait for winter any more to have ice cream. If we wanted homemade ice cream our dad would go to Cold Storage and bring in a big block of ice and Jimmy would chip it up to use in the ice cream freezer.

After we moved into town our dad went to work at the BIA school (Bureau of Indian Affairs) on Mt. Edgecumbe. He would still fish in the summer time, but the rest of the time he was a teacher. He taught Gas & Diesel Shop and also Carpentry. Each year the students in his senior carpentry class would build a complete house. They would learn all they needed to know about being carpenters by practicing on the house they were building.

The beginning students would build smaller items, usually some furniture to sell or to put in the houses that the senior class built. Our dining room table was built by one of his classes. If you wanted something built you would buy the wood and tell them what you wanted and they would make it. The table was light colored wood and was round, with many extra leaves that would extend it to seat about 16 people. One of the legs was a bit uneven, or our house was, and we had to stick a bit of cardboard under that leg whenever we moved the table so it wouldn't rock.

21
LIFE IN TOWN

In town there were more kids to play with. Two of the girls in my class, Marcia and Phyllis, lived across the school yard, next door to Market Center. They had a game of jacks and they taught me to play. We would sit by the hour on the porch and play jacks. I got to be very good and in my memory I was the champion of the fourth grade. I hope that others don't remember differently.

The floor in our house was old linoleum at first and it made the ball bounce funny, but I would find the smoothest place I could and practice and practice. We had many rounds that we could play, after the first one. We had claps, one clap after the ball bounced before you tried to pick up the jacks, then two claps and up to five, which was the most we could manage. There was under the bridge, where you scooted the jacks under one hand that formed a bridge by putting your thumb and fingers on the floor and raising the middle of your hand. Another was to slide the jacks into your cupped hand, instead of the bridge but I forget what that was called. Then there was Around the World - pick up the jacks and circle the ball with the handful of jacks before catching the ball. There were so many variations that we could play all afternoon and not repeat one. Whoever had completed a round first got to call out the name of the next round that we would play. When you dropped a jack, or missed picking up the correct number, or moved another jack that you weren't supposed to be picking up, you lost your turn and the next player got to try.

Some days we would swing or slide, or play on the monkey bars at the school grounds. I tended to get seasick from swinging too much on the swings and I wouldn't feel well, but I did it anyway. We would sometimes ride our bikes on the playground, or ride up and down the quiet streets. Going to Totem Park was fun; we would pack a lunch in a paper bag and set off for the afternoon. The first time that we went to Totem Park we all stopped and tried to run up the rock in front of Sheldon Jackson College. We parked our bikes and got as far back from the big rock as we could, and ran as fast as we could till we hit the rock. Then we got about half way up and began to slide back down. There was nothing to hold on to, and we fell to the ground laughing.

We tried and tried, but never did get all the way up the face of that rock that day. I had on saddle shoes and they were slick on the bottom so I had no traction. There was a little path up the side of the rock and we went up that way and looked around to see everything from our perch. We could see the bay and the roads along the bay, and most of Sheldon Jackson College from there. After a while we slid down the face of the rock and continued on to Totem Park, to ride our bikes in the partial darkness of the big trees and look at the totem poles again.

You went between the first two totem poles and you were inside the park. We spent many days exploring there. You could walk out onto the beach at many places and sometimes we would spend time on the beach; sometimes inside the park, other times we would go up the little river that flowed at the end of the park. We would eat our lunch and be very careful not to leave any trash behind. There never was any litter in the park.

When we were going past Sheldon Jackson College on the way home my friends asked if I wanted to see the museum there. I hadn't been to a museum before, so of course I wanted to see it. One Saturday we rode our bikes up the hill to the museum, parked them carefully out of the way of people who would be going in, and walked into the cold, dim museum. It was built of cement and was eight sided, with a skylight on the top for letting in some light.

There were displays of Indian and Eskimo items, with notes beside them to tell a little about them. There was a man there who asked us what we would like to see. I didn't know what I wanted to see so I told him we'd like to see everything please. He laughed and said he would try and show it to us.

The first thing he pointed out was up near the ceiling, it was an animal skin kayak with the figure of a man in it. The figure was dressed in traditional Eskimo clothes and he had a paddle like he was actually paddling. He said that it had been made a long time ago and that the museum was the best place for it, because then more people could see it. We looked at things on the wall, things in cases and on shelves, but soon my friends wanted to go home. I wanted to stay and stay but they didn't so we got ready to leave. When we were going out the door the man there said to be sure and come back any time and look at more things. I was glad to hear that, because there were so many things I wanted to look at more closely. When we got home I told our mom that I had been to the museum that day and she told me to not make a pest of myself. I was always careful to not make a pest of myself, for I was sure that pests were awful things. The next Saturday I was up early, for it was summer and I wanted to go back to the museum.

We never were allowed to sleep in at our house and were up by six a.m. every day. We cleaned the house every Saturday morning and I wanted to get my chores done as fast as I could so I could go back to the museum. I started early on my room, making my bed and straightening my drawers like we did every Saturday. Then after breakfast I helped with the chores in the rest of the house.

After chores I went over to get my friends but they couldn't go to the museum with me that day. I wanted so badly to go; I had lots of questions about what I had seen, and wanted to see more. I ran home to tell our mom that I was going to the museum, and she once again said not to make a pest of myself. I said I wouldn't and off I went. I tried to run up the big rock a couple times but didn't make it, so went right up the side path and announced for all to hear "I'm going to the museum again!"

There was no one to hear but that was okay with me - I was going, so I slid down the rock and skipped up to the museum. The door was open and I went right in. The man there seemed to be glad to see me again, and this time there was a lady with him. I started to walk slowly around in the museum, looking at the books, the shells, the spears, all the baskets, all the different things that were there. The lady asked if I wanted to know anything and I would ask her questions about the items and she would tell me wonderful stories. I asked her how many times we could come to the museum and she said as often as we liked, but only on certain days. The museum was open on Wednesday, Friday and Saturday. Now I knew what I wanted to do with those summer days - I wanted to come to the museum. I asked her if there were any more museums in Sitka but she said this was the only one. I thought that was too bad, because by now I really liked museums.

I spent the rest of the morning there, which wasn't very long because I had to stay home and do my chores first, and I didn't even think about lunch, until the lady told me I would have to go home because they were going home to eat their lunch and wouldn't be back until 2 o'clock. I didn't want to walk home, just in case our mom wouldn't let me come back, so I practiced running up the face of that big rock until I was tired, ate some crackers that were in my pocket and then climbed the little path to the top of the rock and sat and watched the boats go by in the bay.

I was sitting there and a boy ran up the rock and scared me - I hadn't heard him coming. He said he lived in a house on the Sheldon Jackson College campus. He was a year older than me and he knew a lot of interesting things about Sitka. His dad did work around Sheldon Jackson and he told me that the students there came from all over Alaska because their towns didn't have schools to go to. There was a high school and a college there. I told him that when I was finished with grade school that I would go to high school there, so I would be near the museum, but he told me that I couldn't, because there was already a high school in our town. I told him I would anyway and if he said I couldn't he would have to get off my rock, so he stopped saying I couldn't go to school there. He told me it wasn't really my rock, anyway

We talked for a while more about all the things he knew about Sitka and Sheldon Jackson and then I thought it might be 2 o'clock so I wanted to go back to the museum. He said he would go with me to see it because he hadn't been there. I was surprised because he lived so close by. We had to wait a few minutes for the man and lady to come back and open the museum so we sat on the steps and waited. There were some crows walking about on the lawn eating something and I found a few cracker crumbs in my pocket to feed them. He said not to feed the crows because they were pests, and that worried me. I was wondering if our mom meant for us not to be crows when she told us not to be pests, but I was pretty sure that wasn't what she meant.

But by then the museum workers were back from lunch and they unlocked the big heavy doors so we could go inside again. The boy hadn't seen the things in the museum so I told him all that I had learned from the man the day before, and from the lady that morning. We walked slowly along, looking at each item. When I got to something I hadn't learned about we would ask questions and learn more. It was such a fun day that I was sorry when the lady told me it was four o'clock, as I had told her earlier that I had to leave to go home at four.

She asked us to sign our names in the book at the front of the museum. She said everyone that came there signed their name and showed us names of people that had come from far away to look at all the things in the museum. I thought that was pretty important for a museum to have people come for other countries. The boy showed me where his house was and then I went home to help with dinner. I wanted to tell everyone about the museum but we were busy making dinner and then doing dishes.

After dinner I went out in the yard and sat on the bottom of a skiff that was turned upside down in our yard. I thought about all the things I had seen, and planned when I could next go to the museum. I liked to sit outside in the evenings; I would put on my sweater and stay out as long as I could. I liked the sounds of the evening, the birds hopping about or ravens flying over, and I liked to feel the cool air on my face as I sat and thought about things.

On Wednesday I wanted to go back to the museum again and got up early to do my chores. I asked our mom if I could go and she said I could, which surprised me, but I was glad she let me. I got there just when they opened and the same man and lady were unlocking the door. The man asked me if I was going to come every day and I said that I would if they didn't mind. They laughed and so did I although I didn't know it was funny, because I really did want to come every day. I liked them very much and they were always kind to me.

I spent all day there again, although this time I brought a sandwich in my coat pocket. When it was 1 o'clock they had to go home for lunch; I said that I had my lunch and I must go eat it in my secret place. So up the rock I ran, almost making it to the top and then climbed the little path, unwrapped my sandwich and sat and ate my lunch and watched the boats. It was raining but I didn't mind; I had my coat and scarf on so I was warm. I stayed again from two until four o'clock and when I left I said that I would see them again on Friday. They laughed again and said they thought I would find more interesting things to do.

During the next summer I would spend a lot of time there, all day long on Wednesday, Friday and half of Saturday. I never tired of seeing the things in the museum and after a few weeks the man and lady would let me look at some of the things in another room. They showed me how they fixed things that were broken and how they kept track of all the items in the museum. I wanted to know how they found all the things there. They told me that people would send things in when they found something interesting that had to do with Alaska, and that many of the things had been given to the museum by Dr. Sheldon Jackson, who had collected those items many years before. I wanted to find something interesting to put in the museum, but I didn't know where to look.

It was an exceptionally happy summer for me, the summer of the museum. I spent two and a half days a week at the museum- just half a day on Saturday because of all those chores. Some days I was allowed to help with the chores at the museum and when I was very careful they would let me help clean items or dust the shelves. I was very good at sweeping and helped to keep the floors and the entrance swept. Each day they were open I would be sitting on the steps waiting for them to come and open the great heavy doors. They told me that the building was made of cement because then it could not burn down and destroy all the treasures that were there. I was glad, because I remembered very well what it was like to have a fire burn up everything that we owned. I was especially glad that is was fire proof because of the man in the kayak. I knew he wasn't really a man, but he seemed like one to me and I didn't want him to burn up.

22
BEARS, PLANES AND A NEW BOAT

Soon after we moved into the big house in town Jeff would limp and cry because his foot hurt. He would not want to put his shoes on or go to school, and so our mom took him to the doctor to see what the matter was. The very next day after the doctor visit they both got on the airplane and flew to see the doctor in Seattle. I was sent across the street to stay with Kathleen Brandt and her kids. It was just next door, but I felt lonely, and didn't know if our mom and Jeff would ever come back, or if they would have to take Jeff's foot off. I didn't know how he would manage to walk if he didn't have his foot. I would try to stay awake at night to think of some way to help Jeff if he got his foot taken off.

At Kathleen's we could play upstairs in her big house, or make forts in the yard. I had a good time there, but wanted to go back to my own house. Sometimes in the afternoon Kathleen would let me go over to our house for a little while, and I would sweep or do up some dishes if there were any in the sink from when our dad had eaten his meals. After many weeks, Kathleen told me to call the airplane company and see what time the next plane was coming in, because our mom and Jeff were coming back.

I had not used a phone before, so she showed me how. I picked up the phone and listened until a lady asked me what number I wanted, and I said I wanted to talk to the people about the airplanes. There was some noise and then a person said hello to me. I smiled at Kathleen and she smiled back at me -- this was fun! I asked them if they knew what time our mom and Jeff would be coming back on the airplane, and the lady told me they would be there at 2 o'clock. I told her I was happy and thanked her for telling me.

It was still a long time before lunch time so I had to wait for what seemed like forever until Kathleen said I could ride in the taxi out to the turn-around. Kathleen was very kind and would tell me wonderful things and answer any questions I had, but because I was taught not to ask questions, there were things I didn't ask her about, like if the doctors had taken Jeff's foot off, or what they were going to do with his foot if they did take it off.

I told Kathleen that I must go back home before lunch and make sure the house was very clean before our mom got back. I cleaned all the bedrooms, and dusted all the furniture in the dining room and living room. I swept the floors and made sure the magazines on the shelf were in neat piles. I scrubbed the counters and the cupboard doors, and even washed out the garbage can on the back porch. I wanted everything to be shiny and bright when they got home. I swept the porch and set out a cup for coffee for our mom and got the coffee pot all ready to plug in. Then I went back to Kathleen's for lunch and to wait for time to leave for the turn-around.

I was used to walking everywhere, and it was fun to get in the taxi and sit there in the back seat all by myself. The taxi driver asked if I was running away from home, and then he laughed and laughed like he had told me a joke. I laughed too, but didn't understand the joke. I told him I was going to ride to the turn-around and then if he would please wait; Kathleen said that our mom and Jeff would like to ride back with me.

We got there just about the time the big airplane was coming up onto the turn-around, and though I looked and looked, I couldn't tell who was sitting inside those little windows. The taxi driver got out and opened the door for me to get out of the taxi. I told him I was sorry that I didn't have the two quarters to pay for the taxi ride and he told me that was all right, because Kathleen had given him enough money for my taxi ride and for the ride for our mom and Jeff. I was glad, because I didn't know what to do about paying for the taxi ride. I certainly didn't have enough money, because I was given a dime each summer to spend, and I had already spent my dime long ago on a green Popsicle.

Our mom came off the airplane first, and then the pilot came out carrying Jeff. He had a big cast on his foot and he looked sad and tired. But he was wearing a pair of bright orange corduroy pants and I thought he looked very fine for a little brother. The pilot carried Jeff over to the taxi and now I understood why we were riding in the taxi, Jeff was not allowed to walk around on his foot with the cast on it; and he was much too big for our mother to carry all the way home. The doctor had taken a big piece of the bone out of the middle of his foot and it was still very sore. They said he had a cancer on his bone and it had to be taken out or it would spread to all of his bones.

The taxi driver asked our mom which was their suitcase; he put it in the back of the taxi and we rode back to our house. When we got home the taxi driver carried Jeff into the house and put him on the sofa. He helped our mom light the stove in the living room so Jeff would be warm, and then he carried their suitcase into the house.

I was happy for them to be back home, and I would spend a lot of time each day helping Jeff with whatever he needed. I would read stories to him from my school books and help him with his lessons. He wasn't allowed to go back to school for a while, until the cast was off his foot. And then he had to practice walking again, because with the pieces of bone missing he wasn't able to balance himself. So I would bring him things, and sit and play with him when he couldn't get off his bed.

Finally, in the spring Jeff was able to ride his bike again, even though he still walked with a bad limp, and one day we decided to take a long bike ride out past KSEW, the radio station on the very far edge of town, just before the bridge on Sawmill Creek Road. As we were riding down the hill towards the bridge we saw a bear just beginning to cross the bridge and we knew that we had to stop and get out of there. I jumped off my bike, turned it around and jumped back on, pedaling as fast as I could for home. Jeff jumped off his bike too, turned it around and began pushing it back up the hill, as fast as his little legs could go.

Even with his bad limp he quickly passed me up on my bike and he beat me back home, never having stopped to actually get on his bike. Jeff was very afraid of the bears. After that he didn't seem to have so much trouble with that limp.

Not long after Jeff and our mom got back from Seattle, our dad took a plane trip with Jimmy. They packed a small suitcase and we drove to the turn-around with them to watch them get on the plane.

The turn-around is a small airport for seaplanes. The planes land in the ocean, then they spin their propellers a little and this pushes them through the water toward a cement ramp that runs down into the water. When the plane nears the ramp the pilot would put out some wheels from the bottom of the plane and the plane would drive right up the ramp onto a flat spot on the cement. The cement formed a little road in the shape of a circle. The plane would stop at the first part of the circle and let the people out that were coming to Sitka, and let the people on that were leaving Sitka. Then the plane would continue on around the circle until it came back to the ramp and it would go slowly down the ramp, waddling like a big duck with its wings held out stiff. It would get back in the water and after moving a little ways off shore it would speed up until it took off right out of the water.

We watched the plane until it was gone far into the sky and then we walked back to town to our house. Our mom didn't know how to drive a car so we left the car at the turn-around and later a friend would bring it back to our house. We never took the key out of the car, or locked the doors. If someone needed to use your car and you weren't around, they would just get in and drive it, and then bring it back when they were done. Everyone was very careful of each other's cars.

The walk to our house wasn't very long and it wasn't raining so I enjoyed walking along, and I wanted to ask our mom a lot of questions. She had told us that our dad was going to get a new boat, but I didn't know how he would get a boat inside that plane to bring it back with him. She said he was going to the States and would be gone for many days. I knew that California, where we had come from, was in the States, but I hadn't seen any boats there; so many questions in my head.

It seemed like a long time that our dad and Jimmy were gone. Our mom would go to her job in the day time and on weekdays Jeff would go across the street and stay with the neighbors, because he wasn't old enough to stay by himself. I had my chores to do but when they were done I could go to the museum on Saturdays, or I could play on the school grounds.

At lunch time I would make sandwiches and soup and Jeff and I would have lunch together. I would sometimes read a comic book to him after lunch, or a story from one of my school books. I did the lunch dishes and he would lie down on the sofa and take a nap. Then I would go across the street and tell the neighbor that he was having a nap and I would stay in our house with him until he woke up. By then it would be time for our mom to come home and we would fix dinner. We had interesting things to eat during the time that our dad and Jimmy were gone. We would sometimes have chicken pot pie, or macaroni and cheese - things our dad didn't like to eat.

We had a regular schedule of things that we would eat for each meal when our dad was home. Sundays we had roast, with potatoes and carrots cooked in the same big pan as the roast. Our mom would take us to church, but our dad didn't go, so he stayed home and cooked dinner. There would be mounds of fresh baked rolls to go with the roast, all of it ready to eat just as we came home from church. The house smelled delicious on Sundays.

Monday was meatloaf night, with baked potatoes and green beans. Tuesday we had liver and onions, and Jeff didn't like that. I liked the liver and onions and was glad, because we were required to eat all that was served to us, and only what was cooked for that meal. The only thing I didn't like was lima beans, but our dad ate those for Saturday lunch and we didn't have to eat them if we would make ourselves a sandwich, and by lunch time on Saturday I was always at the museum with my sandwich wrapped in waxed paper, in my coat pocket.

Wednesday night was pork chop night, with lots of mashed potatoes and creamy milk gravy made in the pork chop pan. We also had biscuits with the pork chops, and canned corn. Thursday night we had fish for dinner, usually halibut, but sometimes salmon. Our dad would cook the fish in a big pan and make baked potatoes and peas to go with the fish. Friday we would have fried chicken dinner. We also had mashed potatoes and gravy with the chicken, and corn again for our vegetable. Every meal for each day of the week was the same thing; we didn't change any item of the dinner, so we knew just what we would be having to eat each day.

Our dad liked pickles and things like that with each meal, so we would have bowls of sweet pickles, dill pickles, watermelon and kelp pickles, and pickled peaches, and we had canned tomatoes with each meal. The canned tomatoes were like our salad -- we would dip a big fat tomato out of the can and put it in a small bowl, just the one tomato, and put one bowl beside each plate for a salad. I liked to taste the cold sweet tomatoes, and would take a bite of hot food then a bite of cold tomato or pickle.

Our dad also liked fresh bread and butter with each meal, and we had to make sure the bread was very fresh. When he would take his slice of bread he would lift up two slices, take the one under those two and put the first two back on the pile, so he made sure he got very fresh bread that had not sat in the air on the table.

Saturday night was hamburger night at our house. Our dad would clean off the top of the big cook stove. First he would scrub and scrub it with a special big gray brick, back and forth, back and forth, until the top was nice and smooth and clean. Then he would take a wet rag and mop up any little pieces of stuff that had been scraped up by the brick. After this the top of the stove was shiny and clean and he would cook the hamburgers on it. Next he would chop onions into small pieces and mix them in big bowls of hamburger, then form the hamburgers into balls.

He would make a big stack of waxed paper pieces, just a bit bigger than the hamburgers were to be. He would put down a piece of waxed paper on the counter, put a hamburger ball in the middle and put another piece of waxed paper on top. He would take a plate and push it down on the top waxed paper, squishing the hamburger nice and thin and even. He would take off the top waxed paper from that hamburger and use it for the bottom paper for the next hamburger. He repeated this over and over until he had several big stacks of hamburgers on platters, with waxed paper between. Then he would butter the buns and toast them on the top of the hot stove, flipping them up onto more platters on the warming shelf on the stove.

Then it was time for our friends to come by and eat hamburgers. It seems that no Saturday went by without at least twenty people coming to eat. When they started arriving, our dad would begin cooking hamburgers. While he had been fixing the hamburgers and the buns I had been setting the table. I put out plates and silverware, big coffee mugs and lots of things to put on the hamburgers; mayonnaise, mustard, relish, pickles of all sorts, onions that our mom had chopped, and ketchup, which our mom called "catsup." There were napkins at each plate and extra napkins in a bowl in the middle of the table. Our dad could cook a lot of hamburgers at one time and as someone would finish their hamburger he would bring another and another until they could eat no more. Friends would come from town, from out of town; there would be teachers from the BIA school, doctors, ministers, fishermen, aunts and uncles; everyone would come and eat hamburgers.

As people would begin to finish their dinner I would help clear the table and set more plates and cups on for the next ones to eat. Then I would begin to wash the dirty dishes in the corner sink in the kitchen. At first I had to stand on my box to reach the sink, and I would climb up and down many times in one night getting all the dishes washed. The water was always nice and hot because the stove was turned up high to cook the hamburgers and it heated our water too.

After everyone who was visiting had finished eating then Jimmy and I would get to eat. Jeff was allowed to eat with the first group that ate because he had to be in bed earlier than we did. I liked to sit at the table with Jimmy and eat my hamburger; I would swing my feet under the table and listen to the adults as they talked in the living room. After Jimmy and I finished (Jimmy would eat two hamburgers but I could only finish one) we would clear off the table and put out bowls for ice cream, BIG bowls, and our dad would call out for everyone to come and eat ice cream. Those were good Saturday night dinners, and we did it every Saturday that our dad was home.

While our dad and Jimmy were gone to get the new boat we missed all the friends that would come over for those Saturday night hamburger dinners. One day, our mom told Jeff and me that we would go down to the boat harbor after she got off work and see the new boat coming in. I was to wash Jeff's hands and face and get him all cleaned up and then when it was time to leave we were to walk down to her office and wait for her to get off work.

Jeff and I sat on the big front steps of the Coast and Geodetic Survey building where our mom worked, waiting for her to finish. We watched some boats coming up the channel and saw people coming and going at the post office next door. Then we all walked out to the new boat harbor -- which was a ways out of town. We liked to walk, even though Jeff walked slowly because he still limped after his foot surgery. There were lots of interesting things to see on the way and I enjoyed the slow walk. Sitting at the boat harbor was our car. Someone had driven it down there so it would be there when our dad and Jimmy came back.

We waited and watched as the boats came into the harbor. I didn't know what our new boat would look like and I was surprised when our mom pointed to a very big boat and said that it was our new boat. It was a very fancy boat, and much bigger than the ones we had before.

It had the four fishing poles on it like the other boats, and it had a very big cabin, with lots of pretty windows. It was painted white on the hull and was all plain wood on the cabin, a gleaming shiny wood that our mom said was teak.

We waited at the float until Jimmy had tied up the boat and then we went aboard, to see our dad and Jimmy and look at the boat. I was glad to see Jimmy; I had missed him a lot during those weeks they had been gone to Washington to buy the boat. Inside, the cabin was very big, with seats on three sides, a very big wheel, and a table that folded down in front of the seats at the back of the wheelhouse.

When we went below, it was much bigger than our other boats, and our dad told us it was called a cabin cruiser. We liked the bigger boat and the table up in the wheelhouse so we could sit and play cards or write things on our pieces of paper, or watch out the windows to see the scenery. The other boats our dad owned only had a wheelhouse just the size for one or two people and when we were in the cabin below we could only see a little bit if we pressed our faces against the portholes. This was much better.

After a while our dad was all finished tidying up the boat for the night, and we helped to carry their bags up to the car. One of the things they had was a very big foot locker, and it was so heavy that Jimmy and I could not pick it up together. Our dad picked it up and swung it up on his shoulder and carried it to the car. Jimmy said there was a surprise inside.

Jimmy carefully carried a big glass ball float to the car. It was so big his arms almost couldn't go around it and he had to walk slowly. I wanted to know where he got it, and how heavy it was, and what he was going to do with it. I had so many questions for Jimmy that day! The glass floats are found in the water in Alaska after they have broken off the nets of Japanese fishermen many hundreds of miles away. The currents in the ocean drift the glass floats all the way over to Alaska, and sometimes you can find them along beaches or just floating in the water.

Our mom had several that we had gotten out of the water while fishing, but the biggest one was only about a foot across. This new one was over two feet across and a pretty dark green. It was very heavy, and Jimmy told me how they found it.

Our dad had been taking a nap after lunch and Jimmy was piloting the boat, watching for logs or other things in the water that you must not run into. He looked to one side as they passed an object and he thought it was a glass float. He got the binoculars out and looked again, and it was the biggest one he had ever seen. Not being as careful as he should have, he swung the boat around too quickly and it tipped quite a bit, which woke up our dad. He jumped out of the bunk to see what was the matter, he thought they had hit a log. Jimmy turned the wheel back quickly again and the boat tipped the other way, just as our dad was in the galley, and to keep from falling he put out his hand to steady himself - but what he steadied himself on was the hot top of the cook stove that they had just used to cook lunch. He burned his hand very badly, and was bandaging it as Jimmy finished maneuvering to get the big glass float.

They had a hard time getting it on board, as they had no net big enough to capture it with, so Jimmy got in the skiff that they towed behind the boat and pushed the float up against the boat to be able to lift it into the skiff. Then our dad pulled the skiff up close to the end of the boat and Jimmy held the float up for our dad to take it on board. They put it next to one of the bunks and piled some things around it so it wouldn't roll around in rough weather. It was the grandest float I had ever seen, huge and clear and green, and it sat in the dining room all the years we lived in Sitka.

When we got home, our dad opened the big foot locker he had brought with him on the boat. It was filled with every kind of fruit you could imagine! There were strawberries, oranges, apples, bananas, and even cantaloupes and watermelons. Our dad had gone shopping after they had bought the new boat and had filled the foot locker with a treasure of fresh fruit. We put the fruit in our refrigerator and had wonderful treats for many days. The fruit was sweet and delicious, not like the things we would get from the stores in Sitka. Most of those fruits had come up from Seattle on the barge and were many weeks old when they finally got to us, and had been kept so cold that some of them had squishy places that had been frozen. They didn't taste nearly so fresh and sweet as these that our dad brought back.

The next day we all rode in the car down to the boat harbor to clean up the new boat and to go for a short ride on it. It was named the Polly Jane, and was a very pretty boat. It didn't look at all like the other fishing boats in the harbor, and I was quite proud that we had such a fancy boat. In the early morning I had helped our mom to pack a picnic lunch for that day. We finished our breakfast and washed up the dishes. Then we turned the stove up high, and fried chicken and made fresh rolls.

Our mom would pinch off little bits of dough from the big bowl of dough she had made the night before and roll them around in her hands to make perfect little balls that she would place in the big baking pan. When it was full, she set it on the warming shelf at the back of the stove until the rolls were as tall as the top of the pan. Then she would put them into the hot oven and bake until they were very big and fluffy. We wrapped the pans of rolls in big towels and put them in a basket to take on the boat picnic. By then the chicken was crispy and delicious smelling and we had made a great big bowl of potato salad. Our dad liked onions and dill pickles in his salad and we chopped them very fine and added them at the last.

There were some brownies that we had baked and an angel food cake because our dad loved it. We took a big bowl of sliced fruit to put on the slices of angel food cake. We also put in jars of dill pickles, watermelon pickles, kelp pickles and the little green sweet pickles that Jeff loved. There were deviled eggs and jars of olives. It was going to be a good picnic.

But first we had to clean up the boat. We washed and swept and scrubbed. I was very good at washing windows so I got the job of washing all the big windows, and there were a lot of them. While we worked on the boat, friends would stop by to take a look and talk about how wonderful it was. Our dad was very glad to have another boat after the Ella June had burned up in that awful fire. And the Polly Jane had a diesel engine, which was safer.

After several hours we finished all the cleaning, the ropes were wound into neat little circles on the deck, and everything was bright and shiny. When our dad was ready to start the engine, he had all of us get out and walk a ways down the dock until he said it was safe to come back on board. He waved his hand to us and we ran back and climbed on board. He didn't want any of us to blow up if the new boat exploded! He did that same thing always after the Ella June exploded, even though the *Polly Jane* had a diesel engine, and diesel doesn't explode.

Jimmy untied the ropes to the bow and stern of the boat, put one foot on the deck of the boat, pushed against the float with the other foot, and jumped on the boat, and we were off. I really wanted him to teach me to cast off a boat like that, but he said my legs were still too short to do it, and he didn't want me to fall into the water.

It was fun to ride through the harbor and wave to our friends from our new boat, and we took a nice long ride out to Silver Bay, where we anchored and ate our lunch at the fold-down table. After lunch we all took naps in the bunks, because we had been up so early getting ready for the picnic and then had spent all that time cleaning the boat up. After a while I heard the engine going on the boat and realized we were almost back to Sitka and the boat harbor. It had been a good boat picnic day with lots of sunshine and seagulls, and we had even seen some seals along the way.

At Christmas time that year we had a new aunt and uncle coming to dinner. Our mom's brother, Uncle Ivan, and his wife Aunt Norma, had moved to Sitka. Now we had two Aunt Normas. Uncle Ivan and Aunt Norma lived on Mt. Edgecumbe with their little baby daughter Cindy. Sometimes I would ride on the shoreboat to visit them. Aunt Norma would make coffee and put extra milk in it for me to drink. I didn't like coffee but she thought it was so much fun that I never told her I didn't.

She had fancy magazines that had pictures of ladies in new dresses and hats. We would look through the magazines and make up stories about the ladies in the magazines. Sometimes we would cut out the pictures and pretend they were paper dolls. When we were done with that we would give them to Cindy and she would crinkle them up in her little baby hands.

Christmas was a busy time, with lots of baking and friends coming over. Our church had a big Christmas pageant, and we all had to learn pieces to say during the program. I always got a long poem to memorize. I liked to learn the poem, but I didn't like standing up in front of people to say it.

Jimmy's birthday is December 19 and we would have a small family dinner for his birthday, with chocolate cake for dessert. Our birthday dinners were always whatever was on the regular menu for that day, and Jimmy's birthday that year was on a Monday so we had meatloaf, with baked potatoes and green beans. Our mom baked a cake with frosting for dessert on our birthdays. Jeff's birthday is on Christmas day, so he always had turkey for his birthday dinner.

We spent weeks baking breads and cookies, pies and cakes. Our dad made candies, and divinity was his specialty. He made it with nuts and without nuts, with maraschino cherries or gumdrops, and sometimes with red or green food coloring. He whipped and whipped it until it would stand up in stiff peaks, then dropped big spoonfuls of the candy onto waxed paper to sit and cool. I loved the airy bubbles in the divinity and my favorite was with nuts in it.

Sometimes our grandma would send a big box of walnuts to us from California. We would take the hammer, a board and the nuts out into the shed and crack them open. Jimmy showed me how to hit them on the pointy end to make them split right in half. Then we would take little picks and pull the nut out in one piece. If any broke we put them in a different bowl for chopping for cookies or candy. It was cold in the shed and our hands would be red and sore by the time we were done cracking that big box of nuts.

Two or three days before Christmas we would go out in the woods and find the perfect tree. We would hunt and hunt, looking at each one we found to make sure we got one that was just right. Not too tall - not too short - not too wide - not too skinny. At last we would agree on a tree and our dad would chop it down. He would pull it through the snow to the car, put it on the top, and tie it down with ropes that he had brought from home. We would drive back into town and often we would see our friends coming home with their Christmas trees on their cars or in their trucks.

When we got home, our dad would untie the tree and bring it in the house to put in the tree stand. The stand had a row of lights around the edge and he put bubble lights in the stand. It looked like a row of candles around the bottom of the tree. Once he had sawed the bottom of the tree flat and gotten it into the stand, he would put strings of light all over the tree. Next our mom would wind silver tinsel around and around the tree. Then we would begin to put the ornaments on the tree. We had some very old ones, from when our mom and dad were kids, and some from when they were first married, and five little angels on clouds that were made of angel hair and were my very own ornaments. I would hang them up very carefully each year. We would hang long strands of icicles on each branch, making sure that we put on only one strand at a time. At last the tree was done and our dad reached up high and put the star on the top.

Earlier in the week I had gone over to visit Aunt Norma, and she was decorating their tree. She had put the lights and ornaments on and was adding the icicles. She had ten boxes of icicles and I didn't know how she would get them all on the tree. She had the kind of tree with branches that stuck straight out and she put one strand after another on the branches, right next to each other, until each branch was almost covered with silver. I liked the way it looked, so different from our tree.

People in town had strung bright Christmas lights back and forth across the streets in town and had put candles in the windows of the stores. It all looked very festive, and there was fresh snow on the ground.

Two days before Christmas, our mom began her big cooking spree for the Christmas dinner. She started making pies: pumpkin pies, mince meat pies, apple pies, vinegar pies, lemon pies - so many pies! She had a special cupboard in the back porch that was almost as cold as a refrigerator, and she would put the pies in there after they were done. She didn't put meringue on the lemon and vinegar pies until Christmas day, so they would be fresh. She put waxed paper over the top of each pie to keep it clean.

Then she would bake loaves of bread and put them in paper bags, some to give away and some to eat. The day before Christmas, she would cut up the bread for the stuffing, boil eggs for deviled eggs, and make cranberry sauce. No matter where you looked there was something good to eat. There were plates of cookies set out for our friends that stopped by, and tins of cookies packed to give away as gifts. On Christmas Eve we all got in the car and went around town to give out cookies to friends, then home for hot chocolate and cookies.

Christmas day was the big cooking day, with guests starting to arrive right after breakfast! We would get up very early and make our beds and comb our hair, then we would go into the living room and open our presents. After presents there was a big breakfast of ham and eggs, toast and sometimes orange juice. Jimmy and I would clean up the living room so there would be places to sit, while our mom did the dishes.

She had been up at 4 a.m. to get the huge turkey ready to bake. She had mixed all the ingredients together for the stuffing in a big wash basin and had stuffed the turkey full. There was too much stuffing to fit into the turkey, so she put the rest in a pan to bake in the back of the big oven. She had started the dough for the rolls, and it was sitting on the warming shelf of the stove, rising taller and taller.

Our table could seat 16 people and often there were more than that for dinner. The table would be loaded with every good thing you could think of to eat. The big golden turkey would be brought in and placed at the end of the table. Plates were passed around to our dad and he would cut thick slices of turkey, put them on the plates and pass them back around. The turkey would often weigh over 25 pounds and there was plenty of meat for everyone to have all they wanted. There were mashed potatoes, deviled eggs, Harvard beets, stuffed celery, olives, at least 6 kinds of pickles, fresh rolls hot out of the oven, candied yams, two kinds of cranberry sauce, green beans, baked beans, gravy and stuffing. I always sat next to Jimmy and we would eat and eat until we could hold no more.

After dinner we would help our mom to clear the table, rinsing and stacking the plates in piles to be washed. The glasses and silverware we put right in the sink and one of us would begin washing dishes. We used up many dish towels drying the dishes, but it was fun to work together in the kitchen. There would be big cups of coffee for all the adults to drink - and when the dishes were all done we would start bringing out the desserts, making a very pretty table full of cakes, pies and cookies. Everyone would get a small plate and take whatever they wanted from the dessert table.

After the dessert dishes were once again done, Jimmy and I would go to our rooms and look at our new gifts. Jeff still had his cast on his foot and he would clump into my room and we'd play some games while the adults talked and played cards long into the night. It was a long day and lots of fun, and it was also fun to climb into bed in nice warm flannel pajamas and drift off to sleep, remembering all the fun things we did and the good food we ate.

Our Christmas tree would stay up until December 29, and then we would take it down and clean the entire house, from top to bottom. All furniture was moved and cleaned behind, floors were mopped and waxed, walls were scrubbed, closets were cleaned out - every single thing in the closet was taken out so we could clean the walls, shelves and floors. Windows would be washed, and curtains taken down and washed and ironed. Everything in our house sparkled so that we entered the new year clean!

23
Picnics and Hammers

At the end of summer, after I finished fourth grade, we all rode the shoreboat over to Mt. Edgecumbe, where we went to a big all-day picnic. This was a special picnic for the families of everyone who worked for the BIA school. We got up early and did our chores, making our beds very carefully and putting everything away that was out of place so the house would be neat when we got home.

I liked riding the shoreboat. Many of our friends were on the boat, going to the picnic also. There were games to play, and contests for everyone. There were long tables full of food, and three men stood at big outdoor stoves cooking hot dogs and hamburgers. At first we walked around just looking at everything there was to do. Our mom, dad and Jeff stayed together, and Jimmy and I were allowed to go where ever we wanted to.

Jimmy showed me where the contests were being held, and he wanted to try some. He found a nail-pounding contest for me to enter. There was a group for each class, and I got in the group for fourth graders. All of the other kids were in my grade at school, and we all were each given a big hammer and some nails. We stood near a long board that was put up on sawhorses. I had helped our dad to do some work on our house and I knew how to use a hammer, but this one seemed very heavy. We were told to get a nail out - they were very long nails - and that when told to start we should start pounding. The first one that pounded in three nails would be the winner.

Jimmy would stand nearby watching, and he told me to always try and hit the nail right flat on the head, not to let the hammer slide to the side. The judge shouted, "GO!" and I tried to remember Jimmy's advice. I hammered and hammered and the first nail went in, then the second! I wanted to stop and see what the other kids were doing, but Jimmy was yelling, "Keep pounding! Keep pounding!" so I picked up the third nail and whammed at it. When it was all the way in the board I heard cheering; I looked up to see what they were cheering for, and it was me! I had beaten all the other fourth graders in nailing the three nails in. The judge came over and held my arm up high in the air and told everyone my name, even though everyone already knew it, and declared me the Champion Nail

Pounder of the Fourth Grade. I was very proud, and he gave me a piece of paper saying that I was the champion. I showed it to Jimmy and he said I had done very well.

Then he wanted to join the races with other boys, so I watched as they took turns running up and down the big cement running lanes. Sometimes Jimmy would beat all the other boys and I would clap and cheer, and sometimes he would be the second or third one and I would still clap and cheer. I liked to see him run so fast.

The last race he was in was a gunny-sack race. Each boy got inside a big gunny sack and pulled it up to his waist, and held onto it to keep it from falling. One boy was practicing and fell and hurt his mouth, so the other boys had to wait a while until a doctor had come over to see how that boy was doing. While they were waiting Jimmy let me try on his gunny sack. It came almost to my neck, and Jimmy said he could tie it on me and I would be a sack of fish! This made us laugh, and after that, all day long we would laugh when we would think of it.

Then it was time for the race and Jimmy climbed back in his sack and got in line with the other boys. He told me he was going to try to win by taking small jumps, because sometimes when you take large jumps you tangle up your feet. Sure enough, hop hop hop hop, and Jimmy was ahead of the other boys. He kept up his short little hops, bouncing up and down so fast that it made me laugh, and he was the winner by a long ways. I ran up to hug him and he took his gunny sack and put it over my head and said, "Let's go to eat lunch little fish sister." I was very happy.

A big siren sounded, and we all went to find our moms and dads and eat our lunch. I was very hungry and wanted a hot dog and a hamburger. When it was my turn to be served I asked for one of each, and the man serving laughed and said that pounding nails must make little girls very hungry! I got potato salad and pickles and some green onions on my plate and we sat at long table and ate our lunch.

Then we got in line again and each got a big piece of chocolate cake and two scoops of ice cream. Jimmy showed me how to make chocolate soup. First we smashed our cake into small bits, and then stirred and stirred until it was mushed into the ice cream. We turned around on the picnic table and sat with our backs to the table, ate our chocolate soup, and listened as a band played. I think it was the Mt. Edgecumbe BIA High School band that played that day. They would march back and forth along the tables and people would clap as they went by, and Jimmy and I would eat chocolate soup and smile. One time Jimmy waved his spoon at the band and a boy waved back.

It was finally time to go home. We had been there almost all day. Our dad carried Jeff to the shoreboat, and we rode across to our car that was waiting by the post office. On the ride home I was very tired from such a big day of fun, and as soon as we had our baths we climbed into bed for a good sleep. But before I went to sleep, I put my Nail Pounding Champion paper on my desk where I could see it when I woke up in the morning.

24
OH THAT PARROT

That next fall I was in fifth grade and we had an interesting teacher. We didn't seem to do very much in most of our classes, but we surely did concentrate on spelling. Mrs. Mitchell would give us the spelling lesson for that week, and we were to write all the words ten times each - but not one word at a time, ten times, but the entire list, ten times over. We had to memorize all the words in order and when it came time for our spelling test Mrs. Mitchell would start the test with any word on the list she wanted; from that point we had to write the rest of the list, then begin from the top of the list and complete it to the word she had picked. I think it was more of a memorization test than a spelling test, but that is the way she did it every week.

Recess was a lot of fun that year, for I now had lots of friends and we played our games together. In the spring we would play hopscotch and jump rope. In hopscotch we would try to pick the best 'lager' that we could find. Sometimes we used stones, but those bounced too much. The luckier ones had a chain, the kind you might put keys on and hook the ends together. These would throw well, and would stay put where they landed, not skipping over onto the line or bouncing out of the box. It was easy at first to hit the boxes, but as you got to the other end it was harder to not have the lager slide. We drew our hopscotch in the dirt in a certain section of the playground, and there were several games of hopscotch going on at the same time. We took a stick and retraced the lines for each recess; that way we could tell if someone stepped on a line and lost their turn.

Jump rope was fun, with funny rhymes and games that we played. I liked to jump single, but some of the girls could jump Double Dutch, where there were two ropes turning and you had to jump very fast to keep your feet from being tangled up. We all took turns jumping and when someone missed they had to turn the ropes until someone else missed; then they could get back in line for another turn at jumping.

We had special songs that we sang was we jumped rope.

Benjamin Franklin went to France
To teach the ladies how to dance.
First the heel, and then the toe,
Spin around and out you go.

~

Chocolate bears and gingerbread cats,
All dressed up in whipped-cream hats.
Danced in the garden under the moon,
Beat sweet rhythms with a wooden spoon,
Whirling, turning, jumping to the beat,
Melting down to their ice cream feet.

When the baker ran to see,
They ran beneath the gum-gum tree,
Running in between the rows,
Tripping over ice cream toes.
There were 1, 2, 3 . . .

~

Cinderella dressed in yella,
Went downstairs to kiss a fella,
Made a mistake and kissed a snake.
How many doctors did it take
1, 2, 3, ...

~

Grace, Grace dressed in lace.
Went upstairs to powder her face.
How many boxes did it take?
1, 2, 3 . . . . .

I eat my peas with honey,
I've done it all my life.
It looks a little funny.
But it keeps them on my knife.
How many peas can I get on my knife?
1, 2, 3, ...

~

Ice cream soda, lemonade, punch;
Spell the initials of my (your) honey bunch.
A-B-C-D . . . .

~

Mabel, Mabel, set the table,
Just as fast as you are able.
Don't forget the salt, sugar, vinegar, mustard,
red-hot pepper!

~

Miss Lucy had a baby
And she named him Tiny Tim.
She put him in the bathtub
To see if he could swim.
He drank up all the water.
He ate up all the soap.
He tried to eat the bathtub
But it wouldn't go down his throat.

Miss Lucy called the doctor,
Miss Lucy called the nurse.
Miss Lucy called the lady with the alligator purse.
In comes the Doctor, in comes the nurse,
In comes the lady with the alligator purse.
Out goes the doctor, out goes the nurse.
Out goes the lady with the alligator purse.

~

Teddy bear, teddy bear,
Turn around.
Teddy bear, teddy bear,
Touch the ground.
Teddy bear, teddy bear,
Show your shoe.
Teddy bear, teddy bear,
That will do.
Teddy bear, teddy bear,
Go upstairs.
Teddy bear, teddy bear,
Say your prayers.
Teddy bear, teddy bear,
Turn out the light.
Teddy bear, teddy bear,
Say good night.

~

Not Last night but the night before.
Twenty-four robbers came knocking at my door,
They called me out for the world to see,
And this is what they said to me--
Spanish dancer turn around,
Spanish dancer touch the ground,
Spanish dancer do a kick,
Spanish dancer do the splits!
Spanish dancer, turn around.
Spanish dancer, get out of town.

My favorite game, though, was jacks, and we played by the hour. There was a cement porch by the kindergarten room, it was great for playing jacks on. You had to have a good flat surface for the jacks. There was also a little roof over the porch and it would keep the rain off us during rainy recesses. But some days that cold cement would scrape our hands until they were almost too sore to write in class after recess.

It wasn't too long after I started fifth grade that our mom took Jeff to the doctor again. He was tired and had a high fever, and would cry a lot. She took him to the doctor at the big hospital on Mt. Edgecumbe, and when she came home that night she didn't bring Jeff with her. I was very worried, because I didn't think Jeff should be left alone at the hospital by himself. Who would fix his food, did they take a bed to the hospital for him, and who would make his bed; who would wash his clothes or fix the hot water for his bath? All these things worried me very much, and I thought that I should have gone with them to the hospital so I could have stayed there to help. I didn't know if they had a special bed for him at the hospital or if he would even have a bed at all.

I knew not to bother our mother with a lot of questions, so I would sit very quietly and try to hear what she was telling our dad. I was relieved to find out that he was in a room with a lot of other little boys and that the nurses brought him food when he was hungry. Our mom said he had rheumatic fever and I didn't know what that was, but figured that it must be very bad, because when I was sick and couldn't walk when we still lived in California I did not have to go and stay at the hospital.

Every day after that our mom would go over on the shoreboat as soon as she was done with her job. I would have to fix dinner each night, but I already knew how to cook everything we ate, and sometimes Jimmy would help me with lifting the big pans on and off the hot stove. I would set the table at noon when I came home for lunch, after I washed the lunch dishes. Then when I got home I would start frying the chicken or the liver, and peel the potatoes. Jimmy would put the pan of potatoes on the stove and take them off, and pour them into a big colander to drain the water off. Then I would put them back in the pan and put them on the warming shelf, and when our dad came home from work he would mash them for dinner. I was not tall enough to mash the potatoes, even if I stood on my box. I would figure out how long it would take to make biscuits and while they were baking I would fill the pickle dishes and put them on the table in a nice design. It was strange to not have our mom and Jeff eating dinner with us, and it was a very long time until Jeff came home from the hospital.

Our mom would come home late at night, and sometimes she would mop the floor or do some other work before she went to bed. I wanted to help her all I could, but I didn't know how to mop the floor. Sometimes I would practice to see if I could get it nice and clean, but it was very hard to do. She would tell us stories about the other little kids in the ward with

Jeff. She said that at meal time the nurses would bring a cart with all the meals on it for each little boy. They would put the same thing on each plate but some of the other little boys didn't like the things they served.

One boy would not eat the banana because the hide was so tough, he said. Our mom showed him how to take the peeling off, and he liked it better then. But none of the other little boys would eat the peanut butter that came in a little plastic cup on their plate. Our mom would show them how to spread it on their bread for a sandwich but they would just shake their heads and push it away. They did not like the way it looked, so they would not put it in their mouths. They hadn't seen peanut butter before.

After Jeff finally came home he had to spend many more weeks in bed. He had to rest a lot and still our mom wanted him to get his school lessons done when he could, so once a week his teacher would come to our house and talk to him and give him lessons. The other days I would go to his class after school and the teacher would give me his lessons for that day. I carried them home very carefully and piled them on the table beside his bed. I would peek in first to see if he was sleeping, and if he was I would wait until he woke up and then take his lessons in.

I liked to help him with his lessons and if he had words he didn't know I would help him sound them out. I would bring anything he wanted so he could do his lessons. It was almost the same as correspondence courses except for the teacher that would come to our house every week.

Before Jeff had gotten sick our dad had decided to fix up the inside of our house. It was full of very small rooms and he wanted to make the rooms bigger, and to move some of them around. After he would come home from work and dinner was over he would begin building. He took down some of the walls of the tiny rooms and made bigger rooms of them. There was a door that went out the front of the house, but we never used it very much. It had steps that went down to the front yard and they were rickety and broken, so he hammered the whole porch and steps off the front of the house and closed up the door.

Where the living room had been he made a bedroom, and where the dining room had been he made another bedroom that was to be mine. My bedroom had been where the new dining room would be, and the living room was going to be connected to the dining room to make one big room. Also he was going to connect the kitchen to the dining room on the other end and it would be nice and open.

While he was building there was sawdust everywhere, and it often was hard to keep the house very clean. The first thing he did, after closing up the front door, was to take the carpet out of the living room. It was hollow and echoey in there without a rug, but much easier to keep cleaned up without it. He would bang and saw and cut on the walls until they were all down, then he would begin to build up new walls where he wanted them. It was fun to walk between the rooms when the walls weren't finished, sort of like walking through the bars of a cage.

When our dad was building he never had to measure any wood he was going to cut. He would just look at the place where he needed to have a board and he would then go and cut it, and never would it come out wrong. His friends like to try and trick him, and often when they would come for Saturday night hamburgers they would call out measurements to our dad. They would say, "7 3/8 inches" he would then raise his hands in front of him, and come to a quick stop at the measurement they had called out. They would bring their tape measure - he didn't have one - and measure the distance between his hands and it would be exactly what they had called out. They would laugh and call out another measurement, "18 1/16" inches, and he would do the same thing, with the same results.

He never moved his hands back and forth to get the right measurement - he made one move and stopped there - and it was always right. Sometimes they thought if they would catch him doing something else and call out a measurement that he wouldn't get it, but he never missed. He could drop his hamburger flipper and put his hands out for a measurement at a moment's notice and always get it right. It was great fun to watch them try and stump him and they never could.

He built all the kitchen cabinets in our house without ever measuring a door or a single board, and each cabinet was exactly the same size as the other. He built many tall dressers and they were perfect in every detail; all the drawers slid just right, everything fit together perfectly, and he never measured one piece of wood. He never had an electric saw or any fancy tools, just a hammer, a crow bar, a plane, a hand drill and a hand saw. Everything he built was done with those tools. He would call up the lumber yard and order the wood he wanted and all the supplies, and they would come in a truck to our back door. They would unload all the supplies into the shed behind the house and our dad would start on another project.

He loved to remodel the house, and sometimes on Sundays while we were at church, he would begin tearing down the walls again. His friends said that he should put zippers on the walls so it would be easier to move them. In all the years that we lived in that house my bedroom was in every location except where the kitchen and the bathroom were. I had built in desks, window seats and beds, in different rooms at different times. I liked all my rooms and would have been happy to leave them alone and not remodel, but our dad liked to do that.

We had a big green parrot that lived in a cage in the corner of the dining room. My friend Phyllis's dad had given the parrot to us when we moved into town. His name was Perry and he was very clever. To make him stay inside the cage our mom would put a clothespin on the latch to his door, but he would chew and chew on it and soon break it off and lift the latch and climb up on top of his cage. He would fly around the house and when our dad was cooking, Perry would land on his shoulder and jabber. One time he bit our dad's ear and it made our dad jump and Perry fell to the stove, burning his feet. Our dad put him in a pan of cold water and then rubbed something on his feet. For several days Perry sat on the bottom of his cage like a chicken, until his feet weren't sore anymore.

Perry could talk, and we would teach him lots of things to say. He could whistle like he had seen a pretty girl bird going by, and that always made our friends laugh. Before he had lived with us or Phyllis's dad, Perry had learned a number of "bad" words that our mom did not allow in our house. She decided to teach him to sing "Jesus Loves Me", a song we sang at our Sunday School. Every time when she was mopping the floor she would sing it over and over and finally Perry would sing it too, but he added his own touches. He would sing a few words of the Sunday School song, and then a few swear words, more of the song and then more swear words. We wanted to laugh, but knew better than to laugh where our mom could hear us, so Jimmy and I would go outside into the shed and laugh and laugh at how funny Perry would sing his wicked Sunday School song!

Sometimes Perry would sleep on his perch, using just one foot. He would curl up the other foot and then forget that he had one foot off the perch already, and would fall off the perch. This was always in the middle of the night, and then he would swear, using all the words he knew, sometimes over and over. We would have to hide our heads under our pillows to keep from laughing out loud at him.

Perry loved to fly around the house, but for some reason he liked to chase me more than anything else. He would aim for my head and squawk really loud. I would cover my head and run for my bedroom, with Perry right behind me. When I was sweeping the floor he would use his foot and toss big bunches of his sunflower seeds out onto the floor I had just swept. Then he would take some of his water and splash it about with his beak to make the floor wet. He was a very naughty bird.

He especially liked to come to the table and eat with us. I was glad that he didn't sit next to me, because I was afraid of him. He had his own little dish that sat on the table between our mom and our dad, and they would put pieces of food in it for him to eat. He loved pickled peaches, and if he didn't have a bit of pickled peach in his bowl he would walk right across the table, dragging his tail in anything and everything, and nip a bite right out of the serving bowl. Our dad thought this was very funny, but our mom was not so pleased. Later, when our grandma came to visit us and saw the bird sitting on the table she was very surprised and perplexed; she didn't want a bird walking all over the table while she ate!

Our dad drank coffee with each meal, and would slurp it when it was hot to cool it off some, or he would pour some from his spoon back into the cup to cool it. Perry would listen, putting his head to one side, and then after a while he could make the same sound as our dad slurping or of the coffee splashing back into the cup. In the mornings when he wanted to get up, he would make the coffee sounds, and if that didn't bring someone to take the cover off his cage he would try out a few swear words.

His cage sat by the window, and when he would see the crows flying by he would look up at them and shout "Dirty Birds! Dirty Birds!" I don't know who taught him that. If he got too noisy our dad would put him back in his cage and latch the door, then cover the cage with a big thick blanket, so it would be dark and Perry would go to sleep. But before he would go to sleep he would call out, "Heeeeeellllp. Heeeeellllp, 'in a funny little voice, like he was far away. When our grandma came to visit us, she laughed at that, but she still was not pleased that Perry came to the table to eat with us.

25
COMPANY IS COMING

One day our dad told us that our Grandma and Grandpa were coming to visit us for a couple of months. Jimmy and I were excited because we hadn't seen them for a long time. Jeff didn't remember them, but he was excited too.

We scrubbed and cleaned the house extra carefully before they arrived. My mom said we had to have everything in order and we worked hard at it. We usually cleaned the whole house very well on Saturdays, getting every speck of dirt we could find.

This was not our regular Saturday schedule of cleaning. We had a bright blue rug in the living room and it was my job to sweep it clean. The only way we had to clean it was to sweep it with a broom. First I would dust the whole room, all the shelves and pictures on the wall and the knick knacks on the shelves. Then I would get a big pan of water and put it on the rug, being careful not to spill any when I carried it through the house. I would dip just the end of the broom into the water and begin to sweep. I didn't put too much water on the broom or it would make dark water spots on the rug, but just enough water so that when I swept, the dust wouldn't blow around the room. I would sweep and sweep until I had cleaned the rug completely. I swept the dust off the carpet onto the dining room floor and picked it up with a dust pan. After sweeping the rug then I had to dust again, in case there was any dust from the sweeping. I had to wash the front of the fish tank and wash the windows in the living room. Then it all sparkled.

My next chore was to take everything off the counters in the kitchen and scrub them spotless. I had to empty the canisters by pouring the contents into big bowls, and then wash and dry the canisters, and put the contents back in. I had to wash all the fronts of the cupboards till there was not one spot left. After that, I had to take the big metal garbage can that sat on our back porch and scrub it clean. Sometimes it didn't smell very good, so I had to rinse and rinse to get it shiny clean. Our mom said you should be able to eat off her floor or out of her garbage can, but I never wanted to. I did make that garbage can sparkle though.

After the garbage can was clean and had passed inspection I would set about cleaning the laundry porch, straightening the shelves and washing the outside of the washing machine and the refrigerator. By this time the others had finished their chores too and my mom would shoo us all outside while she mopped the floors. Jeff never had chores to do, but everyone else did. I was glad when she said it was time to scrub the floor, for I would take my sandwich that I had made after breakfast and start out for the museum. But this Saturday was different; our mom said we had to do extra chores to be ready for our Grandma and Grandpa when they got there the next day. We did all the regular Saturday chores and then started on the extra ones.

The small shed at the back of the house had two rooms in it; the bigger front room was for our dad, his tools and supplies and the back, smaller room was for us kids. We kept our comic books there and anything else we wanted to play with. There was a small table in there and a few outdoor toys. We had to sweep it clean that day and stack the comics neatly. We even washed the window in our part of the shed.

Our dad was grumbling about cleaning up his work area; it seemed to always be in a mess. He had his tools and lots of wood, and every time he would work on a project he would mess up the workshop again, with tools everywhere! Now while we worked on our club room he worked on the workroom. He stacked some tires in one corner, hung all his tools on the nails in the wall, stacked the lumber up carefully on one side, and let me sweep up the floor. We had finished with the club room and so had no other chores left to do, and I wanted to help get things ready for our grandparents.

I didn't mind not going to the museum that day, because having company from the States was a great treat. I couldn't reach the window in the workroom, so I was allowed to stand on the workbench and clean the window from the inside; Jimmy stood on a box and cleaned it on the outside. Soon that shed was as clean as our house. Our mom was still mopping the floors, so we sat in the club room and read comics for a little while when we finished all our chores.

Then our mom said it was time to bake a nice cake. I got out the ingredients for her and we made an applesauce cake, which was my very favorite. First we lit the kitchen stove and heated the oven, and at the same time it heated our hot water. It was a very big wood stove that was converted to use fuel oil instead of wood. There were two big 55 gallon drums that sat at the end of the shed, and they were filled with fuel oil by a big truck that came from Service Transfer, which was a gas station and moving company. Their big truck would pump the tanks full and then we would have heating and cooking fuel for a long time.

The cook stove and a heating stove in the living room had lines running to them from the tanks. You would turn on the fuel with a knob on the stove for a minute or so, until there was some oil in the bottom of the stove, and then throw in a match to light it. The amount of heat was controlled by the knob. If you turned on the fuel and forgot to light it right away the bottom of the stove would fill with too much fuel to light and you would have to dip it out with paper towels. It was a messy job because you had to reach your arm all the way to the bottom of the inside of the sooty stove and you came out a mess, not to mention that you had to pick up those fuel oil soaked paper towels. Then you had to light the stove carefully in case there was still a little too much oil in there.

When the stove was hot we would turn the knob down and put the cake in to bake. Because the fire box was on the left side of the stove, that part of the oven got hottest, and partway through baking something we had to turn it around so both sides would bake evenly. If you didn't turn it soon enough, one side of the cake would be much higher than the other, or the cookies would be burned on one side and uncooked on the other side of the pan. And once the oven got to the correct temperature you had to know what setting to turn the knob to so the heat would stay at that temperature. Usually everything cooked pretty well in that oven.

While the cook stove was on, it would also be heating the hot water. There were water pipes that ran round and round in the fire box and it would heat the water in the hot water tank, which sat in a hallway just behind the stove. If the cookstove was on for too long the hot water would get too hot, and the tank would begin to clank and bang. Then we would let a little of the hot water out of the faucet, or someone would take their bath if it was nighttime. This method of heating water would not be so good in an area where the weather was very warm and you didn't have your stove on very often, but in Alaska it worked fine. We had to have the stove on most of the time anyway so we always had a fresh supply of hot water, and if we needed more we could turn the stove up for a while.

Our applesauce cake came out perfect. We put a pretty crocheted tablecloth on the table and set out cups, saucers, plates and forks. Napkins were folded carefully and placed next to the stack of plates. The coffee pot was filled and ready to go, and then our dad and mom went to the turn-around to pick up Grandma and Grandpa. It was hard to wait for them to come back from the airport, even though it was really only a short time that they were gone. We were excited to see them after all this time.

I was sitting in the big chair in the living room, thinking about what to do next to pass the time, when I heard the car drive up. We knew we must be little ladies and gentlemen and stand quietly when company arrived, so I helped Jeff to stand straight and tall, and we all stood in a row when the door opened. In came our Grandma, and she was carrying a surprise for me in her arms. She had my wonderful doll Bunny!

She had carried her carefully from California all the way on the planes. I was so excited I began to cry as I hugged my Grandma and Bunny at the same time. I knew I was too big to cry, and I wasn't being brave, but I was too happy to care. I had no idea that Grandma was bringing Bunny with her. My Grandpa stood behind her and in his big voice he laughed and laughed because he was so happy. He picked me up and swung me and Bunny around and around and we all laughed and laughed.

I was too excited to sit and eat my cake when it was time - I just wanted to dance and hug Bunny, then hug Grandma and Grandpa, then dance and hug Bunny some more. What a day that was! I suppose we had dinner, I suppose we did the dishes, I suppose the adults sat and talked, I suppose that we took our baths and got ready for bed as usual, but I can remember only that Bunny came home that day, the happiest day I had known.

Late into the night Bunny and I talked and talked. She told me of her adventures, of seeing my cousins when they would come to visit our grandparents, of the sunshine in California, of the long plane trip, the many different kinds of planes they had ridden on. I told her of Sammy Sue and how they would be great friends, of all the places we had lived, of the boat fires and the adventures we had, of school and whales and boats and libraries and museums. I finally slept, with Bunny on one side of me and Sammy Sue on the other.

EPILOGUE

I lived in Alaska through my high school years. I did get the fur parka from my Aunt Norma and wore it for many years until it literally fell apart. I still have the mukluks.

Don and I met in Neal Anderson's drug store, where I worked at the soda fountain, during my Senior year of high school. I graduated in 1964 and later that year I moved to Texas, where Don had moved to be near his father, and we got married in Arlington, Texas. We moved back to Sitka in search of a better job and our first daughter was later born there. Our last two children were born in Wisconsin. Our family had many adventures, moving back and forth across the country. We've lived in the desert, 20 miles from the Mexican border, in Kansas, Wisconsin, central and Eastern Texas and up and down California and now we live in Bellingham, WA where we have the fun of living near two of our grandsons. Our youngest grandson lives in West Virginia.

Our dad, Bud Dunlap, passed away in 1972 in Vacaville, CA. Our mom, June Dunlap, moved back to Alaska after that and lived there for over 20 years, and passed away in 1996, in Virginia Mason Medical Center in Seattle, WA.

My oldest brother, Jimmy, lived most of his life in Alaska, with a short time spent in Georgia. He took Perry the parrot with him. He has four children, Buddy, Billy, Hilary and Fred. He passed away in 1999.

Jeff married and moved to Santa Cruz, CA and lived there with his family until late in his life, when he moved to Nampa, ID. His children are Neal, Ryan and Amanda. He passed away in 2009 after a long illness.

Over the years Bunny has continued to travel with me. She spent some time in Alaska before rejoining our family once again in northern California, when my children were in early grade school. She now spends her "retirement" in a rocking chair, and is loved by all who meet her. She has been my special friend all these years.

.

ABOUT THE AUTHOR

I asked my grown children to write this section – you will see me through their eyes.

JoAnn Dunlap Bayne spent her earliest years in California, and was raised on the islands and waters of pre- and post-statehood southeast Alaska. A painter, photographer, and quilter, she raised her three children across the U.S., making life an adventure in each new location. She now lives in northwest Washington with her husband and lifelong partner in adventure, where her three young grandsons cannot believe their good luck to have her.

Normally when you read about an author, you see where they were educated, and all of the awards they have won. Those may be great, but this author is my Mom. There isn't an award for always having dinner ready when we got home. I haven't seen an award ceremony for throwing the best birthday party of the entire school year - as judged by my kindergarten peers.

What I have seen is how much she cares for all of us. She has set an example with her nearly 47 years of marriage to my Dad. To this day I'd rather have a home-cooked meal over going out to eat, because of the wonderful meals my Mom makes. She has always been there with good advice on any situation. Now that I'm a parent myself, her good advice continues to be helpful, and I hope to pass that along to my children.

She has lived her life as an example - how to stretch a dollar much further than one might think humanly possible, how to be a giving person, and I know that there will always be chocolate chip cookies in the cookie jar.

She has always been there whenever I have needed her. She is amazing, loving, caring, and giving, and I still call her up often just to talk. She is the most amazing quilter on the face of the earth, and she is always remembered by everyone who meets her. The author? The most wonderful Mom ever.

JoAnn embodies many things and has accomplished so much in her life that it is difficult to include so much in a space so small. But I shall try here to list some of the more notable highlights: She is an extraordinarily accomplished and talented quilter, an avid reader, pianist, artist, mother of 3 grown children, grandmother of 3 boys (Jahn-Zyel, Ben and Donnie Ray), author, baker and teacher. She has done everything from entering projects in local county fairs to creating handmade felt stockings for her family members at Christmastime. Her favorite meal is 7-layer Mexican dip and homemade apple cake (hold the frosting).

walkingtoalaska@gmail.com

13290618R20121

Made in the USA
San Bernardino, CA
18 July 2014